ImagiNation

ImagiNation

The Golden Age of Toronto Kids' TV

Ed Conroy

DUNDURN PRESS

Publisher: Meghan Macdonald | Acquiring editor: Kathryn Lane
Cover design and illustration: Scott Woods
Interior layout: Laura Boyle

Library and Archives Canada Cataloguing in Publication

Title: ImagiNation : the golden age of Toronto kids' TV / Ed Conroy.
Names: Conroy, Ed (Cultural historian), author.
Description: Includes bibliographical references and index.
Identifiers: Canadiana (print) 20250236559 | Canadiana (ebook) 20250237059 | ISBN 9781459755918 (softcover) | ISBN 9781459755925 (PDF) | ISBN 9781459755932 (EPUB)
Subjects: LCSH: Children's television programs—Ontario—Toronto—History. | LCSH: Television broadcasting—Ontario—Toronto—History.
Classification: LCC PN1992.8.C46 C66 2025 | DDC 791.45/6—dc23

We acknowledge the support of the Canada Council for the Arts and the Ontario Arts Council for our publishing program. We also acknowledge the financial support of the Government of Ontario, through the Ontario Book Publishing Tax Credit and Ontario Creates, and the Government of Canada.

Printed and bound in Canada.

Dundurn Press
1382 Queen Street East
Toronto, Ontario, Canada M4L 1C9
dundurn.com, @dundurnpress

Dedicated to my mum, who encouraged me to read books, and to my wife, daughter, and son, who encouraged me to write them.

The child is in me still ...
and sometimes not so still.

— **FRED ROGERS**[1]

One thing I've learned is that there's a push and pull by two forces. There's the force of so-called "good," of people that want to teach kids things through television and don't want kids' brains to rot if they watch TV, and then there's the commercial forces. And those two forces tend to be at cross purposes.

— **JOSH MORRIS, creator of *It's Alive!* (1994)**[2]

C is for Cookie, that's good
enough for me.

— **THE COOKIE MONSTER**

Contents

1980s

1990s

Introduction

I HAVE ALWAYS BEEN FASCINATED BY VISUALS, ESPECIALLY the ones we were exposed to during our formative years. Consciously or unconsciously, good or bad, imagery we experience during youth, in books, magazines, movie theatres, and especially on television screens, stays with us our whole life. It burrows deep into our psyche and helps inform our world view. Perhaps that is why there was so much hysteria when television arrived: the fear that its visual power would warp children through pervasive advertising and images of violence. But what if television's inherent powers could be used for good? To educate and inform and ultimately make the world a better place? Once educators got a hold of the medium, television as a societal benefit seemed a distinct possibility.

Born in Toronto in the late '70s, I was blessed to experience a truly golden age of local children's television. The problem with a golden age, as they say, is that you never know when you are living in one. Growing up, I absorbed television culture like a sponge. During that era, we had limited viewing options, a dozen or so channels, and we couldn't control what was on when (at least, not before the advent of videocassette recorders, i.e., VCRs). I and legions of others watched hundreds of programs out of sheer boredom — whatever was on was the only thing on. It wasn't until years later that I began to appreciate the artful vision of those local kids' shows we watched after school, or as the sun rose early on Saturday mornings, or under duress in sweaty classrooms on enormous television sets wheeled in like manna from heaven. As I grew older, I was compelled to learn more about the television of my childhood. Outside mere nostalgia, its provenance genuinely intrigued me. I wanted to determine what was real and what might have been fevered, Triaminic-induced dreams; to uncover more about how it all began, who made this golden age happen, and, most importantly, why it seemed that Canadian broadcasters were better at it than anyone else.

One of the great challenges in documenting our recent cultural past is a lack of interest in popular culture and its rich history. Television ranks among the most disrespected and misunderstood of cultural industries, due to a myriad of reasons, including but not limited to the ephemeral and disposable nature of the medium, its voluminous back catalogue, and the entrenched belief that as an art form it is not worthy of serious study. As Jennifer VanderBurgh correctly observes in *What Television Remembers: Artifacts and Footprints of TV in Toronto*, "Television has been systemically undervalued in Canada as a cultural venue of importance."[1]

In 2006, I started a side project called Retrontario (retrontario.com) to redress this imbalance in my own small way. A new and exciting video-sharing platform called YouTube had just bloomed, and its corners were overflowing with vintage video content that highlighted regional television productions. Turning to the vast archive of VHS and Betamax videotapes I had accumulated through years of garage-sale and thrift-store sleuthing, I began to digitize and upload a vast swath of off-air home recordings featuring neglected Toronto- and Ontario-based television ephemera such as commercials, public service announcements, station identifications, sign-offs, and chunks of local children's television programming.

Almost immediately I was overwhelmed by the positive reaction. Not only did this illustrate a huge desire for this particular blend of nostalgia, but the open comments section positioned below the site's video screen served as a practical oral history, providing crucial historical and social context to the videos themselves. Through analyzing that past, might there be some benefit in plotting a course for the future? The storyteller-by-way-of-archivist within me was inspired to capture even more of this fast-receding history, beyond the mere sharing of old video clips, as stimulating as that was.

I began my research by interviewing many people involved in the production side of (mostly) Toronto television and was lucky enough to have my work published on digital media sites such as blogTO, and in print in the *Toronto Star*. While I covered a great many flavours of local pop-culture history, it was always the pieces about children's television that seemed to attract the most attention (or, to use the favoured parlance of online publishers, clicks). As Retrontario, my self-financed archival project, expanded its online footprint to other social media platforms such as Facebook, Twitter, and Instagram, its reach increased, as did my stated modus operandi to "celebrate the neglected corners of Ontario's rich televisual history; to put back into circulation material which rightly or wrongly had fallen into a black hole and was, for all intents and purposes, lost."[2]

In 2023, I was invited by the Museum of Toronto (then known as Myseum of Toronto) to curate an exhibit that aimed to take a closer look at the history of children's television in Toronto. Part of the museum's mission was to "fill a gap in the city's cultural offerings,"[3] and this invitation afforded me the opportunity to take an even more dedicated look within a genre for which there existed no definitive history. The resulting exhibit, *Mr. Dressup to Degrassi: 42 Years of Legendary Toronto Kids TV*, ran from May until October 2023 at the museum's 401 Richmond Street West location:

> The TV shows of your childhood hit closer to home than you might think. From 1952 to 1994, Toronto was a global player in a golden era of children's television programming. For over four decades, our city brought together innovative thought leaders, passionate creators and unexpected collaborations — forming a corner of the television industry unlike any other in the world. Toronto etched itself into our collective consciousness with shows like *Mr. Dressup*, *Today's Special*, *The Friendly Giant*, *Polka Dot Door*, *Degrassi*, and more.[4]

We unleashed an atomic blast of unfiltered nostalgia: puppet replicas of Casey and Finnegan and their treehouse from *Mr. Dressup*, the castle wall and miniature furniture from *The Friendly Giant*, the magical *Polka Dot Door*, a

In 2023, the museum installation *Mr. Dressup to Degrassi: 42 Years of Legendary Toronto Kids TV* featured re-creations from many classic Toronto children's shows such as the Casey and Finnegan puppets and the treehouse from *Mr. Dressup*.

Today's Special display case brimming with classic tie-in merchandise, LPs, a bank of period-appropriate television sets looping episodes of *The Kids of Degrassi Street* and *Degrassi Junior High*, and an assortment of original puppets used in *Today's Special*, *Bookmice*, and YTV's The Zone and supplied by the puppeteers who created them: Noreen Young, Nina Keogh, Bob Dermer, Jamie Shannon, and Jason Hopley.

Monitors throughout the museum replayed a range of classic series clips and new interviews with notable talent such as Phil Guerrero (YTV's PJ Phil), Brenda Kamino (*Mr. Dressup*), and the late Nerene Virgin (*Today's Special*). There were puppet-making stations, a robust visual timeline, and live Q and A and trivia events all summer with performers from many of the featured shows. Our exhibit elicited a tremendous response — the *Toronto Star* called it "a treasure trove of nostalgia"[5] — and an outpouring of goodwill. We heard from many guests that such a chronicle of Toronto's role in children's television was not only warranted but should also be permanent. People left with big smiles, or misty eyes. Or both.

During the exhibit's staging, I learned more about CBC's first head of children's television, Dr. Fred Rainsberry, a true media pioneer and one of the most influential figures in the development of children's television in Toronto. It became evident that in the 1950s he alone was instrumental in bringing educators into the fold of television production and shaping the landscape at the CBC that ultimately manifested our gilded trifecta of TV icons — the Friendly Giant, Mr. Rogers, and Mr. Dressup.

The story of children's television tends to be the same the world over — a never-ending struggle between educational needs and entertainment needs, public broadcasting against commercial broadcasting, rote didactics versus free-spirited imagination. In Toronto, the CBC and TVOntario forged the promise of public broadcasting, while CTV and YTV advanced its commercial possibilities. They each contributed to the genre of children's television, some more than others, and some with much greater care. However, all their output bears historical assessment and is also historically relevant, especially in the context of the time it was made.

While the U.S. and the U.K. enjoy cottage industries commemorating their classic pop-culture properties, with retro books, websites, merchandise, and home entertainment releases on physical media proving wildly popular, Canada lags far behind. In 2023, however, the feature-length documentary *Mr. Dressup: The Magic of Make-Believe* directed by Rob McCallum won the People's Choice Documentary Award at the Toronto International Film Festival. The film's warm reception exposed a growing interest in the stories behind the success of Canadian kids' TV.

Much of Canadian television is tied up in archaic and prohibitive rights issues that prevent programs from being repeated on current streaming services or made available online. Added to this, the archival situation is dire. Until the mid- to late 1960s, most children's television was broadcast live with no documented recordings. Even when videotape technology arrived, keeping recordings was a cumbersome and expensive undertaking; numerous tapes were wiped and reused. Low-budget children's series suffered the worst fate as they were mostly assessed as a throwaway regulatory obligation with no future value. Although syndication and international sales led to greater archival care of certain titles, as of 2025 the vast majority of programs discussed in this book are inaccessible outside of unofficial uploads on YouTube (guilty as charged, @Retrontario!) or fuzzy home-recorded VHS or Betamax tapes that occasionally resurface at garage or estate sales. Beyond the accessibility of the programs themselves, there is barely any reference material, especially for large swaths of TVOntario curriculum-based television programs.

Toronto is globally recognized for producing revolutionary comedic television shows and stars — Lorne Michaels (the creator of *Saturday Night Live*), *Second City Television* (1976), *The Kids in the Hall* (1989), actor Jim Carrey, stand-up Russell Peters, and perennial reality-TV host Howie Mandel, to name a few — and innovative newscasting production methods as cultivated by Moses Znaimer at his celebrated stations Citytv (1972), MuchMusic (1984), and Bravo! (1995). Titans of media theory such as Marshall McLuhan, Harold Innis, Edmund Snow Carpenter, Northrop Frye, and Ursula Franklin all contributed to what is known as the Toronto School of communication theory. Why is it that our pioneering work in the field of children's television is so overlooked? Indeed, in 1996's *Mondo Canuck*, authors Geoff Pevere and Greig Dymond say, "In the world of children's entertainment, Canada is something approaching its own Hollywood: it enjoys world renown and near-global market saturation. It is looked up to and envied, and it has been far more often challenged than surpassed."[6]

Considering that some of Toronto's most recognized international celebrities — Drake, Ryan Gosling, Eugene Levy, Catherine O'Hara, John Candy, Dan Aykroyd, Mike Myers, Sarah Polley — began their careers working in local Toronto-produced children's television, its historical oversight even on a commercial level is glaring. In her article addressing some of the causes and remedies, "'Missed Opportunity': The Oversight of Canadian Children's Media" (2016), York University professor Natalie Coulter declares: "The first thing to do in exploring this omission of children's media within the field is to take stock of what is missing, to illustrate the depth and richness of the industries here in Canada."[7]

I have long felt an obligation to take more stock. To create something that better contextualized the rich history of local television shows and networks and presented them in roughly chronological order. In 1988, Fred Rainsberry published the seminal *A History of Children's Television in English Canada: 1952–1986*, an invaluable text that I highly recommend to all budding students of the discipline. While assembling that volume in the early 1980s, Rainsberry interviewed many of the people involved in the creation of local children's series from both behind and in front of the camera, most of whom are no longer alive. Thanks to the help of his son Paul Rainsberry, I was able to access many of those tape-recorded interviews, which provided key and mostly never-before-featured information and thoughts from the creators themselves. During this book's research and writing, I interviewed many more who contributed greatly to children's television in Toronto for additional clarification and rumination, although with so many no longer with us, I wish I had started the endeavour much earlier.

Fred Rainsberry's 1996 obituary read, "The lives of all Canadian children have been immeasurably enriched by this gentle, loving man,"[8] a powerful reflection that has stayed with me throughout this project. When television began in Toronto, the industry was made up of a nexus of misfits, professionals, educators, artists, dreamers, and chancers, who over time moulded the medium into a recognized and respected form. They had big hearts and bigger ideas; no manuals, no precedents, and not much money. A tribute to their collective stories is long overdue.

Retrontario.com — reconstructing our televisual past, one tape at a time.

Now I can present my updated research: a comprehensive chronology of Toronto's children's television phenomenon, from its humble beginnings until the year 2000, the first time any such work has been attempted. It has been an unbelievable honour to assemble the material you hold in your hands, which gave me the opportunity to relive my childhood.

I hope it does the same for you.

Viewer Discretion Is Advised

IMAGINATION IS INTENDED TO BE A CELEBRATORY, COMPREHENSIVE chronology of the very best offerings of live-action children's television created in Toronto between the years 1950 and 2000. Every attempt has been made to include correct titles, spelling, running times, years of production, and cast information, where known. After reviewing stacks of old TV guides, newspaper listings, and online entries, it is safe to say there is much conflicting information out there, and that's before you factor in people's fuzzy thirty-forty-fifty-year-old memories. Because television is deemed an instantly disposable medium, and storage is expensive and resource consuming, not even the broadcasters kept much of their own history from the last century. When it comes to educational television, scant information about provenance was available at time of release, never mind retained for researchers to pore over decades later.

I have endeavoured to include an entry for every notable live-action children's television series created in Toronto during those first fifty years on the air, but may have inadvertently neglected a few. In my defence, for some series there now exists nothing more than a title listing in a TV guide. Also, when writing about any art form, there will be subjective observations on quality, or lack thereof. I offer my humblest apology if your favourite childhood program isn't included here. That also applies to many behind-the-scenes people who warrant mention and attention for their hard work. If anyone has been overlooked, please get in touch so that I may rectify future dispatches on the subject.

I've adhered to Toronto's geographical parameters as rigidly as possible. As such, there are a few important Canadian children's series that do not have dedicated entries by right of their regional status. As much as I would love to include more detailed histories of series like *The Hilarious House of Frightenstein* (Hamilton); *You Can't Do That on Television!* (Ottawa); *Harrigan* (Kingston); *Big Al's Cartoon Capers and Ranch Party*, *Camp Cariboo*, *Romper Room* (all Kitchener); *The Silver Basketball* (Peterborough); *Let's Go!* (Winnipeg); *Size Small* (Saskatoon); *Harriet's Magic Hats* (Edmonton); *Danger Bay* (Vancouver); and *Chez Hélène* (Montreal), I believe they merit positioning within the context of their own unique localities. That said, there are of course exceptions, like *The Forest Rangers*, which was filmed in rural Ontario locations like Bracebridge, Tottenham, and North Bay, but conceived, written, and edited in Toronto, hence its inclusion here.

I have also chosen to highlight live-action series, as opposed to animated series. Frankly, the history of animation in Toronto — via pioneers like Al Guest and Jean Mathieson, Nelvana, and many others — is another (enormous) volume altogether, and although there is some crossover with live action (Nina Keogh worked on *Rocket Robin Hood*!), for the most part it is self-contained and absolutely worthy of its own dedicated tome. Additionally, I have steered clear of game shows, made-for-TV movies, and short-form interstitials, again, with a few exceptions. Sorry, *Just Like Mom* fans!

The year 2000 seemed appropriate as a cutoff for a few reasons: That was the year in which the Canadian Radio-television and Telecommunications Commission (CRTC) in Ottawa approved licences for 283 new digital television channels. It was a watershed moment; access to hundreds of specialty channels resulted in a decline of the medium's formerly inherent quality — locality. In tandem, the internet went mainstream. No longer an exclusive domain of geeks and hackers, the so-called World Wide Web provided a shiny new content delivery machine to the masses. First in 2000 when "webcasting" became a trend, combining old broadcast principles with new-age web interactivity, and later with social media sites like MySpace and Facebook and finally YouTube in 2005, heralding the age of user-generated content. When first-generation iPhones became available in 2007, television was no longer the most important communications tool; rather, it had become a support organism in a very busy ecosystem.

Although the practice started as far back as the 1970s, by 2000 international co-productions were no longer rare, but rather industry standard, diluting much of television's homespun local character and resulting in a very homogenized product. I am not providing a qualitative judgment on the value of children's television programs that came after the year 2000, but rather an honest observation. Your mileage may vary.

"Kids TV" or "children's television" refers to programs created for young audiences from two to eleven years of age, and teens from twelve to seventeen years of age. You will find variations of "kids," "children," "teens," and "tweens" used throughout, as at various times the definitions shifted among television executives and producers. I have tried to note certain series where a specific age bracket, e.g., eight to twelve, was targeted.

Television in Canada officially began on September 6, 1952, in Montreal at CBFT-TV, a French-language service of Ici Radio-Canada Télé, owned and controlled by the Canadian Broadcasting Corporation (CBC). Two days later it was joined in Toronto by CBLT-TV, CBC's first English-language service. Until 1960, all new privately owned television stations were CBC affiliates. You will find references to "the CBC" throughout, as these made-in-Toronto programs were broadcast to the entire affiliate CBC network across Canada and not made specifically for their Toronto station, CBLT-TV.

Now with all that out of the way, let's change the channel to something much more interesting!

1950s

1

Let's See (1952)/Uncle Chichimus (1953)

IT ALL STARTED WITH A LITTLE GREEN PUPPET.

In 1950, freshly graduated from the University of Toronto, future Academy Award–winning director Norman Jewison took a fateful meeting with Stuart Griffiths about getting a job at Canada's first television network, the Canadian Broadcasting Corporation (CBC). Griffiths was a thirty-one-year-old media visionary who rose through the radio side and was appointed program director of the CBC's first English-language television station, CBLT-TV, located on Jarvis Street in the Church and Wellesley neighbourhood in Toronto, Ontario. Noting Jewison's ambition, Griffiths conceded that the CBC was years away from properly launching a television service. He suggested Jewison go to London, U.K., immediately and get some instruction from the British Broadcasting Corporation (BBC), which had been making television since before the Second World War.

Jewison duly relocated to London and began to absorb all he could about this new medium through fellow Canadian Bernard Braden, who had made it big in London as host of a popular BBC children's show, *Bedtime with Braden* (1950). Braden gave Jewison an opportunity to help write scripts and learn the basics of camera placement. Summoned back to Toronto in 1952 by Griffiths, Jewison was enrolled in a crash course on television production hastily organized by the CBC. CBC's Canadian network broadcasts were provisionally scheduled to begin in September of that year: the French service from Montreal on September 6, 1952, via affiliate CBFT-TV; and the English service from Toronto two days later on September 8, 1952, via CBLT-TV.

The National Broadcasting Company (NBC), the oldest broadcasting network in the U.S., had sent a team to train the first generation of Canadian small-screen directors on how to correctly stage a television production. "The weeks before we went to air were terrifying," Jewison wrote in 2002. "We were crazy with excitement and fear."[1]

Jewison was assigned the role of floor director for CBLT-TV's opening-night broadcast on September 8, 1952. Moments before the signal switch was activated and the English service went live, a technician removed the photo slide of CBLT's station logo, which was positioned in front of a camera, to give it a last-minute wipe down with a cloth. Jewison recalls producer Murray Chercover admonishing the tech and barking at him, "Don't do that!"[2] Unfortunately, the damage was done. When placing the slide back in front of the camera lens, the technician positioned it upside down. The first transmitted image that blazed across Toronto screens was a technical gaffe. "I can't remember what we did, or if we shot the poor guy responsible," recalled Jewison many years later.[3] After quickly cutting away from this error, the very next image viewers saw was that of a grotesque little puppet called Chichimus, operated by John Conway, who welcomed viewers into the wonderful world of local television courtesy of the CBC.

Toronto native Conway had been fascinated by puppets since childhood. After receiving his Master of Arts degree in English from the University of Toronto, Conway became an English professor at the University of British Columbia. His love of puppetry brought him back to Toronto in 1950, where he formed the York Puppet Theatre troupe. While in British Columbia, Conway had created a supporting puppet for his shows named King Chichimus, the Bold. The name came from combining a comic-sounding word "chich" with the Latin "imus," for maximus, "the mostest."[4] In the year leading up to the inaugural broadcast, the CBC had hired Conway and members of the York Puppet Theatre to perform while they ran camera tests — dry runs for the children's programs that might soon be produced in its studios. The puppets gave the production team something to light, stage, and shoot.

As the launch date approached, Griffiths and fellow CBC executive Mavor Moore saw great promise in the puppet character of Chichimus and the

Puppeteer John Conway with his unique creations Uncle Chichimus and Hollyhock.

artistic ambitions of Conway. They developed a short fifteen-minute program based around him that would anchor each nightly broadcast with a comedic preview show. Titled *Let's See*, the show started each night with the caustic Chichimus highlighting that evening's lineup. He was joined by meteorologist Percy Saltzman. The two would chat about current affairs and the day's big events, then Saltzman would provide a local weather forecast. Opening night at CBLT-TV was quite a show. After the logo snafu, Conway's Chichimus act recovered the channel's composure with a humorous sneak peek at all the evening had in store. The first night included a live in-studio performance by pianist Glenn Gould and a sensationalist report by Lorne Greene on the daring escape from Toronto's Don Jail of the notorious bank-robbing Boyd Gang. However, Chichimus had stolen the night's accolades.

Through Chichimus, Conway was satirizing what he called "the old school," Toronto's conservative ruling class. To his mind, Chichimus was "very formal about everything. A scholar of all sorts of antique and arcane lore. That's perhaps where the nostalgia came in. He represented an older generation of Ontario."[5] *Toronto Star* writer Ed Hausmann once described Chichimus as "a balding Canadian curmudgeon."[6]

Chichimus soon became the CBC's first bona fide breakout star. Conway and Saltzman had such great chemistry that their a humorous nightly fifteen-minute-long improv session often overshadowed the more prestigious productions that followed. Chichimus began to receive fan mail, mostly from Toronto-area children. Although considered an adult program that dealt in satire and current events, *Let's See* was adored by kids. It soon became apparent that Chichimus needed his own show. During that first year on-air, the CBC had not yet created a dedicated children's department. Producers Joanne Hughes and Peggy Liptrott had been placed in charge of nurturing a late-afternoon schedule, but there was no real guiding ideology or plan. At the time, producers of children's programs were unburdened by bureaucratic meddling and were free to experiment with their own ideas. This freedom also allowed them to seek out the best performers for future children's content.

Griffiths had noted one of the earliest successful children's series in the U.S. was *Kukla, Fran and Ollie* (1947), which ran on WBKB-TV in Chicago and was later picked up by the NBC in 1949 for wider transmission. The series featured popular radio comedian Fran Allison interacting with a pair of puppets. The show followed the Punch and Judy format, which had been popularized during the Victorian era, although its roots went as far back as seventeenth-century Italy. One person operating two puppets — one male, one female — engaged in slapstick and exaggerated physical comedy, within the confines of a small booth. As Conway worked to expand the Chichimus character and to flesh out the show's concept, he soon realized Chichimus's Punch needed a Judy. Conway created a female puppet to play Chichimus's niece, Hollyhock. That made him an uncle and provided the new show with a title — *Uncle Chichimus.*

Although the show was broadcast in black and white, Conway painted his puppets in extraordinary colours to emphasize their personalities. Chichimus was forest green with sky-blue lines on his face, while Hollyhock was dark yellow. Conway had picked up this technique during his training with Muriel Heddle's Royal Canadian Puppet Ballet.

Initially Ross McLean served as producer on *Uncle Chichimus*, while Norman Campbell took the role of director, followed by Jewison. Seeing as the interplay between the human Saltzman and puppet Chichimus had been received so well on *Let's See*, Jewison suggested Larry Mann be added to the cast. Mann was renowned for his ability to create infinite characters, making him a perfect foil. Jewison later recalled,

> We always managed to put in physical business, which John was very good at because they were hand puppets. They worked with real props. Hollyhock was always making spaghetti, she was always cooking something or knitting or something physical. [Chichimus] was always on the phone and using real props. And Larry Mann was so malleable. I mean, he could do any accent at all. And we used Larry in many different ways. It was really an interesting combination.[7]

Although they were drawing inspiration from the Punch and Judy formula, a conscious decision was made to break the puppets out of the booth — no one else was doing that with puppets on television. "One thing that made *Uncle Chichimus* different from any other puppet show at that time on the air, and they were all very popular in those days, [was that] we took him out of the proscenium."[8] Jewison would stage long and elaborate tracking shots that took the camera down a hallway, through a set of doors, and into a studio set where Chichimus would be playing piano. All done live, with ropes and wires. Although ostensibly a children's program, the mischievous team of Jewison, Campbell, and Conway tried to insert as much subversive content into the show as they could get away with. As Jewison recalled,

> It was wonderful because I found that with puppets we could get away with black satire and double entendres and so on. We could get it past the censors, and we could get away with stuff you

> could never get away with if you had been working on *The Big Revue* (1952). In other words, through the mouths of puppets, we were able to become quite caustic and do political satire and inside stuff. Much like *Kukla, Fran and Ollie* did in Chicago.[9]

One extended storyline saw Chichimus start his own television network — the Chichimus Broadcasting Company (CBC). "We were able to satirize our own network, and there were a few times Ottawa got upset. We got angry memos,"[10] said Jewison.

Although it was superficially a one-note puppet show for kids, Rainsberry held the series in high regard due to its inherently subversive nature:

> Chichimus did many things — he once flew to the moon, he was a detective, he was an actor, hockey coach, and everything else that Conway and Mann could poke fun at. It was a clever and witty show, but it was something more — it was the only properly done show of gentle satire ever aired on Canadian television that reached out and was acclaimed by the public at large.[11]

Disaster struck *Uncle Chichimus* on January 20, 1954, when a briefcase containing both puppets was stolen from Conway's parked car on King Street West. Since the broadcast was live and Conway had no duplicates puppets, Mann was forced to host the show solo on January 21. He pleaded with viewers for any information that might lead to the return of Chichimus and Hollyhock. Indeed, the show and its characters were so beloved by the city that *The Toronto Daily Star* ran a headline on its January 20 cover announcing "Uncle Chichimus, Hollyhock Kidnapped."[12]

While Conway began building new Chichimus and Hollyhock moulds, studio director Frank Fice hatched a brilliant but necessary plan to incorporate the real-life mystery into the show, buying them time. Conway appeared on-air as himself, offering a three-hundred-dollar reward for the safe return of the puppets, while Mann played several roles, including a policeman, a news reporter, and a hard-boiled private investigator. Engaged viewers sent even more cash to the CBC, increasing the reward. When the new puppets were ready, the story concluded with Mann's reporter character being gunned down in a hail of bullets as he was about to reveal the identity of the kidnapper. As the *Toronto Star* later reported,

> It was the only time before or since that any television performers, Canadian or otherwise, ever warranted such headline treatment. No ransom note was every found, nor were the culprits ever apprehended. To this day, the case remains in those dusty files marked "unsolved."[13]

Puppeteer John Conway, Uncle Chichimus, Hollyhock, and Slimey the Frog appear in this promotional card from Ottawa Gas, given out at the Ottawa Exhibition in 1962 or 1963 to promote *Cartoonerville* (1961).

Not long after the kidnapping storyline was resolved in June of 1954, CBC program executives decided to transfer producer McLean over to the more prestigious nightly current events show *Tabloid* (1953), which featured Chichimus's old sparring partner, Saltzman. More troubling, they wanted it to take over *Uncle Chichimus*'s plum 6:30 p.m. time slot. Conway was given the opportunity to carry on the series in a revised format but declined. He was exhausted from two years of daily live television and frustrated with the constant revolving door of production people. Jewison by this point had been promoted to producing the live entertainment series *The Big Revue* and *On Stage* (1954). Conway left the CBC to form his own production company — Chichimus Films, Ltd.

Chichimus was resurrected in 1957 for the short-lived *The Adventures of Chich*, a twenty-six-episode series that Conway produced himself and sold to the CBC. It featured Chichimus interacting with other puppets performing classic fairy tales. The show did not perform well and was not renewed for another season. In 1961, Stuart Griffiths invited Conway to work at CJOH-TV, Ottawa's affiliate to CTV, Canada's first commercial network. Conway appeared on a series called *Cartoonerville* (1961) as both Chichimus and Hollyhock, and a new character called Slimey the Frog where the puppets filled out time between old Betty Boop cartoons. It was an ignominious end to the character who helped launch television in Canada.

Conway left show business and returned to teaching English at various Ottawa-area high schools. Because most of the early *Uncle Chichimus* shows were broadcast live, there is no visual record of many of its pioneering techniques. Respected American puppeteer George Latshaw (who had been a guest on *Uncle Chichimus* in 1953) claimed that much of the radical styles of filming puppets for which Jim Henson would be credited for inventing in the 1960s had actually been done by Conway in the 1950s.[14]

Jewison recalled Conway could at times be difficult to work with:

> John being, at times, schizophrenic, he would really kind of slide into Chich's character. You didn't know who you were talking to. Were you talking to John Conway, or were you talking to Uncle Chichimus? It was very, very strange. I'll never forget. Whenever he got upset, he just said [in the style of nasally Chichimus], "If anybody wants me, I'll be in my room." And that's the way we ended all kinds of shows. Because he used to get furious, very testy. Furious with Larry! With Hollyhock! And everybody. Mad all the time.[15]

Conway later expressed that he shared something in common with his creation:

> I suppose I am like Chichimus in the way that I am something of a scholar myself. You know, I am rather fond of the classics such as Milton and Shakespeare and Wordsworth. [Chichimus was] a bit quixotic, you know. He's tilting at windmills most of the time, but that doesn't matter.[16]

2
Space Command (1953)

CBC'S VERY FIRST ENGLISH IN-HOUSE DRAMATIC SERIES WAS a science-fiction spectacular billed as a "pro-social action show full of tension, drama, and jeopardy." It aired live on CBLT-TV on Friday nights — it was later moved to Saturdays — and was kinescoped so that it could be distributed to other CBC affiliates including CBOT-TV in Ottawa, CFPL-TV in London, and CBMT-TV in Montreal. The kinescoping of live broadcasts involved creating a film print by shooting the screen of a studio monitor. This allowed series to be "bicycled" to other stations for subsequent broadcast. Unfortunately, kinescoping was never intended as a reliable archival practice.

Space Command followed the continuing adventures of the XSW1 spaceship and its crew on their mission to explore the galaxy for extraterrestrial life, while teaching the audience educational material about astronomy, science, and medicine. Although expensive to produce, the series favoured dialogue and informative content over space battles and aliens, and was often criticized for being too talky, although the special effects by John Lowry were noteworthy.

The cast included Harry Geldard as XSW1's Captain Steve Cassel, Robert Barclay as Lieutenant Frank Anderson, and James Doohan as Phil Mitchell. Notable guest stars included Barry Morse, who played Lieutenant Philip Gerard in *The Fugitive* (1963), and William Shatner making his first onscreen appearance with Doohan. The two would later explore the galaxy together again in 1966's much better remembered *Star Trek*. Creator Alfred Harris told the *CBC Times*,

> The series *Space Command* … is designed primarily for the younger members of the TV audience. It will follow closely the known facts and plausible hypotheses. The first few scripts will deal with sunspots and their possible effect on

> space flight and space stations. Later in the series such themes as evolution, space-medicine, the meteorite danger, the origin of the asteroid belt, and many others will be projected into the future and developed.[17]

Space Command ran until 1954, chalking up 150 episodes. Despite being kinescoped, only a single episode of the series is known to exist — sadly for *Trek* fans, not the one with Shatner.

3
Telestory Time (1953)

THE VERY FIRST SERIES DESIGNED FOR A PRESCHOOL AND primary audience was a 15-minute-long show called *Telestory Time*. It featured honey-voiced Pat Patterson reading a story while artist George Feyer sketched scenes, and Doris Ord played the electric organ. The show was created and written by Patterson, host of the CBC Radio show *Pat's Music Room*, and Dorothy "Dodi" Robb, at the time a writer/producer for the MacLaren advertising agency in Toronto. Feyer was a well-known commodity thanks to his work as a cartoonist at *Maclean's* magazine. Patterson and Robb weaved tales for preschoolers, and Robb estimates she wrote over four hundred original stories for the series: "I didn't want to ever write another one about a talking rabbit or rivers again."[18]

Telestory Time was a crucial training ground for many young CBC directors, including Norman Jewison, Henry Kaplan (*Dark Shadows*), Peggy Liptrott (*Polka Dot Door*), and Norman Campbell (*Fraggle Rock*). According to CBC's subsequent head of the children's department, Fred Rainsberry, the format was visually overwhelming for young viewers. The storyteller, artist, and organist all competed for viewer attention, resulting in a televisual cacophony: "These were the early days of television when we had much to learn about mobility of camera and the value of close-ups to strengthen relationships — in this case, between the storyteller and the viewer."[19]

During this primitive era of television production, the floor camera would typically be locked into a medium shot for the duration of a live show. *Telestory Time* also suffered from a bloated budget, owing to the crowded talent pool, and was ultimately withdrawn after two years on the air. The understanding and application of how to produce effective programming within the children's department at the CBC was rapidly evolving by the time Rainsberry arrived in 1954:

> As we learned more about production techniques, we were able to implement our policies about child development and its relationship to the use of television for children. It became a challenge to integrate the native talents of performers, writers, and producers into more effective children's programs.[20]

4

The Howdy Doody Show (1954)

ON MARCH 29, 1954, CBC'S TOP EXECUTIVES STUART Griffiths and Mavor Moore offered Fred Rainsberry the position of Supervising Producer of Children's Television. Rainsberry was tasked with developing the guiding principles that would produce a cohesive lineup of children's television programming. It was a critical role that needed a strong advocator, and

Rainsberry was determined to create programs that were pedagogically robust and that pushed against the continuous pressure to commercialize.

Rainsberry hailed from Enniskillen in southern Ontario and studied English and philosophy at the University of Toronto. He became a schoolteacher, working in Belleville and then in Toronto. He did his postgraduate studies in philosophy at Michigan State University, earning a Ph.D., and later taught at Yale. Rainsberry published several articles that exalted the potential of television in education. He disputed its negative reputation amongst academics and argued passionately against censorship while encouraging parents to watch TV with their children.

Upon taking the role at the CBC, Rainsberry implemented a policy of hiring professional educators for all children's productions:

> At that first meeting with the creative people, I particularly recall insisting, as a good educator should, that professionals have input into program planning. I wanted to draw upon the authority of respected librarians, musicians, and other experts with whom we would be expected to work.[21]

Rainsberry's proposition was critical to the evolution of children's programming at the CBC and beyond. Until the arrival of Rainsberry, employees on the production side tended to come from radio or live theatre. Television had been viewed with great suspicion by many in academia, and even those who saw its potential lacked the connections within the industry that would allow them to influence its development. Thanks to Rainsberry, educators in Canada now had a seat at the table of the nascent medium.

As he began to plot out a schedule that balanced the educational needs of a child with the programs he had available to work with, Rainsberry realized that he had been stuck with a vulgar endeavour the CBC had already committed to produce prior to his arrival: a Canadianized version of *The Howdy Doody Show* (1954) intended to replace the diminishing returns of *Uncle Chichimus* (1953). In the U.S., *The Howdy Doody Show* was created by Victor F. Campbell and E. Roger Muir for the NBC television network in 1947, and, owing to its immense popularity, it had become the template for most children's shows across North America. It starred "Buffalo Bob" Smith, who appeared beside the freckle-faced marionette Howdy Doody (named after the western expression "Howdy Do?"). Both characters originated on the radio, where Smith's bombastic delivery of "Say, kids, what time is it?" became the rallying cry for a generation. The answer? "It's Howdy Doody Time!"

Dr. Frederick Rainsberry, the inaugural head of the CBC children's department, manifested the arrival of quality Canadian children's programming through his insightful hiring of Bob Homme, Fred Rogers, and many others.

The program was deeply rooted in the mythology of the American frontier and the Wild West, with generous helpings of the circus — it was all cowboys and clowns. There was a menagerie of puppets, villains, and human guests who all lived together in Doodyville, an elaborate set located at Rockefeller Center in New York City. It famously housed a studio audience of thirty children on bleachers who became known as "the peanut gallery." (Incidentally, it was that peanut gallery that inspired Charles Schulz to name his Charlie Brown comic strip *Peanuts*.) Howdy Doody characters introduced short, serialized clips from western films, sang songs, and integrated advertising from Kellogg's, Ovaltine, Colgate, and Macy's department store into each day's raucous live show.

Rainsberry was horrified by the series' blatant commercialism, wanton use of weaponry, and dependence on violent western films. Mercifully, the CBC deal with NBC allowed modifications to be made to the format. The purchase of a series name and basic elements was rare then but has since become common in the industry and is known today as "formatting." Mostly applied to reality and game shows, formatting occurs when a series' basic

An original toy doll of Howdy Doody, who remained the same in the Canadianized version of *The Howdy Doody Show*. Howdy would go on to inspire the character of Woody in Pixar's enormously popular *Toy Story* series.

concept or skeleton is sold from its country of origin to another, where it can be augmented with local cultural references and locations. Usually, but not always, the title is kept, as in *The Amazing Race* (U.S., 2001), *Big Brother* (Netherlands, 1999), and *The Office* (U.K., 2001). The Canadianized *Howdy Doody Show* was given a top-down overhaul that changed its central theme from the Wild West to the Great White North, eschewing cowboys, horses, and six-shooters for coonskins, beavers, and canoes. Buffalo Bob became Timber Tom, and the whole bang-bang anarchic Americana vibe was dialled back to a much cooler, calmer Canadiana.

Doodyville was rebuilt to spec in CBLT-TV's Toronto studio with its own peanut gallery. Select characters from the U.S. version were retained, including the central character of Howdy Doody, the no-good Phineas T. Bluster, Clarabell the miming clown, and Cap'n Scuttlebutt (although in the Canadian version he was cast as a live actor instead of a puppet). New puppet characters included a parrot named Percival and Haida, princess of the forest. All cowboys were scrapped, and forest rangers took their place. *Space Command*'s James Doohan was first offered the lead role of Timber Tom but declined due to the show's daily commitment and lower-than-scale salary. Peter Mews accepted, but he wasn't available for the first few weeks of shooting. William Shatner was cast as Ranger

Bob to fill in until Mews was ready. During production, if Mews fell ill or was absent, Robert Goulet appeared as charming French Canadian "Trapper Pierre."

Uncle Chichimus director Frank Fice and writer Cliff Braggins were ported over to *The Howdy Doody Show*, and joined by writer John Gerrard, who is credited by Rainsberry as being the show's greatest attribute and who went on to write *Whistle Town* (1958) and create CFTO's *The Professor's Hideaway* (1961). Alfie Scopp was cast as sensitive Clarabell the clown, while Uncle Chichimus's old partner in rhyme, Larry Mann, was the pirate-attired buffoon Cap'n Scuttlebutt. Husband and wife puppeteering team Hal and Renée Marquette were put in charge of creating and operating all the series' puppets, while Jackie White voiced Howdy Doody. Quentin Maclean provided a non-stop musical score as the show's resident organist.

The shoot-'em-up western serials were removed entirely, replaced by serene silent films of nature, historical re-creations, or travelogues that Timber Tom or other characters narrated by answering questions yelled out by kids in the peanut gallery. As the series progressed, characters were connected with certain genres. So, for example, if films about Indigenous culture were shown, they were presented by Princess Haida. Mr. X was another new puppet, created solely to present films about history. He was a mysterious old man cloaked in black, a time traveller who explored the past in his spaceship, the Whatsis Box. The character was cut as he was considered too frightening. But evidently Toronto-born CBC producer Sydney Newman felt there was much more mileage in the Mr. X concept. In 1963, when he was hired by the BBC to rebuild their Saturday night family schedule, Newman pitched them an educational science-fiction series about an old man who travels through time in a police box. He called it "Dr. X," which was later changed to *Doctor Who* and became a wildly popular series that is still in production today. During his lifetime Newman never mentioned the show's obvious debt to *The Howdy Doody Show*'s Mr. X. It's possible that he unconsciously recalled Mr. X's conceptual framework when devising his own.

The Canadian version of *The Howdy Doody Show* ran successfully for five years, until 1958 when it was cut back to three days per week (Monday, Wednesday, and Friday) and a potential replacement series — *Whistle Town* — was tested alternately on Tuesday and Thursday. *Whistle Town* was created by

Howdy Doody writers Braggins and Gerrard and contained a novel gimmick: Its primary setting oscillated between the town's toy shop (Tuesdays) and fire station (Thursdays). Rex Hagon (*The Forest Rangers*) appeared as Danny, and Larry Beattie as the toy shop owner, Mr. Bean. John and Linda Keogh created the requisite puppets, including Danny's best friend Foster. *Whistle Town* did not find a mass audience, and both it and *The Howdy Doody Show* were retired from the CBC schedule in June of 1959.

Ruminating on the success of the Canadian *Howdy Doody Show* many years later, Rainsberry observed,

> At this early stage in the development of children's television, the Children's Television Department had already learned that programs need not be pleasing to an adult in order to be entertaining and instructive for a child. If such simple devices as repetition and action have a fundamental appeal for children, may not those same principles be employed in the communication of educational elements in every other kind of program?[22]

5
Hidden Pages (1955)

HIDDEN PAGES WAS A DAILY FIFTEEN-MINUTE LOOK AT BOOKS hosted and created by actor and librarian Beth Gillanders. The program softly persuaded children to read books and visit their local libraries and was similar in style to the popular CBC Radio show *Cuckoo Clock House* (1949).

Each episode of *Hidden Pages* focused on a specific literary theme, using readings and sometimes dramatizations. The first ten minutes were devoted to preschoolers, then Gillanders underwent a costume change before she presented to six-to-eight-year-olds for the final five.

An early concern about television's effect on children was that watching time would replace reading time, causing reading levels to fall. Rainsberry had made it clear that CBC's output would relate to children's in-class experience:

> At the outset, being an educator, I was anxious to ensure that viewing for children out of school hours would not be inconsistent with the creative learning experience which they should be having in school.[23]

The popularity of books featured on *Hidden Pages* showed that television programming could help foster an interest in reading. For Rainsberry, this was a great relief:

> It became clear, within a very short time, that the stimulus of television caused a run on the books at the library. In many cases, the librarians were unable to meet the demands of the children to read the books shown on *Hidden Pages* for several weeks after the program had been seen."[24]

Hidden Pages was originally produced at CBC's Toronto studios at CBLT-TV. In 1957, it relocated to the network's Vancouver studios at CBUT-TV and expanded to a half-hour daily format, continuing until the end of the 1950s.

6

Old Testament Tales (1957)

HUSBAND AND WIFE TEAM VIOLET AND DAVID KEOGH BOLDLY experimented with the art of puppetry as far back as 1925, and by 1928 had established Kay Marionettes, the largest puppet company in Canada. Violet would construct and dress the marionettes and puppets, as well as operate them alongside David, who also provided technical direction. The Keoghs successfully toured Canada and the United States until the start of the Second World War, after which time they formed a new company, Canadian Puppeteers.

Not long after starting at the CBC in 1954, Rainsberry attended an exhibition of Violet Keogh's marionettes held at Simpsons department store in downtown Toronto. Astonished by the beauty and grace of the marionettes, he offered Keogh a job creating puppets for the CBC. A new children's series was in development based on stories from the Old Testament, and the Keoghs' marionettes would be perfect Biblical avatars. The series was to be aired live on Sunday mornings but, as Rainsberry recalled, the production was thrust into chaos due to the frightening design of the marionettes, many of which were unfinished:

> It was a near disaster. [Director] Basil Coleman had been a theatre director, very talented. I remember arriving at the studio and discovering the power of these voices behind these puppets. He'd gotten all the great actors and so on. And I thought, my word, the switch board is going to light up. The children will be terrified. The producer was going out of his mind because nothing was ever ready.[25]

Violet enlisted her son John Keogh to help. Rainsberry later recalled, "[John] said, don't worry, I will take over. And he was there ever after. A very flexible and immensely charming guy."[26] John and his wife, Linda, had apprenticed with John's parents, Violet and David, as well as Muriel Heddle, an American puppeteer who specialized in marionettes and their complex choreography. Heddle had joined Violet and David to form the Kay-Heddle Marionettes company in 1936, performing with the Toronto Symphony Orchestra at Massey Hall, the Toronto Art Gallery, and the Canadian National Exhibition in the late 1930s. Heddle had also trained Chichimus and Hollyhock's puppeteer, John Conway, when he attended the Royal Canadian Puppet Ballet. John and Linda had also studied traditional ballet, while Linda had danced with the Volkoff Ballet.

Old Testament Tales eventually made it to air in 1957, by which point John and Linda had become fixtures within the CBC's children's department through their involvement with the production of *Maggie Muggins* (1955). *CBC Times* featured *Old Testament Tales* in their February 24 edition, writing that

> very few 15-minute television shows require over 12 hours of rehearsal time, but John and Linda Keogh believe that practice makes perfect. Not that they have achieved perfection, but the fact is that their program *Old Testament Tales* has received praise from various religious and secular organizations. So much rehearsal time is necessary, because all the characters are puppets, which the Keoghs and John Botterel manipulate. Not only is *Old Testament Tales* the first live Canadian religious TV series for children, but it is believed to be the only one of its kind in the world. The Keoghs who live at Brooklin, Ontario (40 miles east of Toronto), spend much of their time making the puppets for future episodes. Rarely do they use the same puppet twice, and they are sometimes working on three different sets at once.[27]

7
Maggie Muggins (1955)

MARY GRANNAN, A FORMER TEACHER TURNED PROLIFIC radio host, blazed a broadcasting trail when she began working at radio station CFNB in Fredericton in 1936, writing and reading children's stories under the title of *Just Mary*, the very first narrative radio program for children. Based on the strength of the program, CBC Radio offered Grannan a job at CBC Radio headquarters in Toronto, where she relocated in 1937. In addition to *Just Mary*, Grannan also developed another children's radio series, *The Children's Scrapbook*, and by 1941 was adapting many of her *Just Mary* stories into book format, laying a foundation for Canadian children's literature.

In 1944, Canadian publisher Thomas Allen & Son Ltd. released *Maggie Muggins*, a compilation of Grannan's stories featuring the titular Maggie that had appeared on *Just Mary*. The popularity of the Muggins character led to further stories, and an inevitable radio adaptation thrilled young listeners in the 1940s. Before television in Canada had launched, Grannan had been identified as an obvious source of children's content. As it turned out, she had an aversion to being filmed by a television camera, preferring the anonymity of the radio booth. Grannan did, however, grant the CBC use of her Muggins characters, and provided her full blessing for a television adaptation that she would not appear in.

Maggie Muggins chronicled the dreamlike exploits of the pigtailed, freckle-faced Maggie, who began (and ended) each episode interacting in the real world with her neighbour Mr. McGarrity before disappearing into a fantasyland where she communed with talking animals like Grandmother Frog and Fitzgerald Fieldmouse.

The format was straightforward, and young gun directors Michael Spivak and Norman Jewison jumped at the opportunity to work on a show with so much potential. It allowed them to experiment and try new styles of camerawork, as Spivak explained:

Linda and John Keogh operating animal friends of Maggie Muggins during production of the series.

> What bothered me a lot when I saw that show was that … there was a set which Maggie always approached with camera directed towards the puppets and Maggie's back. She'd always have to cheat. Consequently, every sentence she'd have to say half of it to Fitzgerald Fieldmouse and then turn to address the audience, which meant that the audience felt patronized. The only way to solve this problem physically was to have Maggie behind the puppets. It didn't matter much if the puppets had to turn as long as Maggie always had her face to the camera.… [There was] a treehouse, and so they designed the set with a big knothole in the tree. The look of the show changed from then on and you had a much greater chance to integrate the action because the puppets could go straight up to her face presenting the audience with a continuing uninterrupted relationship.[28]

For their first fully fledged series with the CBC, John and Linda Keogh (see p. 31) built and operated the fantastical animals encountered by Maggie including Reuben Rabbit, Big Bite Beaver, Chester Pig, Greta Grub, Benny

Bear, Leo Lion, Henrietta Hen, and Fluffy Squirrel. Voices for the animals were provided by Linda Keogh, Pegi Loder, and Norma Macmillan, who played Fitzgerald Fieldmouse.

Beth Morris was the first Maggie Muggins in 1955 but was replaced the following year by Deanne Taylor. Mary Long played Maggie from 1959 until the series ended in 1962. Mr. McGarrity was played by three different actors: John Drainie from 1955 to 1956, Frank Peddie from 1956 to 1959, and Doug Master from 1959 to 1962.

8

Mr. O (1956)

THE NEXT PROJECT AT THE CBC FOR PUPPETEERS JOHN AND Linda Keogh was *Mr. O*, a live fifteen-minute series about classical music hosted by David Ouchterlony and soprano Manley Stark, who were joined by puppet personifications of instruments such as Chelly the Cello and Clarence the Clarinet. The puppets were voiced by Len Davidson and Pegi Loder. The majestic imagination and stamina of the Keoghs was truly something to behold; *Puppetry in Canada* described them as "perhaps the busiest puppeteers on Canadian television screens during these years."[29]

9
Junior Magazine (1955)

SINCE THE VERY BEGINNING OF THE CBC'S BROADCASTS IN 1952, short, independently produced educational films had been a bedrock in the children's television schedules. These shorts came from industrial outfits like Crawley Films in Canada, the Central Office of Information (COI) in the United Kingdom, or Encyclopedia Britannica Films and Coronet Films in the United States. Some were silent while others had sound, and they ran anywhere from two to ten minutes long. They covered a wide range of topics, from travelogues to science lessons to traffic safety. Most, if not all, had been created to be shown on 16mm film projectors in schools. Ralph C. Ellis, a Nova Scotian known as the travelling evangelist for the National Film Board of Canada, became the main source of these films for the CBC children's department.

In the early days the shorts tended to litter the schedule as interstitials between programs, with little or no continuity or framing. That changed upon Rainsberry's arrival at CBC, as the films were built into the flow of *The Howdy Doody Show* where the characters discussed them and provided some context. Rainsberry reasoned these films were rendered meaningless when shown without any kind of framework:

> We discovered that the best way to hold a children's audience in a meaningful way was to schedule a daily magazine, or a special magazine such as *Junior Magazine* on Sundays, into which various elements, which formerly constituted independent programs, could now be integrated. Shows like *The Howdy Doody Show*, *Razzle Dazzle*, and *Junior Magazine* all represented a kind of community of young people who

> were friends of the viewers. In many ways, the viewers felt themselves to be part of the community. They shared information presented by role models who would be attractive to them, young people who were meaningful to them as peers.[30]

In 1955, a new program titled *World Passport* was created specifically to screen short educational films. David Clee, an educational specialist, provided context and continuity. It was during the creation of this series that Rainsberry first worked with CBC researchers Peggy Liptrott and Joanne Hughes. They had been among the first to recognize the importance of linking film sequences to broader themes and subjects, rather than using the films simply as filler. This format was further developed in a follow-up program called *Children's Magazine*, which was scheduled to air on Sundays in the early evening. Soon after its release, it was renamed *Junior Magazine*. It provided high-quality and intelligent programming that treated children as bright and curious, and didn't condescend.

Each week, *Junior Magazine* hosts would introduce a variety of films covering an eclectic mix of subjects but focused mainly on travel and family life in different countries. As the series evolved, it began to produce its own short features, eventually adding correspondents from various regions of Canada. The hosts included Ross Snetsinger, Doug Maxwell, Hank Hedges, and John Clark. Snetsinger and Hedges were schoolteachers, while Maxwell was a sports commentator. Clark had recently arrived from the U.K., where he had been a radio personality and star of *Just William* (1946). Over the course of the series the hosts rotated and were sometimes joined by a no-nonsense young journalist named Patrick Watson, an emerging CBC star who Rainsberry had known since his teaching days and who would contribute greatly to the evolution of the CBC. Watson became the co-host of CBC's seminal current-affairs program *This Hour Has Seven Days* (1964), which he would later produce and direct, and in 1991 he would create the popular *Heritage Minutes*, shorts on important Canadians and moments in history, which ran on-air as interstitials between programs.

By 1956, *Junior Magazine* had become a staging ground from which Rainsberry and the CBC children's department could discover new personalities, concepts, and talent. Segments could be tested and serve as soft pilots to gauge the interest of young viewers and the practicality of undertaking a particular production. In 1957, the mellow and understated Friendly Giant, played by American Bob Homme, appeared as a guest on *Junior Magazine*. Impressed with the pilot and Homme's gentle approach to communicating with children, Rainsberry enticed Homme to Toronto and signed *The Friendly Giant* (1958) as a CBC series immediately. The series kept going for four decades, running until 1985.

Rainsberry and the staff on *Junior Magazine* made another major discovery when they invited American puppeteer Fred Rogers to appear on the show. No one could have fathomed how influential Rogers would become and the massive success he would find with PBS's *Mister Rogers' Neighborhood*. Rainsberry noted Rogers's potential after his appearance on *Junior Magazine* and made a point of staying in touch. He did successfully woo him to the CBC for a time (see p. 72).

In 1955, *Junior Magazine* was chosen by the Walt Disney Corporation to be the sole Canadian outlet for its children's films. Beginning with a serialization of *Treasure Island* and then *Long John Silver*, the partnership marked the beginning of a decades-long mutually beneficial relationship between the organizations (and a lucrative one for the CBC) that continues to this day.

In 1959, new segments were added to *Junior Magazine*, including a panel game and a talent showcase called "This Is Young Canada." Music appreciation was also a recurring theme, with special commentary from choir conductor and educator Leslie Bell. In late 1960 and early 1961, a six-part series hosted by National Film Board composer Louis Applebaum featured young Canadian musicians performing with symphony orchestras, including the Toronto Symphony Orchestra.

In late 1962, the time felt right to mature the format of *Junior Magazine* to better reflect the changing, somewhat turbulent times. Many of the film series and shorts had already been moved to *Razzle Dazzle* (1961). In 1964, the show was retitled *Time of Your Life* (see p. 86), completely overhauled with new, more topical content, and aged up to appeal to young teenagers.

10
The Friendly Giant (1958)

IN A CASTLE UPON A HILL NEXT TO A DISTANT VILLAGE, A giant named Friendly is joined by his special friends Rusty, a musical rooster, and Jerome, a dry-witted giraffe, as they tell stories, play music, and enjoy each other's company. A brief, fifteen-minute reprieve from the fast pace of life, the Friendly Giant's soft tones served Canadian children and their parents for decades and laid down a blueprint for Fred Rainsberry's vision of what the CBC children's department could achieve with the right balance of personality, chemistry, and imagination.

In 1953, Robert "Bob" Homme was working at the radio station of the University of Wisconsin, WHA-AM 970. He was a jack of all trades, newscasting, reporting on weather, and hosting a variety of music shows while dodging requests to host a Saturday-morning children's program, as Homme explained in 1982:

> It was always a chore for the program director to find someone to do the kids' show on Saturday morning. And everyone was asked, and everyone tried to get out of it, including me. And I did get out of it. And then one day my wife had a baby. And I found that within about three weeks I was a qualified expert on the subject of children. I had a terrific interest in kids. And the next time he asked me to do the kids' show, I jumped at the chance, and I did it. It was a very quiet show, conversational approach. Informal poetry and stories and music, recorded music.... The usual fare for kids at that time was up and out, pretty exciting and loud, in a sense, presuming a large audience of which each listener was a small part. But I approached it as though there was just one listener.[31]

Homme and his wife regularly drove to Chicago on Sundays to watch live studio recordings of *The Dave Garroway Show* (1953). They marvelled at the imagination that went into the television program's production. During the long drives, Homme mused about creating a television series for children unlike anything else at the time. WHA had informed him that a television licence was forthcoming, and that he should begin planning what a Bob Homme show might look like. One day, Homme imagined himself standing over a miniature village, like a giant. At the time, there were no giants on television (the first of many hooks for the show). Giants scared children, or so the standard thinking ran, thanks to frightening characters like the giant in "Jack and the Beanstalk." Homme imagined his giant being gentle and softly spoken. The title came from his wife, Esther, who suggested that to counter children's ingrained fears, his giant should be friendly.

"Look up, waaaaaay up." Bob Homme as the Friendly Giant, who towered over fifteen minutes of pure televisual serenity every morning on CBC for twenty-seven years.

The setting was another novel hook. Thanks to the popularity of *The Howdy Doody Show*, most children's productions involved a raucous live studio audience of kids — the louder, the better. Homme favoured a far quieter setting. "Bob visualized the intimacy of a family room. Here, there would be no crowds."[32] He chose to set the show in a medieval castle on a hilltop overlooking a village.

Rather than roll a stock opening, Homme favoured shooting the credits live every day, with slight variations but firmly rooted in ritual: first, a welcoming message overtop a slow pan across the miniature community; then, the giant's boot, accompanied by his signature "Look up, waaaay up," followed by a reveal of Friendly's face and an invitation to join him in the castle through the descending bridge. Finally, a request to take a seat and relax:

> The ritual [is] involved in the opening, "Once upon a time, not long ago, not far away," and then it varies from that point on. And then when we enter the castle — "here's one little chair for one of you," "a bigger chair for two more to curl up in," "a rocking chair for someone who likes to rock" … We keep these little rituals to have both the old and the new together.[33]

Homme selected the eighteenth-century English folk song "Early One Morning" as his theme music, and it too was performed live on harp and recorder slightly differently for each show. There was another ritual for the show's closing: a farewell from Friendly, a reprise of "Early One Morning," the raising of the drawbridge, and a cow jumping over the moon.

Homme had hoped to be joined by a giraffe puppet named Jerome. Unfortunately, a flood in the studio destroyed the puppet shortly before filming began, and Homme substituted a replacement based on his son Richard's rooster, Rusty. When Jerome was rebuilt, Homme decided to keep them both. The puppets were built by Dick Bolden, who also voiced Rusty. WHA-AM sports announcer and musician Ken Ohst provided the voice of Jerome. Ohst and Homme had co-hosted a comedy show on WHA where their chemistry and comic timing were legendary. The two shared a similar sense of humour and had been called Wisconsin's answer to Spike Milligan and Peter Sellers from BBC Radio's *The Goon Show* (1951). The use of puppets was crucial to Homme's vision of the show:

> A puppet is a surrogate, usually for children. We think of Jerome and Rusty as being young. In other words, I'm a normal adult. I don't want to pretend that I'm utterly fascinated by playing hide and seek or find the symbol or something.

> So, I must have someone who does enjoy that at the same level that a child does. And then I will relate to the puppets in the way that I will relate to that child. When I see a program in which the adults are pretending to thoroughly enjoy children's games in the way children do, I'm turned off by that. I think it's dishonest, and a kind of dishonesty that's also useless. I don't think it gets them what they think it's getting them.[34]

As with the earlier radio work, Homme believed simplicity was the key to engaging children. He read them stories and played music, because he strongly believed that kids enjoyed listening. To do otherwise would be patronizing, was Homme's thinking. He did not speak at them but rather spoke *with* them as equals, as friends.

Beginning in 1953, *The Friendly Giant* received a boon in transmission when it was picked up by the Educational Television and Radio Center (ETRC), a broadcasting network owned by the Ford Foundation that aired shows across the U.S. (which later became National Educational Television [NET] and was then succeeded by PBS). These broadcasts soon got the attention of Fred Rainsberry at the CBC, who invited Homme to visit Toronto for an appearance as Friendly on *Junior Magazine*. The two had met at the National Association of Educational Broadcasters (NAEB) conference in Connecticut. Rainsberry was enchanted by Homme's persona and wanted to see how his program would translate by giving Friendly a spot on *Junior Magazine* in 1957. Upon seeing him perform live in the Toronto studios, Rainsberry offered Homme a deal to produce thirty-nine episodes exclusively for the CBC. A shrewd businessman and towering negotiator, Homme countered, asking for a thirteen-week contract with an option for twenty-nine more, to which Rainsberry agreed.

Conceptually, *The Friendly Giant* was ideal to serve as a flagship for the fledgling CBC children's department. "He personified our policy and philosophy of children's programming,"[35] Rainsberry told Homme's biographer Grant D. Fairley.

> Philosophically, the program understood the relationship of play to creative endeavour. [Friendly] used visuals to create and invite the responses of children. This was key. Part of the underlying respect that the Giant had with the audience was that he invited their response. This meant that the children were not docile but engaged by the program.[36]

The show was literally transported from the WHA-TV studios in Madison, Wisconsin, to the CBLT-TV studio in Toronto. Homme drove across the border, bringing the castle, the miniature sets, and the puppets in his car. Rainsberry and Homme were in agreement — nothing integral was to be altered. However, Bolden and Ohst, Rusty's and Jerome's voice actors, elected to stay in the United States.

The first producer at the CBC assigned to *The Friendly Giant* was Michael Spivak (*Maggie Muggins*). After auditioning talent from radio and television with children's experience, Spivak selected Joe Murphy to voice and operate Rusty and Jerome. Unfortunately, Murphy was not a natural improviser and read directly from the script, which made the production feel stilted. So much of the magic in the WHA-TV version had come from Homme and Ohst's natural banter. Rod Coneybeare, co-host of CBC Radio's popular children's production *The Rod and Charles Show*, auditioned, although he confessed to being an ineffectual puppeteer, as he later recalled:

> Somebody said to me, "Hey, Rod, I guess you auditioned for Jerome the giraffe, did you?" I said, "What's Jerome the giraffe?" He says, "Well, you know, it's a kid show, this guy from the States, and he's a friendly giant." I said, "Oh, I don't know about that."
>
> I remember the audition because I went up and met this affable fellow that I'd never seen before. And I thought, "Well, this is yet another CBC producer, and he's in an office." And he [Bob Homme] says, "Listen, we got this little puppet here." And he hauls out this giraffe with this long foam rubber neck,

> this silly looking thing. And he says, "Could you put that on your arm and move? You see this little trigger inside there and see if you can make the lips move and talk at the same time?" And I thought, "What is this? I want to get out of here." … First of all it seems so stupid, you know, two grown men in an office. But then I also thought, *I don't know whether I could do it*. I put the thing on and I moved it and I thought, *wait a minute, now I have to speak*. The mouth has to open. I thought, *This is impossible. I can't do this.* And he said, "Could you just try to say anything?" I said, "What kind of voice do you want?" He says, well, "It's kind of like a Jimmy Stewart voice.… It's like your own voice, only just broaden it a bit." Oh, God. And so I looked at it and I made a decision. I said [to myself], *I'm not going to do this*. I knew I wasn't going to get it.… I said, "Look, there's no sense in my doing this here." He says, "Well, why not?" I said, "If I'm doing it, he's on-camera, right?" He told me it was through a window. I said, "I'm not seeing the puppet physically in the setup in the studio." He says, "No, that's true." I said, "I'm looking at a monitor, right?" He says, "Yeah." I said, "Well, it's a totally different thing. It's going to be the right and left. It's going to be reversed." I made up this wonderful story, which sounded like my technical acumen but I was really getting out of it, saving face because I didn't think I could do it. And he said, "Well, you know, nobody's ever come up with that before. That's a good point. Well, gee, thanks for coming in anyhow." So I left. I thought, *Well, that's over.*[37]

Coneybeare got the part. Homme had found his kindred spirit in Coneybeare, who played both Rusty and Jerome. A master of ad lib, Coneybeare could keep up with Homme, and the two were able to riff endlessly. Their conversations felt sincere and were barely scripted. Coneybeare also appreciated the perks of working on a kids' show:

> A kids' show is liable to stay on longer than an adult show. It seemed to us actors, anyhow, [that] the heat wasn't on them, the publicity wasn't so much trained on them, and the brass weren't all that needing to fiddle around with kids' shows. So, we felt that if you get a kids' show, stay on for a while, that's steady bread, you know, you might even get twenty-six weeks. The actor's life is very precarious. And to get thirteen weeks guaranteed in those days, maybe $100 a week or something, if you were lucky, that was really a big deal. Everybody wanted such a job.[38]

Describing their working relationship, Homme said,

> Instead of a nineteen-page script, I prepare a one-page outline, and [Coneybeare] underlines the salient features and pins it up. And we understand each other so well that if a subject is to come up, it doesn't make much difference … who brings it up, whether I ask a question, he answers it, or he has a question, and I answer.[39]

As with the WHA-TV series, the appreciation of books and music provided a perfect forum for Friendly's approach. Concert day was a popular segment presented in the castle's music room on Tuesdays and Thursdays. Friendly would be joined for a live musical session accompanied by the show's resident harpist, John Duncan, and with puppets created and operated by John and Linda Keogh, including the Jazz Cats Fiddle and Angie on harp and double bass, and raccoons Polly and Patty Piper on woodwinds.

CBC's many live television music shows gave Homme access to first-class guest performers including vibraphonist Peter Appleyard, pianist Hagood Hardy, guitarist Bobby Edwards, jazz maestro Moe Koffman, and violinist Bill Richards. The show presented styles as diverse as folk, baroque, Broadway, ancient ballads, and, of course Homme's favourite, jazz:

> We're not concerned with what children like. We're concerned with what they might like. And we want them to like a variety of music and not grow up thinking, *this is my kind of music*. And that other stuff is for someone else. So, we play baroque music. We play music [that] dates back to the twelfth century. Commonly, frequently. We also play folk music of all kinds. And we play very modern music, contemporary music that's written for us. Ah, they're quite, you might say, difficult. And we play pop tunes. We play tunes that the parents will enjoy and try to do it in good taste so that the children, seeing the parents enjoy it, will enjoy it too. And that's a good experience for everyone at any rate.... If you took any part of it, any one little piece and lifted it out of our program and played it in a test to see if this is what kids like? They wouldn't listen to it, much of it. It would turn them off. They wouldn't know what it was doing. But we present it in such a way that, if they like us, they'll like what we like. They can see that we like it and they will accept it, and then they will listen to it and hear it. And if we've done our job, there will be something there for them to enjoy.[40]

John and Linda Keogh's daughter, Nina, apprenticed with them on *The Friendly Giant* from the age of eleven and took over when they retired in 1968. Later, she helped recruit other young puppeteers to perform on the show, including Nikki Tilroe and Karen Valleau. Buster, a rooster with an electric guitar, was operated by Gustáv Hársfai.

Books were featured on the show on Mondays, Wednesdays, and Fridays. The first book Homme read on-air was *Goodnight Moon* by Margaret Wise Brown, a universally acclaimed bedtime story, which has sold upwards of 48 million copies since its publication in 1947. Books were often reread, and Homme felt it important to show that the books were creased and dog-eared, visually communicating they had been read many times. Doug Davidson, *The Friendly Giant*'s producer in 1966, explained why the program's structure was so important:

Nina Keogh, daughter of Linda and John Keogh, operates one of the Jazz Cats. Nina took over from her parents on *The Friendly Giant* when they retired.

> It's not just the easy-going mood. It's the uncluttered, unchanging format. Children know just what to expect and love what is simple and familiar.... We give them just one thing — a story. The conversations and the music all centre around the story. No other children's program has this kind of unity.[41]

Summing up what was most important about the show, Homme told the *Montreal Gazette*:

> It is a total fifteen-minute experience. If the show has any special aim, it's to convey the idea that knowing about music, the outdoors, foreign countries, animals, paintings, books, is a good way to be, that it's fun.[42]

In November of 1966 Homme became incensed when *The Toronto Telegram*'s "Tely's Christmas Fairyland," held on the grounds of the Canadian

National Exhibition, hired someone to appear as "Tely's Friendly Giant," publicizing it in schools across Toronto and across the city's transit network. When Homme reached out to *Telegram* publisher John Bassett, Jr., he feigned ignorance, stating he had never heard of *The Friendly Giant* television series. Homme had long resisted appearing in parades or public events, believing it would destroy the illusion of the giant and the trust he had worked so hard to build with his young audience. Homme did, however, let Friendly provide commentary live from the castle (along with Coneybeare) during CBC broadcasts of the Toronto Santa Claus Parade.

Bob Homme's appreciation of all kinds of music helped inform *The Friendly Giant*, where he hoped exposure to different genres would enrich young viewers' musical tastes.

The Friendly Giant premiered on September 30, 1958, and ran uninterrupted on the CBC for twenty-six years, changing very little from its first episode until its last, barring the switch from black and white to colour in the fall of 1966. Shortly before his passing in 2000, Homme said,

> The program was paced slowly to help build children's attention spans. I was just doing on the show what I did with my own youngsters — talking to them as adults. Our manner was our message. The characters were considerate; they appreciated each other.[43]

11

Tales of the Riverbank (1959)

IN 1958, THE CBC AIRED A CHILDREN'S SERIES BASED UPON the poems of Jean de La Fontaine entitled *Fables of La Fontaine*, produced by French filmmaker Marc Gaudart. Each episode ran for fifteen minutes and employed the talents of real animals, sourced from a farm in Mount Albert, Ontario, including cats, pigeons, pigs, turtles, and horses. Predictably, the animals ran wild on the set, forcing series cinematographer Fritz Spiess to double as a wrangler, attempting (mostly unsuccessfully) to corral them while production delays piled up. Spiess told *CBC Times* he spent

> hours studying each of the animals used in the series to get to know the different problems posed by each — such as a mouse who refused to ride in canoes, a bored monkey who was fascinated by studio wires and rafters, and a rabbit who became so fond of sitting in a jeep that he refused to get out and race with a turtle.[44]

Editors Paul Sutherland and U.K. expat Dave Ellison were also working on the series and wondered if a similar live-action show could be built around more manageable talent. The two began to work on an outline for a children's animal show that starred small rodents. Taking inspiration from the CBC's popular *The Friendly Giant*, they envisioned these animals living in a community of miniature houses and shops, getting around in little cars and boats, and even exploring the depths in a to-scale diving bell. After purchasing a charismatic hamster at Eaton's department store in downtown Toronto, they constructed a miniature set in a rented Etobicoke garage and shot a pilot film entitled *Tales of the Riverbank*, featuring Sutherland as the narrator and voice of Hammy

Hamster. With additional funding from producer Ray Billings, Sutherland and Ellison populated the riverbank with a coterie of rodents including Martha Mouse, Roderick "Roddy" Rat, a guinea pig called G.P., and a turtle named Turtle. Sutherland composed and performed the gentle guitar score.

The pilot of *Tales of the Riverbank* was pitched internally to Fred Rainsberry, who turned it down. He felt children would not accept the fantastical notion of talking animals; *Fables of La Fontaine* had featured a narrator and the animals had remained mute. Undeterred, the pair used Ellison's British contacts and managed to secure a pitch meeting with the BBC in London. The BBC immediately seized on the series's potential. They acquired *Tales of the Riverbank* and bankrolled the high-concept show for an initial order of thirteen episodes with one caveat — Sutherland's decidedly Canadian voice-overs had to go. Popular British children's entertainer Johnny Morris supplied the rodents' voices and additional scripts were adapted by eminent BBC scribe Peggy Miller, who dubbed and narrated European fare such as *The Singing Ringing Tree* (Germany, 1957) and *Belle and Sebastian* (France, 1965).

Ultimately the BBC filmed fifty-two episodes of *Tales of the Riverbank*, running at fifteen minutes per episode and taking two years to produce, double the time a typical children's series should take to complete. They were mostly created in studio with location filming taking place at Wootton Creek on the Isle of Wight. Each episode ended with the narrator saying, famously, "But that is another story."

Tales of the Riverbank became a massive success in the U.K. and was sold back to the CBC in 1961, which, presumably, had accepted that children *do* respond to talking animals. Owing to its shorter running time, *Tales of the Riverbank* often appeared as a film segment within the daily programs such as *Razzle Dazzle*, although it also had a dedicated spot in the Sunday schedule. When CTV debuted in 1960, they outbid the CBC for exclusive rights to *Tales of the Riverbank*, and it appeared on CTV's daily children's offerings *The Professor's Hideaway* and *The Uncle Bobby Show*. Hammy even managed to win the top children's entertainment prize at the Genie Awards in 1963.

In the 1970s, a further series of twenty-six episodes running at thirty minutes each was co-produced in colour by Astral and the newly established

A behind-the-scenes look at shooting the miniature world of *Tales of the Riverbank* (1959).

Global Television Network in Toronto and the ITV network in the U.K., as the BBC had introduced a short-lived policy of not using humans to voice animals. Now titled *Hammy Hamster's Adventures on the Riverbank* (1974), the new show reinstated Sutherland as the narrator on Canadian broadcasts while Morris returned to voice the U.K edition. Again, the series was filmed on the Isle of Wight, but Global's version inserted footage of iconic Algonquin Park wilderness, as well as Sutherland's guitar rendition of Mozart's Andante in C major as the show's theme song. *Hammy Hamster's Adventures on the Riverbank* was far more ambitious than the original, and featured Hammy and his friends G.P. (who now sounded like W.C. Fields), Matty the Mouse (Roddy the Rat rebranded because Astral didn't want a rat co-starring in a kids' show), Wise Old Frog, Turtle, and the omnipresent Owl, all exploring the riverbank by jeep, airplane, sail- and motorboat, hovercraft, hot-air balloon, and diving bell.

An even more modernized Hammy appeared in *Once Upon a Hamster* in 1994. Sixty-five episodes were produced for YTV, filmed entirely on location in Uxbridge, Ontario, and once again featuring Sutherland's gentle and soothing narration.

1960s

12

Just Mary (1960)

MAGGIE MUGGINS CREATOR MARY GRANNAN IS WIDELY considered the first popular children's entertainer in Canada (see p. 32). On the radio, her stories delighted children across the country, and she was a natural resource to tap when television began in the early 1950s. However, Grannan found being in front of a camera debilitating so allowed others to adapt her stories in the production of *Maggie Muggins* (1955). For *Just Mary*, Grannan narrated her own stories off-screen while they were performed live by actors and puppets, which included many detailed new creations by John and Linda Keogh. While the earlier *Telestory Time* (1953) had attempted a similar format, *Just Mary* presented it in a much less cluttered fashion. Adapted Grannan stories included "The Chinese Bracelet," "The Princely Pig," "Golden Shoes," "The Little Good Arrow," "Penny Pink," and "Dolly Petticoats."

13

Junior Roundup (1960)

CANADIAN ACTOR MURRAY WESTGATE, BEST KNOWN FOR HIS role as the Esso pitchman in television commercials during *Hockey Night in Canada*, hosted this weekday afternoon news magazine show, which was split into two parts — the first for younger kids, from preschool to eight years old, and the second for nine-to-fourteen-year-olds. The first segment, called "Bantam Roundup," aired repeats of *The Friendly Giant*, *Maggie Muggins*, and later *Just Mary* for children who had missed the earlier broadcasts due to being at school.

The second part of the program featured a wide range of content and correspondents from across Canada, themed for each day of the week. Monday included a live audience of children participating in quizzes and games with comedians Dave Broadfoot and Jean Templeton, while Tuesday presented science and nature segments from weatherman and Chichimus confidant Percy Saltzman along with Steve Bloomer, another rising star from U.S. television poached by Fred Rainsberry. Wednesday focused on live music and was usually broadcast from Winnipeg. Films from around the world would air on Thursday, while Friday wrapped things up with a kids' news report called "Your World This Week."

Junior Roundup was created by Michael Spivak (*Maggie Muggins*) and Cliff Braggins (*The Howdy Doody Show*) and, by experimenting with cross-country linkups, was the first of its kind in the children's department. Much later, in 1984, CBC's *Switchback* employed a similar regionally segmented magazine format, emanating from network affiliate CBHT-TV in Halifax, Nova Scotia. CBC producer Ron Krantz recalled *Junior Roundup* as a series that perhaps was more appreciated by parents than their children:

> As I recall, *Junior Roundup* was a very ambitious show in the sense that we were putting together a magazine show where regional stations of the CBC would provide specific segments. It didn't work too well from a production, packaging point of view because it just wasn't consistent. Every time you brought things together a little, all of a sudden you were flying off somewhere else.... [My wife] described it as a show that most mothers would love to have their children sit down and watch every day.... I'm not so sure that the kids thought it was a terrific show, although I'm sure it had some excellent material in it.[1]

14
Razzle Dazzle (1961)

BY 1960, PRODUCTION TECHNIQUES IN TELEVISION HAD rapidly evolved, and viewers had become accustomed to a much faster pace of presentation. Studio cameras were no longer locked in place, allowing for more elaborate visual storytelling. More emphasis was placed on the continuity within shows and the short films that used to run silently were now shown with sound and the original narration. Children's shows needed to adapt to keep kids engaged. Under the aegis of Rainsberry, CBC producer William Davidson and his team were determined to create a new style of kinetic magazine show for the daily 5:00 p.m. time slot, a show that would captivate kids, involve them, and peel them away from rival stations rerunning *The Three Stooges* and Popeye and Superman cartoons. Writers Ron Krantz and Cliff Braggins were drafted in to help shape what became the sensational *Razzle Dazzle*.

Davidson recognized that to win over viewers the show needed compelling pacing and novel ways to connect with the young audience. He thought that one way to connect was to make the hosts more relatable by making them younger. This proposition was radical at a time when all children's programming was anchored by older men. Originally, it was decided that the program should focus on three central characters: a girl, her younger brother, and an older boy who would provide a mature figure for the audience. During development, research indicated that children liked animals more than humans, so the older boy became a brotherly type and the younger brother became a turtle. Alan Hamel, a host of *Junior Roundup* (1960), was cast as the wise brotherly type, and Michele Finney, just eleven years old, was the sweet young girl. Finney's resourcefulness and cool temperament (learning sixteen pages of script daily) made her an authoritative role model for young viewers, breaking away from the usual deference shown to adults in every other show. Rounding out the trio, Howard the Turtle was developed as a lovable goof who delivered a stream of puns and corny jokes (referred to on-air as "groaners") that became a focal point of the show. Inspiration for Howard's mannerisms were drawn from a range of fictional animals, from Mickey Mouse to Lassie, but it was John Keogh, the puppet's co-manipulator and voice, that gave Howard a soul, often stealing scenes wholesale from his human co-hosts. Howard didn't move around the set but was animated through expressive neck and head movements. Howard would adopt multiple personas, indicated by a costume or accessory changes, shifting effortlessly from hyperactive DJ Howard Mellotone to the capricious entertainment news reporter Jimmy Fiddle Faddle, to sensitive poet Howard I. Threadneedle.

Other reoccurring characters on *Razzle Dazzle* included the shady salesman Mr. Sharpey, played by Paul Kligman (*Rocket Robin Hood*); Sherlock House, the defective detective; Mr. Igotit, the community shopkeeper; and Howard's nemesis, Percy Q. Kidpester (voiced in person by Ed McNamara), a black-cloaked misanthrope whose appearance on the show guaranteed a chorus of booing. In a 1982 interview Krantz suggested:

> *Razzle Dazzle* also had one other ingredient that I think separated it from any show designed for young people at that time — we simply decided that young people could appreciate satire.[2]

Much consideration was given to the setting of the show, creating a familiar and warm atmosphere dubbed "Razzle Dazzle Alley," a daily gathering place for the assorted cast, guests, and studio audience (referred to as the "peanut gallery," as it was on *The Howdy Doody Show*).

Perhaps the most vital ingredient in the conception of *Razzle Dazzle* was its emphasis on participation. Through endless interactive components, kids were urged to engage with the show by mail or phone, sending in jokes, skits, and ideas for content (which helped the writing staff who had to create five shows per week). The viewers were also encouraged to join the Razzle Dazzle Club so they could receive the *Razzle Dazzle Daily* newsletter and other show paraphernalia like pens, pins, and decoder rings.

Michele Finney and Howard the Turtle (John Keogh) on *Razzle Dazzle* (1961), a wild and woolly children's television series that became a daily ritual for many Canadian kids.

Razzle Dazzle premiered on October 2, 1961, to almost immediate approval from the target demographic. By the end of December, it was watched by half a million young viewers every day. Over a hundred thousand kids joined the Razzle Dazzle Club, and the overwhelming volume of mail — estimated at its peak to be twelve hundred letters a day — prompted production to hire a full-time club administrator. Krantz described the sheer energy and unpredictability each daily *Razzle Dazzle* production wrought:

> It's so difficult to describe now, a live half-hour every day in front of a peanut gallery of fifty kids who did whatever we wanted them to do, who came in every day, live performances, sketches, some excellent magic, some excellent puppeteering. The show very seldom fell apart, although all the conditions were there for it to just go down the drain any day of the week. And for some reason it had such a high energy level and had such a commitment going for it on the part of the performers.[3]

Host Finney became a media darling, gaining her own national fan club, even greeting the Beatles when they played at Maple Leaf Gardens in 1964. *Razzle Dazzle* won a respected Liberty Award for Best Children's Program in Canada in 1962–63, presented by American variety-show host and mega star Ed Sullivan.

Each episode of *Razzle Dazzle* contained a five-minute segment of a serialized adventure story for children. These shorts started with a collection of children's material from Australia and included *The Magic Boomerang* and *The Adventures of the Terrible Ten*. Eventually content from Down Under gave way to a new serialized Canadian story called *The Forest Rangers*, which proved to be so popular with young audiences it was spun off into its own series in 1963.

In 1964, Hamel and Finney were replaced as hosts by Ray Bellew and Trudy Young, and Krantz and Braggins were replaced by writers Michael Spivak, Jerry Ross, and Don Baker. The series eventually wrapped up in 1966, having left an indelible mark on the genre of children's television via numerous novel innovations: the casting of a young host, the use of satire, the creation of a puppet with depth of character, the embracing of interactivity, and the encouragement of viewer mail. Krantz even felt the show helped modernize CBC's special-effects department:

> I think that our special-effects department at the CBC came into its own as a result of the show. They learned to do things that they had never ever been asked to do before. I imagine *Wayne and Shuster* and a lot of other shows [that featured special effects] benefited from that kind of experience.[4]

15
CFTO-TV (1961)

PRIME MINISTER JOHN DIEFENBAKER'S GOVERNMENT PASSED an update to the Broadcasting Act in 1958 that established the Board of Broadcast Governors, a forerunner to the Canadian Radio-television and Telecommunications Commission (CRTC). More importantly to viewers,

Representatives of the Ontario Safety League visit Kiddo the Clown (Trevor Evans) at the CFTO studios in Agincourt, in north Scarborough. Note the poster of Elmer the Safety Elephant on the wall.

the airwaves opened to Canadian stations that were privately held. The CBC no longer monopolized the channels. Applications for new television stations were accepted and nine were given a broadcast licence in the following cities: Calgary (CFCN-TV), Vancouver (CHAN-TV), Winnipeg (CJAY-TV), Halifax (CJCH-TV), Montreal (CFCF-TV for English service and CFTM-TV for French), Ottawa (CJOH-TV), Edmonton (CFRN-TV), and Toronto (CFTO-TV).

John Bassett, Jr., publishing magnate and chief executive of Baton Aldred Rogers Broadcasting, was granted a licence to operate CFTO-TV in Toronto. He had long envisioned a second Canadian network unbeholden to Ottawa as a commercial alternative to CBC. It was christened the Canadian Television Network (CTV) and CFTO-TV served as its flagship. Although television was still broadcasting in black and white, Bassett foresaw the coming of colour and ensured all CTV equipment and technology would be able to broadcast as soon as colour technology was licensed by the Board of Broadcast Governors. Colour hit Canadian screens in 1966, although the impact was muted given less than one per cent of Canadian households had a colour TV set.

CFTO-TV established its studio and transmitting facilities in Agincourt, Scarborough, at 1550 McCowan Road (later renamed, and better known as,

9 Channel Nine Court) and officially joined the airwaves at 10:00 p.m. on Saturday, December 31, 1960, ringing in the new year with a live fireworks display (albeit broadcast in monochrome). The first full day of programming kicked off with a telethon for the Ontario Association for Community Living on Sunday, January 1, 1961.

On January 2, 1961, CFTO-TV premiered its very first kids' show — *The Professor's Hideaway*. Bassett said that his "original philosophy was that CFTO-TV be positioned to our viewers as a family station,"[5] and the channel's licence did require a certain number of broadcast hours be dedicated to children's programming. Initially, CFTO was flush with money and early on the channel did invest in shows for children. However, unlike at the CBC, kids' TV was not considered a long-term business priority and the programming budgets were cut after a few years of broadcasting.

16
The Professor's Hideaway (1961)

THE PROFESSOR'S HIDEAWAY WAS TYPICAL OF WHAT MOST commercial broadcasters offered up for children at the time — entertaining live filler built around product sponsorships and short films, all held together by an amiable grown-up. It ticked a regulatory box, allowed for old content to be recycled and — most importantly — was cheap to produce. Just as the CBC had started by purchasing an established format from the U.S., the popular *The Howdy Doody Show*, and then remoulding it into its own production,

CFTO-TV began by acquiring a format for a New York series called *Magic Toy Shop* (1955), which had a main character loosely based on the Geppetto character from *Pinocchio*. American transplant Stan Francis was hired as host, thanks no doubt to having recently played the voice of Geppetto in the Toronto-produced Rankin/Bass TV series *The New Adventures of Pinocchio* (1960). CFTO-TV's attempt at aping the success of *The Howdy Doody Show* even extended to hiring its head writer, John Gerrard, who was once again required to adapt an American series into something more Canadian.

Having left the CBC, Dodi Robb (*Telestory Time*) joined the writing team assembled by Gerrard and was somewhat redeemed as she had been turned down as a writer on *The Howdy Doody Show*. Robb struggled with the producer's promotion of commercialism over educational content but was able to inject some material that she felt was acceptable. Together with Gerrard and Francis, she retooled the *Magic Toy Shop* format into something different altogether. The Professor was an absent-minded eccentric who broadcasted live every day at 4:00 p.m. from his Hilltop Hideaway laboratory while plotting outlandish outer space or undersea adventures that never actually materialized (instead of making magic toys, although he did that sometimes as well). The presentation format of *The Professor's Hideaway* was reminiscent of *The Howdy Doody Show*, with lightly scripted but mostly improvised skits and crafting sessions in between Popeye cartoons, Three Stooges shorts, and episodes of *Tales of the Riverbank* (1959). Since the entire program was sponsored by Irwin Specialties Ltd. (now known as Irwin Toy), there were toys galore, and at times it could feel like one long commercial.

Husband and wife Hal and Renée Marquette (*The Howdy Doody Show*) were the show's dedicated puppeteers, operating a dog called Samson, two raccoons called X and Y, and many others. The series also featured an array of popular support characters, including Kiddo the Clown and Bimbo, an English-accented clown played by Bobby Ash, soon to be known as Uncle Bobby.

The Professor's Hideaway ran for ninety minutes each day of the week, and even had a bonus Saturday-morning instalment titled *Professor's Cartoon Party* (later shortened to just *Professor's Party*). It was hugely successful, thanks to Francis's charm and upbeat persona and his ability to connect with kids.

An additional daily show was added to the morning schedule, titled *Professor and His Cartoon Friends*. Just a few months into production, Francis told the *Toronto Star* he had one inflexible rule when it came to working with children — "Don't talk down to them."[6] The story also reported that Francis would only sip an occasional beer in case anyone saw him, and he never smoked his cigarettes in front of kids.

By June of 1961, Francis was receiving over two thousand letters per week from viewers,[7] including many mothers asking him to impart positive messaging on-air, such as telling kids not to pick trilliums, or do something educational, such as showing how to grow sprouts from half a potato. However, there were budget issues plaguing the upstart CFTO-TV, as Robb recalled:

> They started up quite ambitiously with Stan Francis as the Professor. As financial things began to get tighter at CFTO — they realized they couldn't afford to do live television — it was just Stan sitting with no props, no anything, you know, carrying maybe an hour or two of airtime. And the same with Bobby [Ash, Uncle Bobby]. *The Professor's Hideaway* was a good show, but then the scripts disappeared as the economics got worse. And tiny poor old Stan, I always felt it hastened Stan's demise from this world — the strain of having to sit in front of a camera with no support system.[8]

In June of 1963 Francis's salary dispute with producers brought an abrupt halt to the show. He was fired by director Murray Chercover moments before going on-air (the same Chercover who had admonished a floor technician for the opening-night upside-down-slide incident, see p. 14). An atypically restrained Kiddo the Clown (Trevor Evans) appeared as the last-minute host, but the press was already sensing trouble at the Hilltop Hideaway. The following day, *The Globe and Mail* reported:

> Since the Professor's image is very close to the real Stan Francis, CFTO-TV's copyright of the character may prove

> worthless. For one thing, children wouldn't likely be fooled by a substitute, and for another, there is nothing to prevent Stan doing a kindly old white-haired codger on another station. Although this will come as a blow to many youngsters, the Professor is most likely gone forever.[9]

Scrambling to find a suitable replacement, the network lucked out with occasional *Professor's Hideaway* guest star Bobby Ash, who suggested creating a brand-new character in lieu of having Bimbo the Clown take over the Hilltop Hideaway laboratory. Ash recalled:

> They wanted me to be a pirate king, or Fireman Bob, or something like that. I said, why don't we just do it like me being just like every uncle would be. The kids would expect him to be wearing a sweater and an ordinary pair of pants and no fancy costume, so I'll just be an uncle — Uncle Bobby.[10]

17
Kiddo the Clown (1962)

TORONTO AUDIENCES WERE FIRST INTRODUCED TO THE INcendiary character of Kiddo the Clown in September of 1962 when he appeared as a guest on *Professor's Party*, before being given his own anarchic slot with *Kiddo Cartoons* at 8:00 a.m. every weekday morning on CFTO-TV a few weeks later. Running ninety minutes per show, the hobo-like Kiddo appeared between cartoons to provide continuity.

A membership card for Kiddo the Clown's fan club.

Kiddo was played by Trevor Evans, who had started his bizarro Kiddo act out west on CHCT-TV in Calgary in 1956 before moving east. Kiddo was described by *Starweek* magazine as "the crazed little guy with the crushed top hat, tattered swallowtails, checkered pants, orange wig and round red nose who kept smacking into doors."[11] His manic energy and truly oddball sense of humour were original and unlike anything else at the time; his popularity soon led to an afternoon show called *Kiddo the Clown*. Stuck in the slovenly basement of an apartment building and with only a mouse for a friend, Kiddo suffered through a daily series of repetitive and bizarre interactions with other building residents while spouting off about Canadian prime ministers such as John Diefenbaker and Lester B. Pearson. Kiddo had a mini orchestra playing in his furnace and an icebox that regularly blasted arctic air through the apartment. This stuff was light years, galaxies even, away from the serenity of the Friendly Giant's castle.

A true anarchic spirit, Evans infused the character of Kiddo with a combination of slapstick and avant-garde, and most of his dialogue was improvised. Despite the popularity of the shows (at one point, Kiddo had three different daily programs on-air), requests for a slightly bigger budget were routinely denied by CFTO-TV executives until Evans had truly had enough. In the unforgettable final episode, Kiddo stood stunned while the walls of his apartment were knocked down around him by Toronto transit workers. They had arrived to lay tracks for the new Bloor-Danforth subway line, which would run straight through Kiddo's basement dwelling. Kiddo turned to the audience and bid adieu.

Toronto television critic Bill Brioux, who remembers seeing the last episode live as a young boy, has called *Kiddo the Clown* "*Pee-wee's Playhouse* in black and white without a budget."[12]

18
The Uncle Bobby Show (1963)

PICKING UP WHERE *THE PROFESSOR'S HIDEAWAY* ENDED, *Playtime with Uncle Bobby* adapted an analogous format featuring cartoons, singers, animals, arts and crafts, magic tricks, and words of wisdom imparted by its exuberant host, Robert "Bobby" Ash. Ash had his lucky break when the host of *The Professor's Hideaway*, Stan Francis, was fired, leaving CFTO-TV with hours of children's content to fill every day as a condition of its broadcast licence. Ash had played Bimbo the Clown on the earlier series and he quickly sold producers on his new character, Uncle Bobby.

Uncle Bobby's long-running CFTO-TV series debuted on September 13, 1963, at 11:00 a.m. and ran for two hours daily. When the station switched to colour in 1966, the show was scaled back to one hour and retitled *The Uncle Bobby Show*. It aired at 11:30 a.m., and was followed at 12:30 p.m. by every kid's favourite lunchtime date, *The Flintstones* (1960). Uncle Bobby's on-air clique included wildlife artist Barry Kent MacKay; magician Ron Leonard and his brother, ventriloquist Cy Leonard; clay artist Ruth Winkler; craft queen Irene Genoe; accordionist Nancy McCaig; Metropolitan Toronto Police officer "Big" Big John Patterson; singer and occasional guest on *Mr. Dressup* Alex Laurier; and cartoonist Les Baxter. As with *The Professor's Hideaway*, the initial script writing was done by Dodi Robb. The series was directed and produced by Elena Jasechko.

"Children are the cleverest people," Ash told the *Toronto Star* in 1969. "You have to be sincere. They can see through you in a minute."[13] Ash created the Uncle Bobby character to be "someone the children could identify with, like a brother or an uncle."[14] Throughout his career he adored interacting with children through magic shows and theatrical performances, and he was well-regarded for his jovial tone. Barry Kent MacKay, one of the show's last surviving cast members, said in 2024 that "Bobby's approach to children's television was very, very special in that he did not speak down to the kids. He was extremely fond of children. He didn't pretend that somehow this all magically appeared in your television. He talked about there being a director or cameraman and he named them."[15] Ash routinely broke the fourth wall, drawing attention to the real-life wizardry of television production, sometimes upsetting guests. Puppeteer Nina Keogh was horrified when Uncle Bobby pulled her up from behind a couch while she was operating a puppet, destroying the illusion of her work.

Ash used a hodgepodge of parlour tricks and circus showmanship gleaned from his life as a travelling vaudevillian in Britain, where he had been a tightrope walker and clown since the age of five. Ash's father had been close friends with Scottish inventor John Logie Baird, who created television in 1926. An extended spell touring the rowdy music halls of Northern England, where he had to sing and dance for his dinner and a drink, gave Ash a darker edge. His hands were badly disfigured from sliding down tightropes. He had survived being a POW twice in the North African theatre of the Second World War, coming face to face with field marshal Erwin Rommel while in captivity. In 1959, he spotted an open casting call from CFTO-TV in a British newspaper. He moved to Toronto and started out at CFTO behind the camera as a floor manager.[16]

With long unkempt hair, a giant Windsor knot, a broad West Midlands accent, and a frenzied style of hosting, he stood in great contrast to squarer contemporaries such as Fred Rogers, Bob Homme, and Stan Francis. Like them, he possessed a Pied Piper–like hold over children, those in the studio audience and those watching at home.

According to MacKay, "Ernie Coombs [Mr. Dressup] clearly respected Bobby Ash. He certainly treated him as a peer, and an equal. But I think *The Uncle Bobby Show* was a means to fulfill an obligation imposed by the regulators to have a certain percentage of children's programming. The budget was minuscule, and I don't think they took the show seriously. Bobby did. Bobby was very into it."[17]

The true star of *The Uncle Bobby Show*, however, was another clown — Bimbo the Birthday Clown — a seven-foot-tall, vaguely nightmarish cardboard cut-out whose appearance marked the "Happy Birthday" portion of the show and was named after Ash's alter ego in *The Professor's Hideaway*. Every episode, Bimbo emerged cackling from behind a studio door, accompanied by his pocket "Peekaboo Twins" mini-clowns, and a gang of crocheted dancing string puppets (Big Daddy Happy, Mrs. Happy, Wilson, Keppel, and Betty), who would rapidly descend from above. This daily ceremony began with Bimbo singing a variation of Jim Reeves's 1953 song "Bimbo," which was a modulated recording of Ash's voice pitched down:

> Bimbo, Bimbo, I'm the birthday clown you know
> Bimbo, Bimbo, here on Uncle Bobby's show
> Bimbo, Bimbo, I would like to say …
> To you and you, a very Happy Birthday
> Happy Birthday, boys and girls!

The Uncle Bobby Show was a great friend to local law enforcement and often featured Toronto and Durham Region police officers discussing safety issues in addition to regular appearances by Officer Big John. A statue of Elmer the Safety Elephant was prominently displayed next to Uncle Bobby's reading chair, and the show regularly ran Elmer's public safety films between episodes of *The Mighty Hercules* (1963) and *Tom Terrific* (1957) cartoons. By 1966 Uncle Bobby was co-hosting broadcasts of the Toronto Santa Claus Parade, where his friend Elmer could be seen walking the parade route alongside the floats.

With sponsorships from Honey Dew beverages and Humpty Dumpty chips, *The Uncle Bobby Show* was at its peak of local popularity during the late 1960s. Uncle Bobby pins became a schoolyard fashion accessory, and Ash dubbed his legion of young fans "Bobby-soxers." During one memorable episode, American dancing sensation Gene Kelly (*Singin' in the Rain*) appeared after doing a spot for CFTO-TV's entertainment desk in the Agincourt studio.

In 1968, a thirty-minute version of the show entitled *Uncle Bobby and Friends* aired across CTV's entire network, providing Ash with national exposure. In addition to his returning CFTO-TV cast, Ash added segments with Bev Marsh signing to the audience, making it the very first children's

Bobby Ash as Uncle Bobby, a whimsical showman who consistently broke the so-called fourth wall of television, like a magician explaining his tricks.

series in North America to incorporate and teach sign language. To capitalize on his elevated profile, Ash released a storytelling LP entitled *The Curious Christmas of Arlington Bloggs* in late 1968, and a follow-up, *Arlington Bloggs: Accidental Astronaut*, in 1969. Ash hoped to create a series of children's books to go along with the records and continue the adventures of Arlington Bloggs. Unfortunately, the national audience did not respond to Uncle Bobby's act as passionately as his local Toronto fans did, and in 1970 the Saturday CTV edition was dropped. Ash refocused his energies toward the weekday program on CFTO-TV and, in 1971, an hour-long Saturday-morning episode was added.

ELMER THE SAFETY ELEPHANT

One of the original twelve Elmer the Safety Elephant busts made for classroom use in the 1960s now resides with the author in Port Perry, Ontario.

Traffic safety mascot Elmer was created in 1947 by Bas Mason of *The Toronto Telegram* and Toronto police inspector Vernon Page, inspired by the lifelong safety work of Inspector Charles Pearsall. Robert Hood Saunders, Toronto mayor from 1945 to 1948, invited them to create a character who could help children learn about the basics of road safety. The animal was chosen because "elephants never forget." Elmer was later redesigned by Canadian cartoonist Charles Thorson, who worked at Disney and claimed to have created Bugs Bunny for Warner Bros. in 1938.

Ontario schools with perfect safety records got to proudly fly the Elmer flag. However, the flag was revoked with just one accident or act of unsafe behaviour. The power of communal pride or shame ran deep in Ontario's schools thanks to Elmer's presence on the flagpole. Elmer was such a mindful motivator that instances of children involved in traffic accidents dropped 44 percent in the years following his arrival in Toronto.

The popularity of the program grew to the point that *The Toronto Telegram*, original owners of the intellectual property, transferred all ownership to the Ontario Safety League, and from there to the Canada Safety Council. Sadly, the currency of Elmer began to fade in the early 2000s, and most schools abandoned the program due to "changing priorities," as they were now having to foot the bill themselves. A radically redesigned Elmer does live on online at a dedicated website set up by the council.

19
The Forest Rangers (1963)

POSSIBLY CANADA'S FIRST ECOLOGICALLY MINDED CHILdren's show, *The Forest Rangers* was initially seen in five-minute serialized chunks on *Razzle Dazzle* (1961), before being given its own thirty-minute slot. Executive producer Maxine Samuels created *The Forest Rangers* with an eye on the international market after noting the success of an Australian adventure series for children called *The Adventures of the Terrible Ten*, which was also serialized on *Razzle Dazzle*. Samuels let Rainsberry know that she thought she could make a similar show set in Canada.[18]

Co-produced by CBC and the British Incorporated Television Company (ITC), *The Forest Rangers* was shot on 16mm film and was the first show produced in Canada to be filmed in colour. However, it was broadcast on CBC in black and white, not switching to colour until 1966, when the CBC's full-colour service began.

The Forest Rangers involved a gang of four young boys and one girl, dubbed the Junior Rangers, who encountered weekly intrigue in the rural community of Indian River, Ontario. They monitored the real Forest Rangers and RCMP through ham radio. The scripts kept to a formulaic adventure storyline with the kids fighting fires, escaped convicts, and illegal poachers. Little was said about their personal lives, although, in another Canadian television first, one of the Rangers had parents who were divorced. The cast included Gordon Pinsent, Rex Hagon, Susan Conway, Michael Zenon, Peter Tully, Graydon Gould, and Ralph Endersby (brother of prolific TVOntario writer Clive Endersby).

In total, 104 episodes of *The Forest Rangers* were produced, and the series was shown in the U.K., West Germany, France, Australia, and Norway. Cast members Hagon and Conway were later selected to be the hosts of *Razzle Dazzle*'s follow-up *Drop-In* (1971).

20
Misterogers (1962)

FRED MCFEELY ROGERS STARTED IN TELEVISION IN NEW YORK City, as a floor director for early NBC shows like *Your Hit Parade* (1950) and the western-themed *The Gabby Hayes Show* (1950). Hailing from Latrobe, Pennsylvania, Rogers returned to the Pittsburgh area in 1953 to help develop a children's series at WQED-TV, which was about to launch as the first community-sponsored public television station in America. Rogers and Josie Carey created *The Children's Corner* (1953), a show that would educate and entertain in equal parts. Both Carey and Rogers believed television could be beneficial to childhood education but felt most children's shows were crass with far too much focus on cheap gags.

Rogers was a musician at heart (he had received his Bachelor of Music from Rollins College in 1951), so while Carey appeared as host, he provided the music. Rogers also oversaw the acquisition of short film interstitials. The night before the station went live, its manager, Dorothy Daniel, gave Rogers a sock puppet, which he later christened Daniel S. (Striped) Tiger. At first *The Children's Corner* did not feature puppets, but Rogers began to use Tiger in place of malfunctioning props — a frequent occurrence as the show had a tiny budget of $150 per episode. Tiger's unplanned appearances proved to be so popular that Rogers introduced other puppets, such as King Friday XIII, X the Owl, and Henrietta Pussycat. Along with the puppets came greater improvisation, and Rogers and Carey adhered to scripts less and less. Rogers operated all the puppets, giving them distinct personalities and remaining hidden behind the scenes.

Rogers was also studying at the Pittsburgh Theological Seminary, feeling his true calling was as an ordained minister within the United Presbyterian Church. As he devoted more of his time toward his studies, the popularity of

Fred Rogers was a natural at communicating with children onscreen and in person, but he needed a little coaxing to hone the character of Mr. Rogers.

The Children's Corner continued to grow. Rogers was becoming frustrated with Carey, whose commitments on other productions kept resulting in her being late or absent. Although Rogers had many ideas on new ways to use television in the pursuit of education, he felt Carey was the wrong onscreen partner for him.

It was around this time that *The Children's Corner* came to the attention of the CBC's Fred Rainsberry, who closely monitored developments in children's television across North America and beyond. Rainsberry shared his interest in the program with the producers of *Junior Magazine*, who duly invited Rogers to do a segment with his puppets Daniel Tiger and King Friday XIII.

After Rogers visited Toronto, he and Rainsberry grew close and kept in touch through phone calls and letters. The "Freds" had a great deal in common, with backgrounds in academia, an interest in the welfare of children, and bright visions for what the medium of television might be able to achieve in the field of education. Rainsberry admittedly had an ulterior motive — he had once observed Rogers interacting with children at an educational conference and been struck by the children's response to his authenticity and charm. Rainsberry strongly believed that Rogers should be hosting his own show.

In the early 1960s, as *The Children's Corner* wound down and he graduated with a Bachelor of Divinity magna cum laude, Rogers finally entertained Rainsberry's proposition. After years of wooing, Rogers came to Toronto to develop a fifteen-minute show that could be paired with *The Friendly Giant* in CBC's morning schedule.

Even after Rogers relocated to Toronto, it was not easy for Rainsberry to convince him he should be front and centre in this new endeavour. Rogers was comfortable puppeteering and playing music; he wasn't expecting to host. According to Rogers, Rainsberry said, "I want you to be on-camera; I've seen you talk with kids.… I want you to look into the lens, and just pretend that's a child, and we'll just call it *Misterogers*. Let's just do that."[19]

Rainsberry placed CBC producer Francis Chapman in charge of not only developing the show, but of developing Rogers himself. He told Chapman that "Fred Rogers was a treasure that ought to be taken care of."[20] Chapman recalled the early reaction to Rogers:

> Initially in the studio, when Fred had arrived and was just starting the new show, there were certain tensions. His sense of mission was very remarkable, a rather rare thing to be found in that environment. For a great many of the people, he appeared to be too good to be true. After a while, he gained the confidence. The people in the studio saw he was indeed genuine.[21]

The CBC provided Rogers with a far greater budget than he had had at WQED, plus he had access to all of the resources the CBC had at its disposal. Chapman recalled how Rogers dealt with the changes:

> There was some difficulty for Fred, I think, coming from the studio in Pittsburgh, which had been a much, much smaller, much more informal affair to the relatively large and structured CBC situation. But he is such a disciplined worker.[22]

With full support from Rainsberry and Chapman, Rogers controlled every element of production, from guests to camera positioning to music selection. In collaboration with CBC producer Bruce Attridge, Rogers was able to build a house for X the Owl, a castle for King Friday XIII, and a fully functioning trolley car. A new beaver puppet was constructed to facilitate discussion on Canadian geographical issues.

The series itself — much like its production — was built entirely around Rogers's persona. The fifteen-minute live show emphasized the importance of

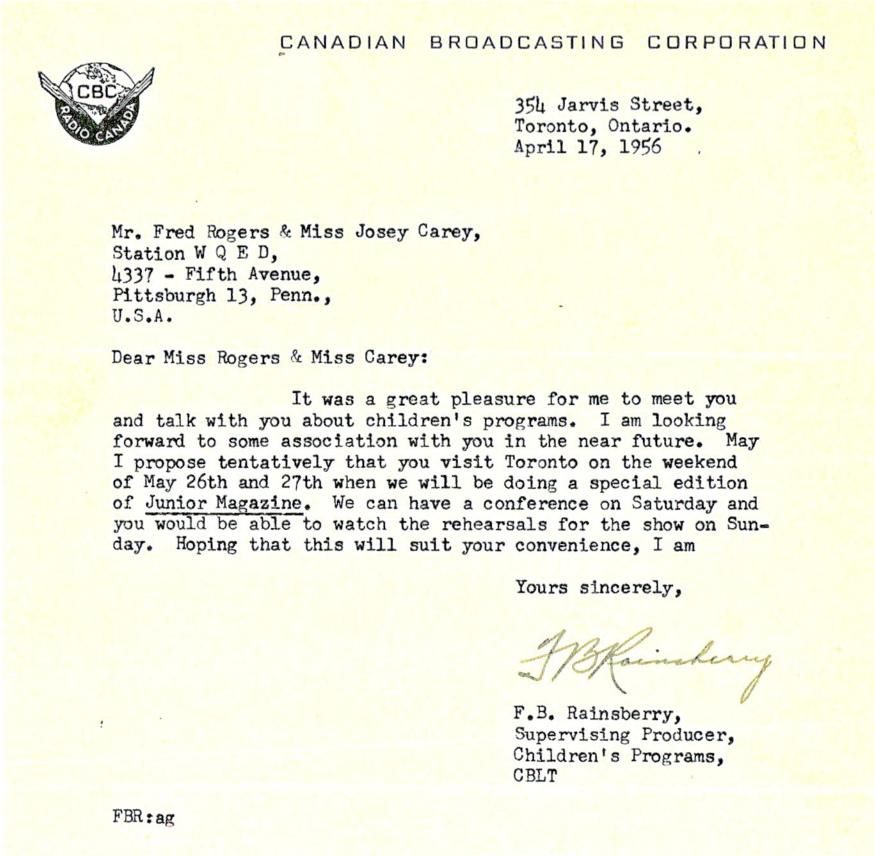

CANADIAN BROADCASTING CORPORATION

354 Jarvis Street,
Toronto, Ontario.
April 17, 1956

Mr. Fred Rogers & Miss Josey Carey,
Station W Q E D,
4337 - Fifth Avenue,
Pittsburgh 13, Penn.,
U.S.A.

Dear Miss Rogers & Miss Carey:

It was a great pleasure for me to meet you and talk with you about children's programs. I am looking forward to some association with you in the near future. May I propose tentatively that you visit Toronto on the weekend of May 26th and 27th when we will be doing a special edition of Junior Magazine. We can have a conference on Saturday and you would be able to watch the rehearsals for the show on Sunday. Hoping that this will suit your convenience, I am

Yours sincerely,

F.B. Rainsberry,
Supervising Producer,
Children's Programs,
CBLT

FBR:ag

Early correspondence between Fred Rogers and Fred Rainsberry, in which Rainsberry first invited Rogers to visit him in Toronto.

imagination with the fantastical Neighbourhood of Make-Believe, an ongoing, soap opera–like presentation featuring both puppets and humans. Transitions to the Neighbourhood of Make-Believe were signalled by the arrival (and departure) of a trolley, and Mr. Rogers would recap the ongoing plot for anyone who had missed a previous segment. Amid the fantastical stories of King Friday and his friends were frank discussions about children's fears and insecurities. The sincerity of Rogers, combined with his focus and intensity, delivered exactly the kind of quality program Rainsberry had envisioned upon their first meeting.

Misterogers was an immediate success, helping form a truly spellbinding block of daily children's programming on the CBC that complemented *The*

Friendly Giant (1958) and *Chez Hélène* (1959, see p. 102). CBC producer Robert Gibbons, who had worked on *The Friendly Giant* and would later work on *Mr. Dressup* (1967), was asked by Rainsberry what he considered the essential qualities of a good children's program:

> I don't think there's a better example than Fred Rogers in *Misterogers*, who has learned the secret that eye-to-eye contact is so important. He actually looks at the child and talks directly to the child, not over the child's head or to some cameraman off to the side like Uncle Bobby. That is just the opposite to a good children's program, in my opinion, as far as caring and aiming the program and the thoughts to the child. He's talking to the cameraman most of the time or to the lighting person or to someone else. He doesn't really seem to care. It doesn't come across as sincerity, whereas [Fred] Rogers does. He speaks right to the children.[23]

After a few years in Toronto, Rogers and his family grew homesick. His old homestead WQED-TV in Pittsburgh was looking for its own flagship children's program and offered him a central role. In 1966, Rogers acquired the rights to *Misterogers* from the CBC and returned to Pennsylvania to produce a new version known as *Misterogers' Neighborhood* (1967), which was later adjusted to *Mister Rogers' Neighborhood* (1970) for the Public Broadcasting Service (PBS) network. The series ran for thirty-one seasons and over nine hundred episodes.

Over the years, the character of Mister Rogers, which Rainsberry and Chapman helped to develop, became an American institution. Much of the Toronto origin story faded over time, and it was wholly ignored in the 2019 film production *A Beautiful Day in the Neighborhood*, which starred Hollywood monolith Tom Hanks as Fred Rogers. Chapman notes what Rogers gained from the CBC:

> When he went back, his demands of the people at Pittsburgh were much higher and, if my memory serves me rightly, he

Ernie Coombs and Fred Rogers on the set of *Misterogers* (1962) with puppets Cornflake S. Pecially and King Friday XIII. When Rogers returned to his native Pittsburgh, he recommended to the CBC that they construct a new series built around his old friend Coombs, which they did with *Butternut Square* (1964).

> actually set about raising money to increase the budget so that it could match the standard [of the CBC show].[24]

Rogers even attempted to buy the sets from the CBC and take them back to Pittsburgh, but he was foiled by bureaucracy. In a 1982 interview with Rainsberry, Rogers observed:

> You know, if it hadn't been for you, I would not have come to use that medium [television] to express some of these things that have become important. And I just find it exceedingly mysterious that an electronic device can communicate a real feeling. And I'm not talking about scripted dramatic presentation. I'm talking about the real thing that comes from somebody's heart.[25]

As planning began on a replacement series for *Misterogers*, Rainsberry asked Rogers about the kind of show he thought the CBC should produce.

How could they possibly follow up his trailblazing act? When pressed, Rogers was unsure of a format, but he did suggest using the talent of one of his own team members, a puppeteer who had relocated from Pittsburgh to Toronto to work on *Misterogers.* His name was Ernest Coombs, better known to legions of Canadian children as Mr. Dressup.

21
Butternut Square (1964)

IN 1961, AMERICAN PUPPETEER ERNEST "ERNIE" COOMBS WAS recruited by his friend and co-worker Fred Rogers to perform alongside him on the CBC's *Misterogers*. Coombs had left an indelible impression on Rogers after they collaborated on a completely improvised live lunchtime series on Pittsburgh's WQED-TV, as well as *The Children's Corner*. Coombs had been working at the station on another show called *Dimple Depot*, where he and his wife, Marlene, operated puppets, wrote, and produced. "I don't know how many people watched [*Dimple Depot*], of course, … but it was an invaluable experience for me," he said.[26] The Coombses relocated to Toronto in 1961. When *Misterogers* concluded in 1964, a replacement series was devised to spotlight Coombs on the recommendation of Rogers, who had decided to leave CBC and continue his career in the States. "Fred Rainsberry wanted us to stay. I couldn't, so I suggested they do a show built around Ernie. He was my extra hand, my assistant puppeteer," Rogers later said.[27]

Like Rogers, Coombs began behind the scenes but was adept at communicating ideas to children, projecting a mild and understated yet playful persona. CBC producers hoped Coombs's talent could be harnessed to replace the neighbourhood-sized hole left by Rogers's departure. Executive producer Bruce Attridge developed the concept for *Butternut Square*, a magical place where people and puppets would come together to dance, sing, and play games, encouraging young viewers to participate. As with *Misterogers*, there were clear distinctions between fantasy play and real life. However, no one had figured out how Coombs could thread everything together. Coombs recalls being in Attridge's office when they hit upon the character who would ultimately become Mr. Dressup:

> When Bruce was first talking about the program, one of the characters that he wanted was somebody who could change characters three or four times in the program. Now, it was a grown-up. Not pretending to be a child but doing something that kids like to do. Being a fireman or a policeman or an accountant or whatever.[28]

Coombs did not recall who assigned the character a name that would define CBC's children's department for decades:

> I can remember sitting in Bruce's office all those long years ago trying to decide what my character would be called. And to this day I can't remember whether I thought of Mr. Dressup, or whether Bruce did. I'd love to find out sometime.[29]

Mr. Dressup was joined by Sandy Cohen, who told stories; Bob "the song trader" Jeffrey, who sang and danced; and The Music Man (Donald Himes), who played piano. Australian puppeteer Judith Lawrence created and operated a faction of puppets, including schoolboy Casey, his dog Finnegan, two pandas Alexander and Miranda, and variety store owner Mrs. Trapeze. The massive village-square set included a shop, a treehouse, park benches, and a series of complex paintings of buildings. When producer Stuart Gilchrist tweaked the format of *Butternut Square* in its second season, he implemented several changes that strengthened the show. Human guests were cut back as more puppets appeared, many created by Nancy Anne Cole, who also appeared as the Puppet Lady. Speaking in 1982, Gilchrist said:

> We would try for a week with a particular theme. Could either be kites, or animals or what have you, but we would try to bring in a great amount of sociological implications, human relations, all of those dynamics, interpersonal relationships one could interpret in an imaginative, creative way for young people. And quite frankly, this was a success. We very soon began to receive responses through the media and through organizations that it was catching on. It was acquiring an audience.[30]

Coombs and Lawrence had such a natural rhythm together that they created a spinoff live act called *The Tickle Trunk* featuring Mr. Dressup with Casey and Finnegan. It played at Toronto's Poor Alex Theatre, located on Brunswick Avenue in the Annex. Years later, Coombs claimed the alluring alliterative name Tickle Trunk (originally called the "Tinker Trunk") had popped into his head while stuck in a Toronto traffic jam at Bayview and Sheppard.

In 1967, at the peak of its success, *Butternut Square* was cancelled. Although the CBC gave no reason, Gilchrist believed the CBC had shifting priorities, and news and current affairs were becoming more important. The elaborate set for *Butternut Square* simply took up too much studio space.

Media reports of the show's impending cancellation resulted in a swift public backlash, and Attridge was pressed to develop a compromise. He suggested getting rid of the square and keeping the living room and Casey and Finnegan's treehouse: "We could keep the components of *Butternut Square* and all of those things we're trying to do. We will use half a studio. And we will change the name. We will call it *Mr. Dressup*, but essentially all of the ingredients will remain."[31] Gilchrist recalls Attridge bargaining, noting that the studio in 1982 was still half the size of *Butternut Square*'s.

22
Mr. Dressup (1967)

THE AVUNCULAR ERNIE COOMBS RETURNED TO TELEVISION as the gentle and accepting Mr. Dressup in *Mr. Dressup* (1967) just weeks after *Butternut Square* (1964) was usurped by CBC's fortified news division. Holding on to puppeteer Judith Lawrence as young friend Casey and his canine Finnegan, pianist Donald Himes, and the erstwhile Tickle Trunk, *Mr. Dressup* moved the communal spirit of *Butternut Square* squarely into a cozier setting (in reality, just a small section of the much larger *Butternut Square* set) with a simplified format and shorter running time of fifteen minutes per episode.

Mr. Dressup and his friends still enjoyed crafts, music, and dressing up to explore everyday experiences. Frequent guests included puppets — Aunt Bird and Alligator Al, Hat-Rack Moose, Hester the witch — and humans — Susan Marcus, Beth Anne Cole, and miming Poco the Clown. Crayons, markers, scissors, and glue were given a daily drill, and the Tickle Trunk's array of costumes and props enabled infinite flights of fancy. The *CBC Times* television listings magazine described every episode of *Mr. Dressup* with one simple sentence — "Trips to the land of make-believe."

As *Butternut Square* was viewed as the heir to *Misterogers*, childhood educators had been involved in every facet of its production. *Mr. Dressup* was designed to take a looser, more relaxed approach, closer in tone to *The Friendly Giant*. The series fostered imaginative play over didactics. While there were scripts, the interaction between Coombs and Lawrence was mostly improvised and, like *The Friendly Giant*'s Homme and Coneybeare, came from great chemistry and affinity. Characters spoke to viewers in the singular, as Lawrence said: "We were not speaking to the whole world. We always thought of the audience as being one child on the other side of the television set."[32] Lawrence as Casey asked Mr. Dressup a lot of questions. "If Casey had been passive, just accepting everything Mr. Dressup said, it wouldn't have been very much fun, or good for the children watching, so it was important that Casey was a bit of an instigator."[33]

Early *Mr. Dressup* producer Robert Gibbons recalled a special on-set moment that signalled to him that the series was on the right track:

Ernie Coombs as the beloved Mr. Dressup first appeared in *Butternut Square* (1964) before getting his own eponymous show in 1967.

> Someone called and said they'd like to bring their child down to see [*Mr. Dressup*] being done in the studio. And we neither encouraged that, or discouraged that.… Because sometimes when a child finally comes in contact with the reality of the set of *Mr. Dressup* or *The Friendly Giant* or the people, they're disappointed. Gee, Friendly Giant isn't a giant after all. And, oh, he's crushed. He's disappointed. So, it's a tender thing we had to judge each case on. But I remember this one time, this lady said she'd like to bring her daughter down. And I said, okay, that's fine. When she came down, we saw the daughter was blind. And it was a very, very tender and emotional hour we spent with her. She convinced us all that she could see *Mr. Dressup* and she could see all the things that they were doing on that program. And so, I realized perhaps maybe for the first time that we really were communicating with our audience.[34]

When interviewing Coombs in 1982, Fred Rainsberry asked him what ingredients made the show (still on-air at the time) so endearing and enduring:

Ernie Coombs as Mr. Dressup, surrounded by good friends. From left: Casey, Finnegan, Hester the witch, unknown, Aunt Bird, unknown, and Alligator Al, all operated and performed by puppeteer Judith Lawrence.

> If somebody tried to ask me to try to define the show, I'd have to say on which day, because there are so many different things we always have. Humour. There's always a little bit of information, I could say education. Sometimes we can have a little bit of suspense if a problem comes up and we wonder what's happening to somebody, or the audience will wonder how we're going to get out of a particular dilemma.... There's a naturalness about it which is I think really important. The fact that we're not tightly scripted, so we stumble our way through in our own words. I think that helps. It seems to the audience that it's really happening at the time.[35]

This simple but resilient format remained largely unchanged for the next few decades, ultimately chalking up three thousand episodes and twenty-eight years on the air. During most of those years it aired during the prime morning slot alongside *The Friendly Giant* and *Sesame Street*, providing preschoolers with an equal amount of cognitive and imaginative play–based television — the Children's Television Workshop (which put out *Sesame Street*) always favoured didacticism through the repetition of numbers and letters, while the CBC's approach was to foster imagination and creativity through costume play, games, artwork, and crafting.

In recalling the success of that era, long-time producer Stuart Gilchrist praised the collaborative environment cultivated by the CBC:

> I think the goodwill and the camaraderie with everyone involved is one of those marvellous things. The Corporation [CBC] had something that I don't think I've ever found since — it had a truly creative environment where everyone could function [at their best].[36]

23
Passport to Adventure (1965)

TORONTO-AREA SCHOOLTEACHER ELWY YOST JOINED THE CBC in 1959 as a guest panellist on *Live a Borrowed Life*, before leaving education to become a full-time broadcaster in the mid-1960s. After working on several different panel shows, Yost was approached to anchor a new kind of daily kids' program. Yost explained:

> A producer named John Twomey came to me and said he was starting a new series that involved movies. He heard I always liked them, and I'd written the odd review. He was starting a new project, *Passport to Adventure*. The idea being to take a feature film and cut it into four parts. The movies he picked were an average 88 minutes long, which made about 22 minutes per night of film, leaving six minutes to pursue the theme and substance of the picture, through interviews and location shooting and all kinds of other educational shenanigans and things. And that ran for two years, and then it was dropped. I think we were killed by *Rocket Robin Hood* (1966), and *Max, the 2000-Year-Old Mouse* (1967). An animated mouse murdered my career.[37]

Chicago native Twomey had been recruited by Rainsberry in 1958 to work on audience research at the CBC, and within a few years he was producing *The Friendly Giant* and *Butternut Square* for the children's department. Films selected for broadcast and discussion on *Passport to Adventure* included *King Kong* (1933), *Abbott and Costello Meet Frankenstein* (1948), *The Invisible Man* (1933), *Lost Horizon* (1937), *The Phantom of the Opera* (1943), *Captain Blood* (1935), *Mighty Joe Young* (1949), and *The Adventures of Robin Hood* (1938). Guests featured included Douglas Fairbanks, Arthur Treacher, and Willard Van Dyke. The films were frequently edited to trim out violence, adult situations, and excessive dialogue that might bore the young audience.[38]

The series title was shortened to *Passport* in 1966, allowing films to be screened that weren't adventures. Yost recalled an episode that featured Canadian actor Elwood Glover as his guest:

> We ran *Jesse James* (1939). And you remember that big scene at the Northfield, Minnesota, raid where Jesse and his brother dive their horses right through a great plate glass window? It's a great shot. The two of them go right through the window. Staggering. And I'll never forget Elwood and

Later to become better known as the jovial host of TVOntario's *Saturday Night at the Movies*, Elwy Yost began his career as local TV's most endearing encyclopedic film fan with *Passport to Adventure* (1965), a weekday serialized movie show aimed at younger viewers.

> I taking sheets of candy glass and smashing them over each other's heads to demonstrate to our viewers right after. I have people still today remembering that, telling me how that intrigued their imagination. It helped them become vastly interested in the whole world of special effects. These things can have lasting impressions, and they can be strongly motivational.[39]

In 1970, Yost left the CBC to join the Ontario Educational Communications Authority (OECA), which would later become TVOntario. With OECA program director Jim Hanley and writer Ken Sobol, Yost reintroduced the format of *Passport to Adventure* as *Magic Shadows* in 1974.

24

Time of Your Life (1964)/ Through the Eyes of Tomorrow (1966)

TAKING A CUE FROM *RAZZLE DAZZLE*'S ALLEY SETTING, *Junior Magazine*'s replacement, *Time of Your Life*, was situated in a coffee-shop setting, the sort of place teenagers in the early sixties hung out in to watch bands. It was a live, sixty-minute variety show that featured music, theatre, topical discussions with guests, and many appearances by young people who were recognized for making a difference in their communities. Michele Finney, now a teenager herself, was poached as host from *Razzle Dazzle* and paired with Peter Kastner, star of Don Owen's *Nobody Waved Goodbye* (1964), a rare early Canadian film meditation on youth rebellion.

Producer William Davidson, with his partner Norman Knelman, had previously directed a quasi-exploitation biker movie called *Ivy League Killers* (1959), an early attempt at getting a viable film industry underway in Toronto. Starring Don Francks, the film was lauded for its realistic portrayal of young people, in this case a gang of motorcycle-riding delinquents. During the early sixties, many young people felt that popular culture, including television, was not reflecting the social challenges they were facing and was therefore not meant for them. In many ways, the content was still stuck in the overly conventional 1950s.

Selected to bring genuine street credibility to *Time of Your Life*, Davidson accepted the challenge and created what might have been the CBC's very first counterculture show. As it fell within the children's department, he escaped the heavy-handed supervision that hampered many of the CBC's prime-time offerings. Davidson had a knack for spotting talent and hired a young Paul Hoffert (later of the Toronto prog rock band Lighthouse) to be the series musical director. Musical guests ranged from the rockabilly sounds of Rompin' Ronnie Hawkins to local heartthrob Robbie Lane and the Disciples. Dramatic plays written by teenagers were performed live, and some were even shot on location with professional actors, usually on videotape rather than 16mm film to help keep costs within the tiny budgets. "Drama was not the exclusive domain of the drama department, though the drama producers were not really aware of this,"[40] wrote *Time of Your Life* director Sandy Stewart.

In 1966, Davidson departed to work on *The Forest Rangers*, and Perry Rosemond took over as producer. The show was retitled *Through the Eyes of Tomorrow*, and Rosemond dropped the music and drama, leaning heavily into current affairs and turning the series into more of an outlet for investigative journalism for young people. He also implemented a policy allowing high-school students to work on the show at every level of production, including decisions on guests and topics. Rosemond is often credited with inspiring a generation of Canadian teens to consider a career in broadcast journalism. *Through the Eyes of Tomorrow* presented a rotating group of hosts, including Paul Saltzman (son of Percy Saltzman, Uncle Chichimus's first onscreen partner), Jennifer Leak, and Rex Hagon. It often courted controversy with footage from the Vietnam War, frank discussions about LSD, and coverage of the destruction of the Black community Africville in Halifax. The final episode in 1969 featured an interview with Jimi Hendrix. *The Friendly Giant*'s Rod Coneybeare spoke of the culture at the CBC that enabled such daring programs for youth to be created:

> I think the business of that day, which is perhaps gone forever at CBC, was how much power a writer and or actor would have in the concept of a show and getting a show on the air with the least amount of committees and the least amount of cooks in the broth. Now that I look back, I realize there were very few people to go through. Shows got on the air, and I think there was a lot more creative control on the part of the actual writers and perhaps performers, certainly writers, than there is now.[41]

IT CAME FROM BUFFALO!

Television signals beamed across Lake Ontario from Buffalo, New York, played a major role in Toronto popular culture that even predated the 1952 start date of our own local television history. WBEN-TV in Buffalo commenced broadcasting in 1948 and prompted many people in Toronto to purchase their first television set. At that time there were only an estimated thirty thousand television sets in all of Canada, most of which were unsurprisingly found clustered near the U.S. border. Even after the launch of CBLT-TV in 1952, it would be another eight years until CFTO-TV and the CTV network arrived, during which time many in Toronto avidly followed Buffalo stations such as WBUF-TV, WGR-TV, WKBW-TV, and WNED-TV, which was New York State's very first non-commercial public television station. These channels brought many U.S. children's shows into the homes of Toronto and remain etched in viewers' memories just as much as our own beloved homegrown series, with titles like *The Jungle Jay Nelson Show*, *Captain Bob Show*, *Bozo the Clown*, *Mr. Whatnot*, and *Buckskin Joe*.

Perhaps the most remarkable was *Rocketship 7* (1962), created by WKBW-TV as an extended promotion for Bell Aerospace, a manufacturer of military aircraft located in Wheatfield, New York. Hosted by WKBW-TV's weatherman Dave Thomas (father of *Buffy the Vampire Slayer* actor David Boreanaz) and his trusted sidekick Promo the Robot, *Rocketship 7* featured an almost entirely educational format, which was unusual for a commercial channel at that time. Astronaut Thomas would screen vintage Warner Bros. cartoons as well as *Gumby* (1953) shorts, interwoven with educational content about science, space, and the aeronautics industry. It ran in the early morning and only ended when Thomas left WKBW-TV in 1978.

A few years after *Rocketship 7*, WKBW-TV launched *Commander Tom* (1965), hosted by another station weatherman, Tom Jolls, as the titular Commander who, alongside his puppet friends Dustmop the dog and Matty the (alligator) Mod, acted out space-based interstitials wrapped around old cartoons and reruns of *The Munsters* (1964) in the afternoon time slot. While *Rocketship 7* maintained its educational bent for the duration of its run, *Commander Tom* slowly shed its militaristic undertones to become more of a cozy *Mister Rogers' Neighborhood* in space. By the early 1980s it had been shuttled to Sunday mornings, where a generation of Toronto viewers were first exposed to *Davey and Goliath* (1961) reruns. Jolls always wore a red Royal Canadian Mounted Police jacket.

As Buffalo's only PBS affiliate, WNED-TV is lovingly remembered by many Toronto viewers for airing their first introduction to *Sesame Street* (1969), or *Doctor Who* (1963), but also for their quarterly fundraising telethons. These often-week-long events were led by colourful Buffalonians like WNED-TV's own Goldie Gardner, who infamously told children watching early-morning broadcasts of *Sesame Street* to wake up their parents and make a pledge if they wanted Big Bird to stay on the air.

Dave Thomas, with Promo the Robot and some puppet friends, on the set of *Rocketship 7*.

25
Barney Boomer (1967)/ Upside Town (1968)

IN 1966, FRED RAINSBERRY LEFT THE CBC. HIS DECISION TO leave was due in part to an opportunity provided by the Rothschild Foundation to help establish a national TV network in Israel. He was hired as a consultant to help create a department that would produce educational television for children, and to recruit Israeli directors and producers. Unfortunately, soon after his arrival the Six-Day War began, and he and his family returned to Canada. Rainsberry took a senior professorship at the Ontario Institute for Studies in Education (OISE), where he continued to inspire students and write about the unrealized educational potential of television. Producer Daniel McCarthy (*The Friendly Giant*, *Mr. Dressup*) replaced Rainsberry as head of the children's department. Keen to make an immediate impact, McCarthy engaged producer Stuart Gilchrist to develop a new daily dramatic comedy show for the 4:30 p.m. slot, moving him off *Mr. Dressup* (1967).

The result was *Barney Boomer*, a strange mix of soap opera and situational comedy, with exterior location shooting done in picturesque Oakville, Ontario. *Barney Boomer* told the story of a young seafaring adventurer who sailed his houseboat into the Cedarville (Oakville) harbour to visit his uncle Captain Boomer, and became involved with the odd townspeople (including *Razzle Dazzle* host Trudy Young playing herself). The studio sets included a lighthouse and convenience store. It was described as *Peyton Place* (1964) for kids.

Gilchrist remembers that, once again, studio space was commandeered by the news division, halting production: "Again we had an unfortunate situation whereby the news department found that they required the studio again. And *Barney Boomer* went on ice for a year."[42] When it returned, original star Heath Lamberts had been contracted to another production and was unable to return, so the lead was recast with John Clayton and the show retitled *Upside Town* (1968). A ten-minute children's quiz show, *Swingaround* (1968), filled out the thirty-minute time slot, and eventually took it over completely. Gilchrist concedes the CBC just did not have the necessary ecosystem to create the show they had in mind:

> We were looking for a program of a strict nature whereby one can employ the economies of production as well as having the continuity. It was ambitious. And looking back now, I suppose it was my own naivete. And I [was] thinking that we could continue with *Barney Boomer* in perpetuity, but we couldn't. It was an exhausting format. As I say, we did not have the type of facility necessary to produce.[43]

The CBC abandoned the concept of a daily dramatic comedy series until 1974, when once again they turned to a trusted *Mr. Dressup* producer (in this case, Don Elder) to attempt something completely different — *Dr. Zonk and the Zunkins* (1974).

26

The Bananas (1969)

THE BANANAS WAS AN UNCONVENTIONAL SKETCH-COMEDY show for nine-to-fourteen-year-olds, described by creator Rod Coneybeare (*The Friendly Giant*'s Jerome and Rusty) as equal parts Second City, *The Goon*

Show, and Charlie Brown. Opening with a visual joke that transposed the CBC's iconic butterfly logo into a scruffy penguin, *The Bananas* was non-stop visual mayhem that showcased the talents of four young comics (John Davies, Francois Klanfer, Bonnie-Carol Chase, and Melody Greer, all selected from a Toronto- and Montreal-wide talent search). The four actors existed within a surreal space called "Bananaland" alongside characters like "Official Certified Genuine Grade-A Gorilla" (a man in gorilla suit), "The Great Announcer" (the disembodied voice of Alan Maitland), and "The Big Mouth" (an oppressive mouth-on-the-wall that exchanges arcane educational information for wheel-barrows of food).

Coneybeare envisioned the show as a catalyst for making kids think more about the world that surrounds them, featuring up to a dozen sketches per episode. *Starweek* magazine suggested "the theme song, for example, is downright inane — but when it's performed by the Bananas it could just be a subliminal satire on all the commercials and musical comedies you hear these days."[44] One recurring sketch involved role reversals where children were portrayed as adults coming home from a hard day's work in the sandbox and admonishing their parents, a trope revisited with much greater success a decade later in the CJOH-TV Ottawa production *You Can't Do That on Television!* (1979).

Unfortunately for *The Bananas*, a few months prior to its release NBC debuted a new kids' show called *The Banana Splits* (1968) in the popular Saturday-morning time slot. It was a psychedelic variety show created by Hanna-Barbera that mixed cartoons, live action, comedy sketches, and music. *The Bananas*' similar-sounding title likely created confusion, and the show was not renewed after the first six thirty-minute-long episodes aired in the Thursday afternoon time slot on the CBC. Coneybeare told *TV North* author Peter Kenter:

> I was trying to create a program that was wry, ironic, and sardonic — something to get the audience to question things around them. It represented a sort of civilized iconoclasm that I believe kids should be exposed to. It was quite successful

with audiences, but it died for lack of funds — it was expensive for the time. We probably should have changed the title after the U.S. program aired, but the CBC really liked the name, so we stuck with it.[45]

27
Adventures in Rainbow Country (1969)

ADVENTURES IN RAINBOW COUNTRY WAS A FAMILY-BASED adventure series with all the panache of *The Forest Rangers* (1963), but with added grit to reflect the changing times. The premise involved a skillful fifteen-year-old wilderness guide Billy Williams (Stephen Cottier) who managed to get tangled up in all manner of outdoor shenanigans, alongside his young sister Hannah (Susan Conway) and their Ojibwe friend Pete (Buckley Petawabano), after Billy's father disappeared under mysterious circumstances in Northern Ontario.

Although it was a ratings success for the CBC, only one series of twenty-six episodes running at thirty minutes each were filmed, as the production team (Manitou Productions) disbanded before any more could be ordered. It was dubbed into French for Quebec and sold around the world, where it found great popularity in the U.K, Australia, and Germany. One memorable episode ("Girl on a Tightrope"), which found young Hannah kidnapped by a deranged circus clown, was watched by more than 4.6 million viewers across the country (according to a Nielsen survey of the most-watched programs on Canadian television published in 1986).[46]

The guest cast included Margot Kidder, Gordon Pinsent, Don Harron, Albert Millaire, and Lois Maxwell (the first Miss Moneypenny from the James Bond films). Conway had also appeared in *The Forest Rangers* and followed this series immediately as the co-host of *Drop-In* (1970).

1970s

28
Sesame Street (1970)

THERE IS NO SINGLE PROGRAM IN THE HISTORY OF CHILDren's television that has had a more pronounced effect on the genre than *Sesame Street*, for an alphabet of reasons. The globally recognized television institution had many architects, but its genesis can be traced back to a 1966 dinner conversation between television producer Joan Ganz Cooney and Carnegie Corporation vice-president Lloyd Morrisett. Cooney was marvelling at the power of commercial television advertising after witnessing a child reciting a beer commercial jingle word for word. Morrisett suggested a new program could apply those same slick Madison Avenue production techniques to teach the basics to underprivileged children in America.

Between 1966 and 1968, research on how to best merge the latest production methods of television and advertising with educational and curriculum goals, sustained by robust audience testing, was conducted by the non-profit consortium Children's Television Workshop (CTW) based in New York City. Cooney became CTW's first executive director after travelling across the United States and Canada researching the current state of children's television along with various academic and social initiatives that might be communicated through the medium. Cooney's findings were published in a 1967 document entitled *The Potential Uses of Television in Preschool Education*, which outlined her vision for in-house formative research and independent summative evaluations that could monitor young viewers' responses and inform future creative work. Cooney's approach became the basis for all CTW productions.

Cooney concluded that "a show devised to present letters and numbers could be done in the format of commercial messages."[1] With an eight-million-dollar combined grant from the Carnegie Corporation, the Ford

Foundation, the Corporation for Public Broadcasting, and others, the CTW set about creating a new, fast-paced children's series that would mix animation, live action, and puppetry. Working titles "1,2,3 Street" and "Open Sesame" were blended to create *Sesame Street*.

Many veterans of CBS's *Captain Kangaroo* (1955) — itself initially seen as an educational alternative to *The Howdy Doody Show* (1947) — helped shape the original concept, including writers Jon Stone and Matt Robinson. Through the CTW's extensive research in television advertising, Stone and Robinson became aware of Jim Henson, whose Muppet troupe was being used to sell junk food though brands such as Frito-Lay and Royal Crown Cola. Joe Raposo, an old friend of Stone, was invited to contribute music.

The creative team was bolstered by child psychologists and educational supervisors at every stage of development. After rudimentary segments were road-tested with a wide range of children, parents, and teachers, it was determined that the punchier animated and puppetry segments performed best, while longer live-action dialogue scenes between the human hosts lost viewers' attention. This four-square method of research-shoot-test-restructure was adhered to for the remainder of production.

Sesame Street premiered across the PBS network in the United States on Monday, November 10, 1969, and could be seen in Toronto via UHF broadcast from PBS affiliate WNED-TV in Buffalo, New York. Its listing in *Starweek* magazine read: "*Sesame Street* is a new daily series aimed at helping prepare preschool children for school, using entertainment techniques common to commercial television."[2] Almost immediately, *Sesame Street* became the most talked about television series on-air, and magazines and newspapers were filled with breathless reports on its effectiveness in teaching children. "My two-year-old son already has learned the alphabet from watching *Sesame Street*,"[3] one Toronto-area parent told the *Toronto Star* in February 1970. The article went on:

> Technically it is the slickest show on television today, abounding in split-second psychedelic pyrotechnics, combining (sometimes simultaneously) animated cartoons, puppets,

> and live performers, making inventive use of sound and edited so tightly that *Laugh-In*, by comparison, resembles *The Ed Sullivan Show*.[4]

CBC's director of informational programming, Knowlton Nash, had begun negotiating for exclusive Canadian broadcast rights ("a superb piece of television,"[5] gushed Nash), although such an acquisition might have been problematic due to the CTW's resolve that the program air free of commercials, twice a day. Prophetically, the *Toronto Star* article also suggested the Ontario government's educational television division, whose Channel 19 would not air until September 1970, would be unable to create a similar program owing to its first year's operating budget of eight million dollars — the exact cost of one season of *Sesame Street*. "Obviously, Ontario's [educational television] programmers cannot afford to duplicate *Sesame Street*, even if they wish to — but they can learn a lot from it for free."[6]

CBC's attempt to acquire *Sesame Street* was impeded when privately held CTV joined the bidding war. The Canadian Radio and Television Commission (CRTC) further complicated issues in February 1970 when it revised its Canadian-content rulings, mandating a minimum of 60 percent Canadian content from all broadcasters. In May 1970, CRTC president Pierre Juneau signalled possible wiggle room by announcing that programs that the commission considered "of significant merit" would qualify as "no nationality," and therefore would not count toward the critical 40 percent of foreign content. CBC took this announcement on good faith, believing that "superior educational TV should know no geographic boundaries,"[7] and promptly upped its bid, winning the prized Canadian broadcast rights to *Sesame Street* at an enormous cost (apparently one of the CBC's most expensive imports ever). There was still the issue of the second daily run, which the CBC did not wish to impose upon its affiliate channels, who were struggling to squeeze in more commercial time during their broadcast hours.

In July 1970, the CRTC changed course and dropped the concept of "no nationality," leaving the CBC "stuck with *Sesame Street*."[8] However, the CBC's incipient relationship with the Ontario Educational Communications

Authority (OECA) and its soon-to-be-launched Channel 19 presented a solution to the second-run issue and an irresistible opportunity for Toronto-based Channel 19. The CBC essentially gifted the second run to the OECA. A similar arrangement was made with ACCESS, Alberta's public broadcaster, allowing it to feature the marquee series at a fraction of the cost. The CRTC did eventually bow to pressure and allow *Sesame Street* a "no nationality" hall pass for its inaugural season.

After a press screening of the first episode in Toronto in September 1970, *Sesame Street*'s executive producer David Connell sought to downplay its reputation as the second coming: "*Sesame Street* is not going to revolutionize the educational world. It's just one little program," he humbly announced.[9] CBC's head of children's programming Daniel "Dan" McCarthy was on hand to publicly ask Connell if he saw any future viability of a Canadianized version of the program "that could be repackaged to show Indian reservations and reflect Canadian bilingualism."[10] Connell mused it was something that might be considered down the line. McCarthy announced that a Canadian-produced children's show similar in scale to *Sesame Street* could never occur due to the costs: "It would require enormous investment … I would like to see more commitment at the taxpayer level. Kids' TV is not at the top of the priority list."[11]

Sesame Street premiered to great acclaim on CBC on Monday, September 28, 1970 (for those who had been unable to watch the cross-border UHF broadcasts from PBS). It proved there was a mass audience for children's programs that achieved their pedagogical objectives through innovative entertainment.

In 1971, when it became clear that the CRTC would not be extending the "no nationality" classification for another season, the idea of the CBC dropping *Sesame Street* from its schedule became a very real possibility. Many of the CBC's affiliates were struggling to air five hours of *Sesame Street* a week, with no commercials (as per the Children's Television Workshop's contractual stipulation), and that counted against their strictly enforced Canadian-content quotas. By 1972, more than half of the CBC's affiliates across Canada had dropped the show. Protests flared up across the country with children, parents, and educators pleading for the federal government to "Save *Sesame Street*!" Animated arguments about the stifling nature of the CRTC's definitions of Canadian content even reached Parliament Hill. CBC's Knowlton Nash recalled the challenge of trying to "Canadianize" *Sesame Street* to placate the CRTC:

> We wanted to insert our own segments into *Sesame Street*, ... teaching preschoolers basic French and showing them lakes and oceans, mountains and prairies, and the fishermen, hunters, city dwellers, and farmers of Canada. But the New York producers were ferociously protective of their successful show. Their apprehension was based on their doubt that we could maintain the same quality of production as the rest of the program. "No bloody way," I had been told when I first proposed Canadianizing it by adding five to six minutes of Canadian material to the show, replacing material on learning Spanish and on Puerto Ricans and Mexican-Americans, which had no relevance to Canadian children. I also wanted to get rid of the alphabet as "Zee" instead of the Canadian "Zed." It was a small point, but it drove me nuts to think of a nation of Canadian children growing up saying "Zee."[12]

Meanwhile, Dan McCarthy had been working behind the scenes with CTW on a favourable resolution. Since *Sesame Street* first aired, CTW had been inundated with requests from countries including Brazil, Mexico, Iran, and Germany to create their own homegrown versions of the series. The first international variant of *Sesame Street* was *Plaza Sésamo* in Mexico, which included a mixture of dubbed segments from *Sesame Street* along with newly created characters and settings. McCarthy spearheaded the second such international hybrid in the form of *Sesame Street Canada*, which also debuted in 1972. For Canadian viewers, the title remained *Sesame Street*, but included the new material, which satisfied the CRTC's Canadian-content quota.

The CBC-produced animated and live-action segments focused on Canadian multiculturalism, bilingualism, Indigenous culture, and history, replacing similar CTW segments that focused on Spanish language and American history. Toronto-area viewers could still see the uncut CTW episodes via WNED-TV's broadcasts from Buffalo. In fact, in Toronto in 1972, *Sesame Street* was the most broadcast series at twenty-four hours per week — seventeen times a week on WNED-TV, seven on Channel 19 (which aired it on both Saturday and Sunday), and five on CBC.

The success of *Sesame Street* and its frenetic tempo erroneously suggested to some programmers that all children's series must engage at a similar speed to attain similar goals. Slower-paced programs such as *The Friendly Giant* (1958) and *Mr. Dressup* (1967) were accused by some of falling behind the times, although that was never reflected in their ratings. In a 1982 interview, Fred Rainsberry reflected,

> The *Sesame Street* thing is built strictly on the conviction that a child grows up, in terms of cognitive development, you see, whereas *Mr. Dressup*, *The Friendly Giant*, and *Mister Rogers* are more playful and more based on personality.[13]

It seemed as if the groundbreaking but hyperactive *Sesame Street* could peacefully coexist in the CBC schedule with its more subdued Canadian cousins.

However, in 1973, the CBC cancelled its long-running Montreal-based French-language children's series *Chez Hélène* (1959), which had appeared in the morning preschool block alongside *The Friendly Giant* and *Mr. Dressup* for over a decade. The head of CBC's children's department, John Kennedy, who replaced McCarthy when he took over the *Sesame Street Canada* project, argued that the newly produced French-language segments in *Sesame Street Canada* had rendered *Chez Hélène* obsolete.

29
Drop-In (1970)

THE 1970S BEGAN WITH A CHALLENGE AT CBC WHOSE TELEvision audience was splintering as dramatically as the era's zeitgeist. The broadcaster needed to recapture the imagination of the nine-to-fourteen demographic, which it hadn't done successfully since the six-year run of *Razzle Dazzle*. It had been retired in 1966, but its spiritual heir had yet to materialize. Producer Ray Hazzan was tasked with the challenge of developing something that could resonate with seventies kids as much as *Razzle Dazzle* had with sixties kids. His arrival at the children's department via the news division brought great promise; he had a knack for experimental approaches to the cut-and-dried formula of news. Hazzan began constructing the show with a pilot summer series called *Dress Rehearsal* (1970), during which the hosts for the new series would be auditioned and selected through viewer voting, a harbinger of reality-based programming yet to come.

Two stars of *The Forest Rangers* — Susan Conway and Rex Hagon — were selected as the hosts of what was now called *Drop-In*. They were occasionally joined by Nina Keogh and her puppets, and young actors Jeff Cohen and Lynn Griffin. The show had a loose format centred on a theme; for example, the magic episode featured disco-age trickster Doug Henning, who dropped in for a groovy, magical visit. Keogh would perform with her puppets or the group might enjoy live musical concerts by guest artists such as Ron Nigrini's Gentle Rock Band (which would sometimes cover Gordon Lightfoot), psychedelic balladeers Perth County Conspiracy from Stratford, Ontario, and even Sharon Hampson (Sharon, Lois & Bram) when she was a folksy solo act.

Re-creations of historical Canadian characters and events with comedians Don Harron and Tommy Tweed were another popular segment, as were extended skits featuring the hosts. Short films of the hosts' visits or "drop-ins" to

An advertisement for *Drop-In* (1970), CBC's groovy new youth show for the 1970s.

various spots across Canada reinforced the show's title and grew more adventurous, with jaunts to Buckingham Palace in the United Kingdom, the Rhine River in Germany, and even the office of the Prime Minister of Canada, where the hosts met and interviewed Pierre Trudeau. The cast eventually grew to include multiple reporters from eight separate locations across Canada, recalling the earlier cross-country flavour of *Junior Roundup* (1960). In 1972, *Drop-In* was taken over by *Mr. Dressup* producer Don Elder. Hazzan had departed to create the Ottawa-based *What's New?*, a current-affairs series aimed at a slightly older teenage audience that used exaggerated puppet caricatures created by Noreen Young. The show possibly inspired the use of grotesque puppets in Britain's biting political satire *Spitting Image* (1984).

UHF — A NEW FREQUENCY

An exciting development for television came in the form of a new broadcasting frequency — ultra-high frequency (UHF). UHF broadcasting had been tested in the U.K. as far back as the 1930s using high-frequency vacuum tubes manufactured by Philips. Postwar, the tubes had flooded the market and were soon exploited for commercial applications, such as radio.

UHF frequencies allowed for analogue television signals to be broadcast in urban areas, although, owing to interference from buildings and other environmental factors, the broadcast range was limited and often fuzzy or distorted by picture interference referred to as "snow." UHF required powerful transmitters and antennas but would theoretically allow for more niche broadcasts from private entities that could not afford the higher-powered VHF signal.

In the late 1960s, the Canadian Radio and Television Commission (later the Canadian Radio-television and Telecommunications Commission, CRTC) in Ottawa began accepting applications for a licence of the very first UHF television station in Canada, Channel 25, which would be stationed in Toronto. At that time, UHF adapters were available to purchase for roughly fifty dollars, and with them Toronto residents could view UHF television broadcasts from PBS affiliate WNED, Channel 17 in Buffalo, New York. Additionally, the Government of Canada had declared that all television sets would be mandated to have a UHF band in addition to a VHF band as of June 1, 1969.

Channelling the past: a 1970s-era TV featuring two reception knobs — one for VHF and one for UHF.

30
OECA (1970)

TELEVISION'S IMMENSE POTENTIAL TO AID IN EDUCATION was noted by select educators from the very beginning of commercial television in Canada. The first educational programs were produced in 1954 by the CBC. Many of the original educational series tended to be talking heads — classroom lessons piped through television signals that didn't make meaningful use of the medium. For many years, schools made little use of the educational material for a variety of reasons, including the lack of budget to accommodate television sets and content that didn't always align with the curriculum. That started to change when local municipalities and provinces began to plan their own boards of education.

In 1961, the Metropolitan Educational Television Association (META) in Toronto was granted a charter by the Ontario Legislature and requested that Channel 19, a UHF channel (see p. 105), be reserved for educational purposes in the Toronto area (it would take another nine years to eventually start broadcasting). META's first programs were produced in co-operation with other local Toronto television stations, including CFTO-TV. In 1963, META produced its first program independently in a studio at the Ryerson Institute of Technology (now called Toronto Metropolitan University). By 1967, META was a full-scale independent producer, and a year later it was producing over sixty programs of its own (the details of which were not well documented).

Bill Davis, Ontario's Minister of Education from 1962 to 1971, envisioned establishing an educational television division within the ministry. Ever the optimist, Davis hoped an educational television station would be broadcasting across Ontario by 1966. Davis selected educator and part-time radio movie-critic Thomas Ranald "Ran" Ide to head the division. Ide had a strong understanding of emerging media and the role it could play in education in Ontario.

In 1966, its first year, Ontario's educational division produced over 150 television programs covering a variety of educational subjects for elementary and secondary school students. The ministry purchased airtime from the CBC and CHCH-TV in Hamilton, Ontario, where programs aired in the morning and early afternoon, aligning with school timetables in the hope they would be used in classrooms. Infamously, Davis received a letter from H.G. Walker, vice-president of network broadcasting for the CBC, stating that "the Corporation is willing to provide the full Ontario network free of charge,"[14] suggesting that the ministry had wasted money in buying airtime on CBC that would have been provided for free.

Education is governed by the provinces, and the federally mandated CBC struggled with meeting the curriculum requirements of ten different provincial ministries of education. After Ottawa decided not to proceed with its plans for an educational broadcasting agency, the Ontario Ministry of Education was able to advance and work out the details for an agency of its own, which would operate in co-operation with the CBC. On January 30, 1970, the CBC's application to the CRTC for the necessary broadcasting facilities was approved. At the same time, the CBC received permission to construct and operate — under contract with Ontario — a Channel-19 transmitter. The transmitter, located at the Jarvis Street tower in Toronto, had an antenna with an effective height of 476 feet.

In March 1970, the Ontario Educational Communications Authority (OECA) was established by an act of the Ontario Legislature. One of the services of the authority was the operation of the new educational television channel — CICA-TV, a.k.a. Channel 19. Ide was named the OECA's first chairman, and CICA-TV began its initial all-day broadcasts on September 27, 1970.

Central to Ran Ide's vision for the OECA was the development of quality content for young people: "If we could devise appropriate programs for children, we would be able to make a positive difference in their chances for success when they began formal schooling."[15] Ide hired many educators, who were placed in key roles aligning with their expertise in an effort to reconcile pedagogical objectives with entertainment for children's programs. Vera Novakowski, who was charged with overseeing teacher education and early childhood education, recalled the OECA's challenge in the early days:

> It was a difficult task to achieve, the blending of curriculum objectives and entertainment. But it was never a problem from my point of view, because I felt that unless the program was entertaining for children and captivated them and caught their fancy and interest, it was a waste of time. It was futile to try to use television as a device to cram children's heads with knowledge. And therefore, the problem really became one of which formats could we use that would enable us to communicate the kind of information that teachers felt was not wasting their time and presenting it in such a way that children would find it challenging, entertaining. That was what we tried to do as we gradually moved out of the more strictly complementary into the more curriculum oriented. Those were our first steps.[16]

Since the licence for Channel 19 was granted in January of 1970, and the proposed start date for the station was September, there was a scramble to acquire programming in time for its launch. One of the most obvious acquisitions was the trailblazing *Sesame Street*, but it was locked into a long-term first-run contract with the CBC.

In 1969, CBC's President George Davidson and Vice-President Eugene Holman had been given a sneak preview and first right of refusal for *Sesame Street*. The two men visited New York and were immediately won over by the production and the Children's Television Workshop team. Signing up on the spot, only later did they discover the fine print that committed CBC to two plays per day, which the large number of CBC affiliates across Canada would never agree to. So the second hour of *Sesame Street* was essentially given to OECA as a way for the CBC to tactfully escape an agreement that never should have been made in the first place. CBC continued to have first-run rights to *Sesame Street*, with the OECA (along with ACCESS, Alberta's public broadcasting network) granted second-run rights, meaning new episodes would air two weeks after premiering on CBC. According to Ide:

> We ended up acquiring *Sesame Street* because it was a successful program that filled a special need. But it was not what we were looking for. It emphasized the teaching of numbers and letters, which it did with a lot of panache ... [but] we were looking for something to meet the needs we felt were not being met in the home.[17]

An early station identification slide from Channel 19.

Emboldened by the critical endowment of *Sesame Street* — when the program was not even one year old — the OECA team sought to create a similar unconventional series that could both serve as a preschool flagship and a mission statement. Little did they know that this expeditiously created series — *Polka Dot Door* — would become one of its most iconic.

31

Polka Dot Door (1971)

BORN OUT OF THE DESIRE TO CREATE A SIGNATURE, PRE-school program that highlighted play and imagination rather than the rote repetition of numbers and letters featured in the blockbuster import *Sesame Street*, *Polka Dot Door* had a great many early contributors, each bringing elements that complemented one another and led to the creation of the network's most enduring and endearing series. Vera Novakowski, head of childhood education at the OECA, recalled,

> [Our] first independent program that went to air in Ontario was *Polka Dot Door.* And it was a major step for us to take. It was an expensive venture. It was something in which we had no experience. We had watched other programs that were being broadcast, *Mr. Dressup*, you know, all the others. We were trying to do something that was unique for TVOntario.[18]

One of *Polka Dot Door*'s many architects was Vera Good, the first female principal in Etobicoke, who ended up at the Ministry of Education just in time for the launch of OECA. Good was an ideal candidate to take on developing a series that would register with preschoolers in their own homes: "We were looking for a series to broaden and enrich the experiences of children," Good explained.[19] After much research, brainstorming, and communication with the CBC's children's department, plus a visit in 1970 with Joan Ganz Cooney at the Children's Television Workshop in New York, Good had compiled vast amounts of information but still had no television program. Later that year, she visited the BBC in London and held meetings with programmers in the children's department. She learned of a BBC series called *Play School* that fit the bill.

Play School was originally created by Joy Whitby in 1964, in response to the shortage of nursery schools across the country. It was further developed by a consortium of educators, children's authors, illustrators, and television professionals. It took a playful rather than didactic approach to artwork, animals, imagination, storytelling, and learning. Production-wise, *Play School* was very progressive, with a revolving line of male and female hosts, including Paul Danquah, the first Black presenter of a children's program in the U.K.

The product, including its construction (a term used in the industry to refer to the many elements of a show's structure and production), appealed to Good and her team, and they purchased ten episodes to air on Channel 19 to fill the initial two-week gap before *Sesame Street* began on October 19, 1970. There was also an option to purchase more episodes in the future.

OECA producer Ted Coneybeare had been with Ontario's educational television division since 1968 and was appointed Education Supervisor, Head of Preschool. Coneybeare reviewed the *Play School* episodes and requested a meeting with one of its producers, who visited Toronto in the fall of 1970. It was during this visit that Coneybeare realized that *Play School* was also available in "program kits," an early name for formatting (see p. 25). *Play School* had successfully sold its program kits to Australia, New Zealand, Spain, Norway, Italy, and Israel. The kits included scripts, music, settings, titles, film segments, and the ever popular "toys" — a group of lovable stuffies and plastic dolls that were often central to each day's episode — Humpty, Jemima, teddy bears Big Ted and Little Ted, and Hamble. Coneybeare committed to purchasing the *Play School* program kits and marshalled a team to oversee its development as an OECA product, comparable to when Fred Rainsberry set about retooling NBC's *The Howdy Doody Show* with a softer Canadian bent for the CBC in 1954.

Producer Peggy Liptrott had been one of the very first women hired to work at the CBC, and, alongside Joanne Hughes, had started the children's department in 1953 before the role was formalized and taken over by Rainsberry. Liptrott was hired to be the producer of OECA's *Play School* adaptation, and was promptly flown to London to review film inserts, which would form the basis of all episodes in its first season. Coneybeare rounded out his team with educational supervisor Marnie Patrick-Roberts, noted professor Dr. Ada Schermann from the Institute of Child Study in Toronto, director Ian Morris, and screenwriters Dodi Robb and Pat Patterson. After all, Robb and Patterson had created Canada's very first English-language preschool program, *Telestory Time* (1953), and more recently had written a successful play for Toronto's Young People's Theatre, *The Popcorn Man* (1970).

The first order of business was to develop a new title that could be used to help promote the launch of Channel 19 set for September 1970, even though the series would not be ready for broadcast until the fall of 1971. Coneybeare's team was considering how to set the Canadian version apart from the British one, and they had roundly decided that a better title was needed.

Play School was set inside a colourful studio space with comfortable chairs, thick shag carpet, and lots of toys and crafts to enjoy. The film inserts were worked into the main flow of the show by the hosts, inviting viewers to look outside through the arched, square, or round window, whereupon a short educational film would play that might explain how a farmer milks cows or how lightning and thunder are formed. Coneybeare's team had decided their version would use a door as opposed to a window as the gateway to and from real life. "The Red Door," "The Green Door," "The Striped Door," and "The Diamond Door" were all suggested, but "The Polka Dot Door" took the win.

Robb began writing scripts, with Patterson adding additional material (together they wrote the first sixty episodes, which were recycled for the duration of the series). As with *Play School*, there was an emphasis on repetitiveness and routine engineered to nurture trust among young viewers. Every episode would feature the hosts introducing the theme of the day, which was particular to which day of the week it was: Monday was Treasure Day, Tuesday was Dress-Up Day, Wednesday was Animal Day, Thursday was Imagination Day, and Friday was Finding-Out Day.

Taking another important element from the *Play School* format, each episode would contain storytime, a segment in which one of the hosts would read aloud from a book and close-ups were shown of the story's artwork. This segment was signalled by the sounding of chimes on a grandfather clock in the set's living area, and a quick lesson in determining what time it was based on the location of the clock's hands immediately followed.

As *Play School*'s stuffed toys and their associated characters were a central part of its popularity, Liptrott and Coneybeare ported over egg-shaped Humpty directly, adding a Dumpty, while Bear was a composite of *Play School*'s Little Ted and Big Ted, and the doll Marigold differed from *Play School*'s rag doll, Jemima. Another new character exclusive to *Polka Dot Door* was Storytime Mouse, a small stuffed rodent who appeared in and around the clock during storytime. In the 1980s, a French Canadian cat named Minou was added to the mix to help children learn simple French phrases.

Beyond the basic *Play School* formula of two hosts — one male, one female — and the stuffed toys, the creative team all agreed *Polka Dot Door* needed an additional element that would help distinguish it from the British show. Robb suggested a new character that embodied imagination, who would appear once a week on "Imagination Day" but would only ever be seen by one host. This new, human-sized personality was baptized "Polkaroo," a portmanteau of Polka from the show's title, and kangaroo, the animal on which early designs for Polkaroo were inspired. The original Polkaroo costume was created by Tanya Petrova, who also designed the Ontario Place mascots Dear Deer, Bashful Beaver, and Rocky Raccoon.

Nina Keogh (foreground) was the first female host of *Polka Dot Door* (1970), seen here with floor director Al O'Malley (left) and producers Ted Coneybeare (middle) and Peggy Liptrott (right).

The character of Polkaroo became the breakout star of the show, and his appearances created an air of mystery as to the true nature of the character, since one host was always absent when he appeared. Upon discovering they had missed him, a host would say a variation of "The Polkaroo was here? And I missed him again?" In later years it seemed the male hosts were always the ones who missed Polkaroo, but Nina Keogh recalls during her time on the show that it alternated. The Polkaroo costume evolved over time and was rebuilt in the early 1980s by Lorraine Cramp, who also designed the costumes for *CUCUMBER*, *Math Patrol*, and *MathMakers*.

Nina Keogh was cast as the very first host and defined the lighthearted hosting template that was followed for the rest of the series. Keogh had recently co-hosted *Drop-In* on the CBC and had spent time operating puppets on *The Friendly Giant* after her parents retired. Gordon Thomson was cast as the male host, but he departed for Hollywood soon after and was replaced by Alex Laurier, a regular on *The Uncle Bobby Show*.

Patterson crafted the original and memorable theme song, which was performed by the opera singer Angela Antonelli. Live-to-tape piano accompaniment was performed by Herbie Helbig and later ragtime virtuoso John Arpin.

In-house art director Dick Derhodge designed a logo based on the title and was then greenlit to create a storyboard for the animated opening sequence:

> After I did the storyboard, I then had to pay an animator. It was two thousand dollars. We shot it in the back of a very narrow restaurant across the street from our original office, which was on Bayview Avenue, close to Eglinton.[20]

Liptrott left the series after one year, and Coneybeare took over as producer. Directors after Morris included David Moore (*Report Metric*, *We Live Next Door*) and Susan Murgatroyd (*CUCUMBER*, *Readalong*). After Keogh exited in 1972, Coneybeare decided to switch up the hosts into separate recording blocks (which captured one week's worth of episodes). This allowed *Polka Dot Door* to become a training ground for future OECA personalities, and to showcase young and diverse Toronto talent.

In 1978, a soundtrack LP entitled *Songs from the Polka Dot Door* was released on the Berandol label. It contained songs written by Robb, Patterson, Helbig, Morris, and Jed MacKay and sung by Rex Hagon, Lynda Kemp, Shelley Sommers, Denis Simpson, Alex Laurier, Carolann Reynolds, Nonnie Griffin, Ken John Grant, and of course Polkaroo.

In 1985, Coneybeare retired, and prolific writer Jed MacKay took over as producer until the show was cancelled in 1993. It was spun off as *Polka Dot Shorts* (1995), also produced by MacKay. The *Polka Dot Door* roll call reads like a who's who in Canadian television between the years 1971 and 1993, including Cindy Cook, actor-singer-writer; Young People's Theatre regular Ken John Grant (*Tell Me a Story*); film, stage, television, and voice actress Nonnie Griffin (*The Care Bears II: A New Generation* [1986]); producer-director-actress Sharon Lewis (*Ready or Not*); actress Malika Mendez (*Read All About It!*, *The Magic Library*); actor Gerry Mendicino (Uncle Taki in *My Big Fat Greek Wedding* [2002]); Canuxploitation regular Candace O'Conner (*Ticket to Heaven* [1981], *The Silent Partner* [1978]); Carolann Reynolds (frequent series host in the early days and star of the *Polka Dot Door* LP); Gairey Richardson (who later took the series on tour in a live stage show [see p. 199]); actress

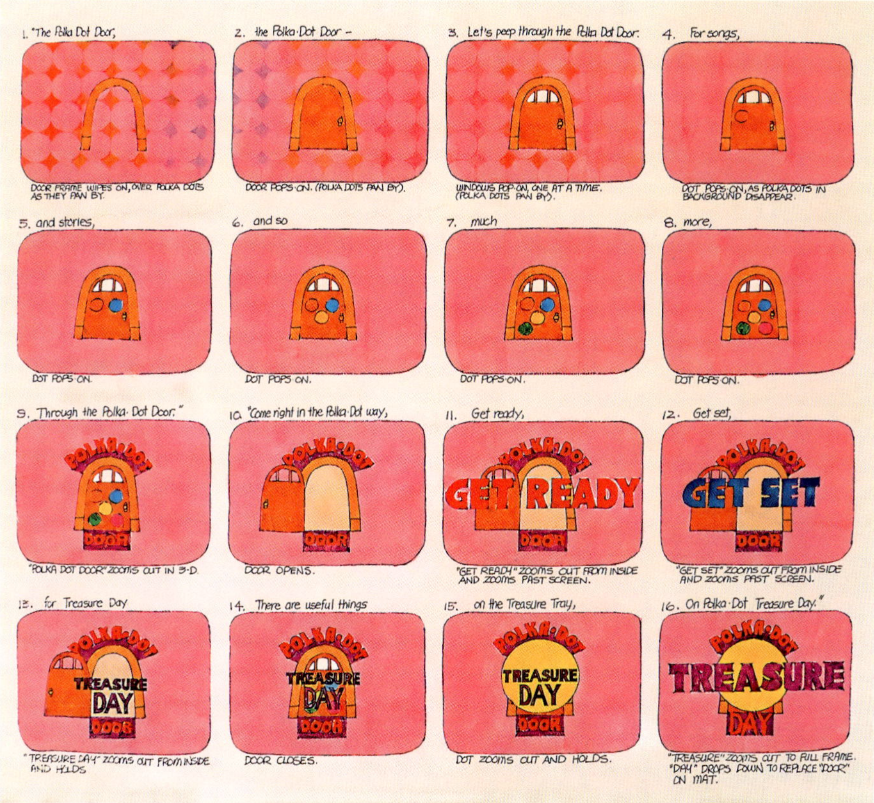

Dick Derhodge's original storyboards for the opening animated sequence of *Polka Dot Door* (1971).

Sherry Miller (*Queer as Folk* [2000], *The Virgin Suicides* [1999], and infamously the Spumante Bambino girl, hawking budget champagne on television during her stint as a co-host); Tonya Williams (Dr. Olivia Winters in the daily U.S. soap *The Young and the Restless*, previously a dancer on Citytv's disco show *Boogie* [1973]); actor Johnie Chase (*Detroit Rock City* [1999], *Dirty Work* [1998]); actor Jim Codrington (*The Ladies Man* [2000], *Tommy Boy* [1995]); actress-singer-author Gloria Reuben (*ER* [1995], *Mr. Robot* [2015], and *Lincoln* [2012]). Future TVO network stars such as Jane Luk (*How Do You Do?*), Heather Conkie (*Dear Aunt Agnes*), Rex Hagon (*The Science Alliance*), Denis Simpson (*Music Box*), and Nerene Virgin all appeared. Virgin was selected as lead on *Today's Special* (1981) based on her work on *Polka Dot Door*.

The educational objectives of *Polka Dot Door* were to stimulate curiosity, creativity, imagination, and "physical dexterity." Motivating children to participate and take an active interest in reading were the secondary goals. An internal network document from 1982 reiterates the major themes of the show:

> Explore, discover, identify, expand on experiences, ideas, objects, concepts, both familiar and unfamiliar. Asking questions is implicit. Presentations will be direct as well as incidental. Each day might include a special "Show and Tell" Time which would take place in the same set location with a special prop to identify the activity.[21]

The Polka Dot way: Polkaroo and the Toys celebrated imagination within, and without, the Polka Dot Door.

A summative evaluation based on a 1980–1982 survey found these goals had been achieved. Many parents revealed their preference for *Polka Dot Door*'s slower pacing, noting that *Sesame Street* left their children in an excited state.[22] Outside of *Polka Dot Door*'s many educational achievements, the series was a sustained ratings success and remained the network's flagship 6:00 p.m. children's series until the early 1990s. Similar to how Uncle Chichimus attained unofficial mascot status for the CBC in its earliest days, Polkaroo became a bona fide local pop-cultural hero, and continues to serve as TVO's seminal symbol, even though the series has been off the air for decades.

32
Guess What? (1971)

AFTER SUCCESSFULLY ESTABLISHING *POLKA DOT DOOR*, PRODUCER Ted Coneybeare and educational supervisor Marnie Patrick-Roberts moved onto the creation of *Guess What?*, a series based around the fascinating personality of Jan Rubeš. Born in 1920 in Czechoslovakia, Rubeš was a bass opera singer who immigrated to Canada in 1948 to join the Canadian Opera Company. He performed on CBLT-TV's first night of broadcasting television on September 8, 1952. He pursued a career in film, television, and radio and is best known for his performance as Eli Lapp, an Amish farmer in Peter Weir's Academy Award–nominated *Witness* (1985), and as Jan in *D2: The Mighty Ducks* (1994).

Rubeš starred as Kazimir Zaremba in one of OECA's first adult series, *Castle Zaremba*, which premiered in October of 1970. A co-production with the CBC, *Castle Zaremba* was structured as a twice weekly thirty-minute soap opera chronicling the lives of new immigrants to Canada and aired on both Channel 19 and the CBC. *Castle Zaremba* was "designed by linguistic experts to be culturally neutral, without any specific first language in mind."[23] Ostensibly the series provided educational lessons in local civics for new Canadians. However, many of the plots attracted negative press attention, including one episode that had a character explain to another how to avoid repaying a loan: "Any time you see anybody coming up to you with a piece of paper, you do the subpoena stomp."[24]

Producers at OECA were so enamoured with polymath Rubeš's many talents they devised a series entirely based around him, exploring some of the multicultural themes first explored in *Castle Zaremba*. OECA internal documents billed *Guess What?* as "a series designed to spark children's curiosity and to help them become more aware of the contributions that other cultures have made to their way of life."[25]

Each episode was set in a room crowded with foreign objects, where Rubeš examined and explored the history of intriguing artifacts from other cultures and long-ago eras. Using mostly song, crafting, and storytelling, Rubeš would pose questions to the audience or invite them to join in singing his songs. Marnie Patrick-Roberts described the series as "a raconteur in an attic."[26]

The structure of *Guess What?* served as a template for many future OECA productions: Each episode ran only ten minutes, as opposed to thirty. Coneybeare and others at OECA felt that shorter programs would allow them to produce much more material, and could be paired with one-minute, five-minute, and fifteen-minute series to fill out thirty- or sixty-minute programming blocks. (The ten-minute format would prove definitive for later series such as *Readalong* [1975]). Many of the international programs, shorts, and interstitials being purchased by OECA from the United Kingdom and Europe had much shorter running times. It remains a very American practice to have television schedules dominated by thirty- and sixty-minute programs that start on the hour and half-hour.

As the fall 1971 season launched, Channel 19's children's offerings included two original productions, *Polka Dot Door* and *Guess What?*, U.S. series *Sesame Street* and *Mister Rogers' Neighborhood* (1970), and U.K. import *The Magic Roundabout* (1964).

A total of forty-nine episodes of *Guess What?* were produced between 1971 and 1973, premiering on Channel 19 on September 13, 1971, and repeated for over a decade before fading into obscurity. A soundtrack LP with a collection of songs from the series was released on the Pickwick label, with graphic design from Dick Derhodge.

33
The Waterville Gang (1972)

THE FIRST CHILDREN'S SERIES FOR CFTO-TV'S PRODUCTION arm Glen-Warren Productions, *The Waterville Gang*, was created by children's entertainer Barry Rosenberg and used colourful puppets to tell stories about a variety of oceanic creatures living below the water. The production was notable for employing chroma-key to create its undersea effects. Puppets were filmed against a blue backdrop, while the puppeteers dressed entirely in blue. This was then chroma-keyed overtop of footage that had been filmed inside a real aquarium, creating a distinctive appearance for the show. It was filmed at 9 Channel Nine Court studio in Agincourt, Scarborough.

Characters included Dodger Dolphin, Angel Fish, Sharky Shark, Eloise "Frenchie" the Seahorse, Sergeant Perch, Pearl Van Oyster, Tucker Turtle, and Ace Seagull. The talented ensemble voice cast featured Billy Van, Len Carlson, Franz Russell, Julie Amato, Sid Brown, and Donna Miller, while puppetry was performed by the Frog Print Theatre puppeteers and included Nikki Tilroe, Johan and Alison Vandergun, Nina Keogh, Roy Small, and Alex Laurier. Both Tilroe and Laurier were regulars at the time on *The Uncle Bobby Show* (also on CFTO-TV), and they would headline together again in *CUCUMBER* (1975).

Nikki and her husband, Bob Tilroe, were key figures in puppetry, especially in Ontario, where they influenced the field through their company, Frog Print Theatre. Originally from the U.S., they moved to Canada in 1968, bringing innovative new styles to the genre by mixing mime, dance, and puppetry. Their contributions extended beyond performance to include training other puppeteers. The Frog Print Theatre, under Bohuslov Olsina's direction, earned significant recognition, including a UNIMA-USA Citation of Excellence for puppetry in 1974 for their live performance of *Mimi and Toto*, which featured music by Heather Conkie. *The Waterville Gang*'s producer/director Milad

Bessada developed the experimental double chroma-key approach, which he later used for certain sketches on *SCTV* (1976).

In total, *The Waterville Gang* produced thirty-four episodes, running at thirty minutes each, filmed in 1972 and 1973. It aired first-run on Saturday mornings on the CTV network and was syndicated across the U.S. and in South Africa. Later, in the early 1990s, it was repeated daily on YTV and gained a new generation of fans with its extraordinary appearance, strange characters, and unique-looking puppets.

34
The World of B.J. Vibes (1973)

THE FIRST OF MANY OECA PROGRAMS THAT AIMED TO INTRO-duce the world of music to children, *The World of B.J. Vibes* was an off-kilter series designed to introduce intermediate students (grades 4 to 7) into the world of music and sound via a groovy disc jockey named B.J. Vibes and played by Gerry Salsberg, who shared his philosophical musing on all things aural. Much more rooted in theory than practice, and more humorous than serious, B.J. attempted to capture the imagination of viewers both young and old and help them appreciate "the organization of sound." The remit was to educate children on the fundamentals of music, while being slightly askew in its presentation. Many segments featured Scanimate, an early form of analogue computer animation developed in the late 1960s by Computer Image Corporation of Denver, Colorado.

The World of B.J. Vibes was very much of its time — the freewheeling 1970s. For example, in the episode "Harmony," B.J. finds it difficult to explain the concept of harmony in terms of musicianship, but when his friend offers him a hot dog without mustard, he is inspired to create "The Hot Dog and Mustard Song," illustrating the importance of the two working together, both literally and figuratively. In another episode, he fends off an attacking vampire by illustrating the subtle sounds that a bat makes.

Paul Hoffert of the Toronto prog rock band Lighthouse served as the show's music director and composer, while Michael Paul and Rock Okada wrote the scripts. Linda Zwicker served as the educational consultant, and it was produced by Sincinkin Ltd. Only six episodes running at fifteen minutes each were produced of *The World of B.J. Vibes*. It aired repeatedly on Channel 19 for over a decade and was sold to many PBS stations, as well as distributed on 16mm film and videocassette to universities and schools across North America.

35
Circle Square (1974)

IN JUNE OF 1962, REVEREND DAVID MAINSE AND HIS WIFE, Norma-Jean, launched a new syndicated Christian television series titled *Crossroads*, which spread the word of the gospel in fifteen-minute episodes that usually aired after the news on Saturday evenings. By 1974, Mainse had established Crossroads Christian Communications and formed a broadcast partnership with Ontario's new independent Global Television Network, which arrived on-air on January 6, 1974. Work began on what was to become Crossroads' flagship series, *100 Huntley Street*, although that did not air until 1977.

Mainse believed children were being underserved by television and began to develop a show aimed to both entertain and espouse Christian values. The resulting series, *Circle Square*, was built around a group of children and puppets who appeared in skits and singalongs. The main characters included Durk (Reynold Rutledge), a gnomic grandfatherly type; Vince (Durk's loyal dog, a puppet); and child puppets Gert and Egbert. The program also contained short, animated segments, including an ear-wormy call-out to viewers inviting them to write *Circle Square* at "2121 Station F, Toronto, Ontario M4Y 2N9" with questions and suggestions. All responders were sent a *Circle Square* songbook so that they could sing along with future episodes. Within the first twelve months on-air, *Circle Square* received over fifty thousand letters.[27]

Circle Square was produced at Crossroads' main production facility located at 100 Huntley Street in Toronto, with location shooting at some of the Circle Square Ranch summer camps that it inspired. It ran until 1986 and was syndicated around the world, most notably airing regularly on the Jamaica Broadcasting Corporation (JBC).

A young Marci Ien was one of the series' regulars and later became a CTV news host and Liberal MP, serving as the minister for women, gender equality, and youth in Justin Trudeau's cabinet. Circle Square Ranch summer camps continue to run throughout Ontario.

36
Dr. Zonk and the Zunkins (1974)

AFTER *DROP-IN* CONCLUDED IN 1974, PRODUCER DON ELDER was requested by CBC children's department head John Kennedy to devise something original that might reverse the diminishing audience in the after-school slot, lost to syndicated repeats of older U.S. prime-time fare such as *The Brady Bunch* (1969), *Star Trek* (1966), and *Ironside* (1967). Favouring a comedic approach, Elder hired Kiddo the Clown himself, Trevor Evans. In the early 1960s, *Kiddo the Clown* had demonstrated Evans's enviable ability to engage children with strange, unconventional comedy that was unlike anything else on television at the time (see p. 63). Evans had since become a television director with his own independent production company (Trevor Evans Productions Ltd.) so was brought on board to develop something scripted, fresh, and funny, aimed squarely at nine-to-eleven-year-olds.

A country-flavoured skit from the truly mind-bending *Dr. Zonk and the Zunkins* (1974), an attempt by the CBC to attract younger viewers with surreal sketch comedy in the coveted after-school time slot. Pictured from left: Fiona Reid, Dan Hennessey, Rosemary Radcliffe, John Candy, and John Stocker.

A fan of surrealist humour, Evans was attuned to the growing interest in Toronto's cult improvisational sketch-comedy shop, Second City Revue on Adelaide Street, which featured comedians on the cusp of landing a break, including people like Jayne Eastwood (*King of Kensington*), Gilda Radner (*Saturday Night Live*), and Dan Aykroyd (*The Blues Brothers*). The club soon moved to Lombard Street, to a building known as "The Old Firehall," where new comedians like Andrea Martin, Eugene Levy, and Catherine O'Hara got their start. The club featured a mixture of talent on loan from mothership Second City in Chicago, and young up-and-coming Toronto talent. Evans saw great potential in the after-school slot at CBC as a training ground for this talent and developed a vehicle to cast these comics and let them loose on television. Inspired by *Sesame Street*'s successful deployment of slick adult advertising techniques pitched down to children, Evans and CBC producer Gerry O'Flannigan hatched an outlandish premise that would allow the Toronto Second City players a chance to do their thing on television, but to a much younger audience than was watching them at The Old Firehall.

Dr. Zonk and the Zunkins centred on a Walter Mitty–like imaginative nine-year-old boy named Billy Meek (played by Robin Eveson) who had two robots in his bedroom, Zooey and Dunkin, also known as the titular Zunkins (operated and voiced by Nina Keogh and John Stocker), who came from a comic book called *Dr. Zonk*. Billy would express his random fantasies, and the Zunkins would manifest them in real life. Essentially, random sketch comedy held together by the thinnest of linking material from a boy and his two robots.

The cast featured John Candy, Gilda Radner, Rosemary Radcliffe, Robert McKenna, Dan Hennessey, John Stocker (doing double duties), and Fiona Reid. Early variations of future *Second City Television* (1976) characters, like Johnny LaRue and Dr. Tongue, are evident in John Candy's *Dr. Zonk* performances.

Maclean's magazine did not mince words in its initial negative review, calling the show "a trendy, media-minded notion of what kids like,"[28] while the CBC's own internal surveying found that most viewers found it childish and unfunny. *Dr. Zonk and the Zunkins* aired on CBC Mondays, Wednesdays, and Fridays at 4:30 p.m. from September 23, 1974, until April 14, 1975.

37
Coming Up Rosie (1975)

PERHAPS SENSING AN ESCAPE ROUTE MIGHT BE IN ORDER, Don Elder and Trevor Evans scripted a spinoff as one of the final episodes of *Dr. Zonk and the Zunkins*, creating a kooky documentarian character played by

Rosemary Radcliffe, who appeared in one of Billy's fantasies. In the aftermath of *Dr. Zonk and the Zunkins*' failure to connect with audiences, Elder and Evans expanded on their soft pilot, devising a more traditional situation comedy that dropped the outlandish robots and random settings. The result was a show that was more popular than *Dr. Zonk and the Zunkins* and far more subversive. Radcliffe played Rosie Tucker, a film-school grad who lived at 99 Sumach Street in downtown Toronto, a dilapidated building populated with charlatans, eccentrics, and other strange individuals. Rosie had applied for a government subsidy and had dreams of becoming Canada's foremost documentary filmmaker. Many of the plots revolved around film production and movie set antics. Elder recalled the promising premise, and its ultimate failure, in a 1982 interview:

> The idea was that through Rosemary's legitimate documentary work she would get a small assignment, say, from the school board to do a little documentary about something that we would be able to, through that device, get out into the world. And had we had the resources and the time ... We had the inclination, but never really worked it properly. And so, the shows, some of them were really very funny, I thought, very, really amusing. And they were done in a style that was current. And my greatest disappointment about Rosie was that it never really pulled an audience as it should have done. And I could never figure out why.[29]

Many of the *Dr. Zonk* cast returned: John Candy played Wally Wypyzypychwk, a Ukrainian who lived in the building and ran a burglar alarm company called Sleep-Tite; Fiona Reid was the manic Mona but left shortly into the first season to play Al Waxman's long-suffering wife on *King of Kensington* (1975); Dan Hennessey was Rosie's neighbour Ralph; and John Stocker played Dwayne the aloof elevator operator. British expat Barry Baldaro portrayed Rosie's associate Dudley Nightshade. Rounding out the *Zonk* alumni were a few new Second City faces including Dan Aykroyd as Purvis Bickle, the building's deranged Scottish superintendent, and Catherine

O'Hara as Myrna Wallbacker, an answering service operator. Eugene Levy turned up as a guest in one episode, although he did not share an onscreen appearance with O'Hara. That epic television coupling began with *SCTV* (1976) and continued as recently as *Schitt's Creek* (2015).

Unlike the rather static *Dr. Zonk*, *Coming Up Rosie* was more indebted to the physical slapstick comedy seen in Evans's *Kiddo the Clown*, with characters racing around the building set and bumping into each other at inopportune times. The writing was sharper too, with rat-a-tat delivery and biting social commentary courtesy of Evans's wife, Barbara Evans; David Mayerovitch; Stuart Northey; and David Thomas. As with *Dr. Zonk*, and owing to the pedigree of the performers, a lot was also improvised.

Coming Up Rosie held onto *Dr. Zonk*'s Monday, Wednesday, and Friday at 4:30 p.m. time slot until dropping to one episode per week in 1976. Aykroyd had departed the cast to join a new late-night NBC comedy variety show, *Saturday Night Live*. The series was popular enough to continue until 1978, when Evans ended it after continually being rebuffed by the CBC on his increased budget requests.

Speaking in 1984, Evans said that with both *Dr. Zonk* and *Rosie*, he had been playing a long game, staging both productions as an opportunity to introduce the after-school audience to contemporary and more mature situations in step with the changing tastes and accelerated maturity of viewers. However, without the budget to build on each successive series, there was no point in continuing:

> It was not a happy leaving. It was a tremendously stressful time. I've called it my Camelot, a dream that could not be fulfilled beyond that point. I preferred a mercy killing because I could not receive more funds from the corporation. I think a series has to grow each year. If you look at *M*A*S*H* (1972), it became a massive hit because each year they were able to top themselves. If you don't increase the budget and inflation continues, you end up with a deficit. And that's really what happened on *Rosie*. We were working on the

same budget from year one going into year four. As my actors were getting better, my writers were getting better, we were growing. I looked at my cast — Dan Aykroyd, Gilda Radnor, John Candy, Rosemary Radcliffe, John Stocker, Dan Hennessy, and Catherine O'Hara. This was their premiere television exposure. These people were growing faster than I'd ever encountered before. The only way to hold them would be to increase the salary and give them a more creative challenge. That couldn't happen. So, I looked at it and I said that the most propitious thing to do is to cancel it. Rocket Richard left at the peak of his career. If it's good enough for the hockey players, it's good enough for me.[30]

38

Report Metric (1973)/ Report Canada (1978)

DEBUTING IN SEPTEMBER OF 1973 AS PART OF THE OECA school block broadcast on Channel 19 and all station affiliates of the CBC Ontario network, *Report Metric* was a new five-minute series hosted by folksinger Heather Conkie. A news and weather telecast, it had the caveat that only metric measurements would be used. Metrication in Canada started in 1970 under the Liberal government of Pierre Trudeau, but the move away from the imperial measurement system took almost a decade to be fully implemented. The series was aimed at getting children used to this new reality by

Host Heather Conkie on the set of *Report Metric*, a five-minute fun and informative look at Canadian life piped directly into classrooms weekday mornings starting in 1973.

using metric to describe weather and the measurement of familiar objects. Daily instalments were broadcast live directly into classrooms across Ontario, reaching over eighty thousand students during the '73/'74 television season, making it by far the most successful OECA school program so far. Director David Moore was credited with creating a popular format that was short enough to hold attention spans, effective in its daily frequency and time of broadcast, and stimulating enough to incite interaction from students across the province who began to mail in their own metric reports, drawings, science experiments, and other creative materials. OECA producer Clive VanderBurgh, who would further exploit viewer mail in his new series *CUCUMBER* (1975), recalled:

> All of a sudden you had all these kids writing into *Report Metric*. Who's going to handle all this mail? We had the public relations department bringing in volunteers dealing with the mail.[31]

This interface with young viewers marked a new era for OECA, which began to build further calls-to-action into future shows, and *Report Metric* remained a teacher favourite as it started each day with a roundup news report for kids. In 1976, a short-lived afternoon spinoff called *Report Music* appeared, in which Conkie discussed music history, theory, and instruments and talked about new releases that might have been of interest to children. Conkie's passion for educational music television was later developed in more detail with programs like *Music Box* (1981) and *It's Mainly Music* (1984, see pp. 202 and 227).

A truly captive classroom audience watches a morning OECA broadcast in the early 1970s.

In 1978, *Report Metric* was tweaked and rechristened as *Report Canada*. While Conkie remained the host and the format's five-minute run time continued, coverage expanded to all of Canada and involved a deeper discussion of history and social issues. Several regular features were developed, including "Kooky Canadiana," which offered tidbits of strange Canadian facts and lore; "Grave Matters," in which Conkie encouraged students to examine gravestone epitaphs; a guessing game that asked the question "Where Is the Frisbee Now?"; and "The Saga of Dora and Dunwit," a bizarre ongoing story about the ghost of a pioneer child and a dinosaur who resurrect spirits of famous dead Canadians to better understand geography and history. Conkie wrote and performed the memorable theme song, which, when watched in class daily, became a widespread earworm:

> Have you ever wondered what came before you, made you who you are
> If you look all around lots of clues can be found, you won't have to look too far
> Mounties and Eskimos, beavers and totem-poles, mountains and prairies, forests to roam
> Artists and pioneers, miners and engineers, oceans and highways help the country to grow
> On Report Canada, we'll find out who we are.
> On Report Canada, discover who you are.

After twenty years on-air, the show was slightly retooled again as *Kids Canada* in 1994, when Jennifer Martin joined Heather Conkie as co-host and the program switched almost entirely to the coverage of social issues. Its time slot remained the same, as did the call-out to viewers and students to send in artwork, class projects, book reports, short stories, photos, and videos. Occasionally Conkie needed to remind viewers of the show's remit, once stating on-air, "Thanks for all your drawings of the Teenage Mutant Ninja Turtles, but please limit your contributions to Canadian things."

39
Inside/Out (1973)

PRODUCED BETWEEN 1972 AND 1973 BY THE NATIONAL Instructional Television Center (NIT), *Inside/Out* was a groundbreaking anthology series that explored a variety of social issues involving children. The series was acclaimed for its unflinching, cinéma-vérité style and won a 1974 Emmy Award for Outstanding Instructional Children's Programming. Its unresolved cliffhanger endings were meant to stimulate classroom discussion. The series was also notable for featuring contributions from numerous television stations across North America, including KETC in St. Louis, WVIZ in Cleveland, WNVT-TV in Virginia, and the OECA (Channel 19) in Toronto. NIT had built a consortium of thirty-two state and provincial educational agencies in the U.S. and Canada to raise the level of budget necessary to make great instructional television (ITV). The entire series ran on Channel 19, and the five episodes of *Inside/Out* created by the OECA — "But … Names Will Never Hurt?," "Getting Even," "Must I/May I," "Strong Feelings," and "When Is Help" — were written by Brooklyn-based Ken Sobol and directed and produced by OECA's Carol Armstrong.

Inside/Out was one of the first, if not *the* first, series that dealt with real kids' problems from their own perspective, and it heavily influenced the documentary-style approach taken by shows like *The Kids of Degrassi Street* (1979). Sobol later adapted eight episodes of *Inside/Out* into a paperback published by Bantam Books in 1974. According to Owen Gottlieb, noted academic and associate professor of interactive games and media at Rochester Institute of Technology, "*Inside/Out*'s powerful, moving children's stories and their aesthetics — both from Canada and the States — are burned into the memories of the Gen-Xers raised on them."[32]

40

Magic Shadows (1974)

BASED ON THE INTRINSIC QUALITY OF HIS *INSIDE/OUT* WORK, Ken Sobol was hired by Director of Programming Jim Hanley to develop further projects at the OECA, the first of which was *Media Circus* (1974). This live-to-air show featured a panel of noted media and literary personalities such as Northrop Frye and Marshall McLuhan sitting in front of a bank of television sets watching and discussing what was airing on the local channels at that exact moment — contemporary media analysis in real-time. With Sobol writing and co-hosting and Carol Armstrong producing, the show was unlike anything that aired on television before (or since). Sobol had spent time screenwriting in Hollywood, as well as reviewing film and television for *The Village Voice* in New York City, and was, according to his son, John, "a massive film buff,"[33] so it was natural that he also gravitated toward another Hanley project, *Magic Shadows* (1974).

Starting in early 1974, OECA aired double bills of classic Hollywood feature films on Saturday evenings under the title *Saturday Night at the Movies*, hosted by the ebullient Elwy Yost and concluding with spirited panel discussions from a field of experts. Along with A-list titles such as *The Treasure of the Sierra Madre* (1948) and *Citizen Kane* (1941), executive producer Hanley was also stuck with volumes of B- and C-list films, as movie studios would only licence titles in bulk packages that mixed both high- and low-quality films together. Taking a cue from Yost's earlier CBC series *Passport to Adventure* (1966), the less-desirable titles were split into segments and run sequentially from Monday through Thursday, with additional commentary from guests and experts like on *Saturday Night at the Movies*. Fridays were reserved for classic western and science-fiction film serials like *Captain America* (1944) and *Flash Gordon* (1936), which were Yost's personal favourites. Sobol devised the themes and topics for every episode of *Magic Shadows*, which ran daily during the week at 7:00 p.m. until 1987. In a 1982 interview, Yost said:

> We have a writer we've been using for ten years. His name is Ken Sobol. He lives in Montreal. He is an ex-American, comes from New York. He's written a book about the life of Babe Ruth and so on. He loves film and has studied film. Very passionate about movies.[34]

OECA producer Risa Shuman, who worked closely with Yost during his tenure, recalls the series ended due to his exhaustive output:

> When Elwy retired from his staff position, he was pooped. There was a deal at the time with ACTRA that on-staff personnel could appear on-camera for nothing. Without Elwy, it would have been financially prohibitive but more important, without him, it just wouldn't work as it was so much his personality. There was a time when Elwy took a sort of sabbatical and we hired Dinah Christie as Elwy's cleaning lady, she would run the projector and read his notes. I think it was for only a month. I don't remember why we just didn't run some reruns, but I do remember how shocked everyone was with how much we had to pay Dinah, even at scale![35]

Magic Shadows is perhaps best remembered for its spooky psychedelic animated title sequence, designed by Sobol's old friend in Hollywood Gary Lund, who had worked with him on the animated series *Fantastic Voyage* (1968). The opening featured a collage of classic Hollywood personalities like Humphrey Bogart and Groucho Marx set to an ethereal piece of music composed by Harry Forbes, influenced by both the Beatles' song "Across the Universe" and the Beach Boys' "Feel Flows."

Impressively, in the span of just a few short months, Sobol was working on *Media Circus* and *Magic Shadows*, and also charged with developing a brand-new educational series led by Ruth Vernon — *Readalong* — which taught the basics of reading and vocabulary comprehension to a young audience. *Readalong* (see p. 150) would become the network's most important children's series since the advent of *Polka Dot Door* (1971).

41
Calling Captain Consumer (1973)

CALLING CAPTAIN CONSUMER WAS AN AMBITIOUS SOCIAL studies program addressing the governing of children's buying decisions, with topics including planning, budgeting, advertising, taxation, pricing, buying, safety, and the history of consumerism, all presented in humorous vignettes. OECA's internal teachers' guide stated:

> This series was designed to help children cope with advertising and consumerism. Should you buy Brand X, or pay a little more for Brand Y? Do advertisements in print and on television tell you all you should know to make a wise purchase? *Calling Captain Consumer* can help students learn how to pick their way wisely through the marketplace.[36]

Produced by Jeremy Pollock, *Calling Captain Consumer* originally aired in the post–*Report Metric* slot in the morning, and was later moved to be part of Channel 19's alternative to Saturday-morning cartoons, The Saturday Supershow, in 1975. In total, forty episodes were produced, ten running at twenty minutes each, and thirty running at ten minutes each. OECA's head of childhood education, Vera Novakowski, recalled the production of *Calling Captain Consumer*:

> The content was strictly geared to themes and topics which didn't necessarily follow a department curriculum. We identified, in the area of consumerism, the kinds of experiences

> children would face in either shopping around town or looking at television and helping them to analyze and understand what forces were at work in trying to captivate them as buyers and not to be so gullible. It was a step closer to direct instructional programming.[37]

The series was very well received, owing to its original concept and humorous writing, and was distributed to many schools in the United States. It had a long run in the Fort Worth district of Dallas, Texas, where it was part of the school board's fourth grade curriculum. In 1989, CBC's affiliate CBHT-TV in Halifax created a popular and long-running consumer advocacy show for children entitled *Street Cents*, with host Jonathan Torrens, although creator John Nowlan cited a 1970s U.K. program called *Pocket Money* as his prime inspiration.

42

Two Plus You (1974)

SET IN A CHILDREN'S TOY SHOP, *TWO PLUS YOU* FOCUSED ON simple mathematical concepts often illustrated through the buying and selling of toys. Store owner Mr. Bean (no relation to Rowan Atkinson's madcap character from the 1990s television series of that name) was played by Alfie Scopp, who had previously appeared as Clarabell the clown on *The Howdy Doody Show* (1954). Allan Levson played his young friend Eric. Prolific character actor Saul Rubinek starred as a burglar robbing the toy store in one of his very first onscreen appearances. Puppeteer Bob Dermer, who would later be central to the cast of both *Readalong* and *Today's Special*, voiced and operated the puppet character of Oswald the Owl. The opening animation was created by Rainbow Animation Limited. Music was provided by Dick Payne, with lyrics by Dick Payne and Clive Endersby, who also got his start at OECA writing several key episodes of the show.

While the series was mostly rote in nature, there were signs of the fantastical approach that would soon become an OECA hallmark, including slightly frightening sequences when the shop was empty, and the toys would come alive. As with *Calling Captain Consumer*, *Two Plus You* was widely distributed to both PBS stations and schools in the United States, where it was used in classrooms, including a Baltimore, Maryland, school that continued to make use of it well into the 2010s.

43
Saturday Morning Supershow (1975)

SATURDAY MORNINGS HAD LONG BEEN VIEWED AS THE MOST significant block of children's programming, starting in the mid-1960s when the big three U.S. networks — ABC, CBS, and NBC — aired old black-and-white serialized westerns and science-fiction programs such as *Flash Gordon* (1936), animated theatrical shorts, and reruns of old prime-time action series like *Gunsmoke* (1955) and *Have Gun — Will Travel* (1957). This began to change with the great success of the Hanna-Barbera animated show *Space Ghost* (1966–67), which opened the floodgates for original cartoon series developed specifically for the Saturday-morning block. Aimed at maximizing toy, food, and beverage sales, these cartoons were often based on pre-existing toy lines or developed in tandem with toy companies.

The 1960s and early 1970s marked the start of an ongoing and still unresolved cultural debate about the effects of screen violence on young people. Fred Rainsberry was often invoked by Canadian newspaper editorials for his belief that television was too often used as a scapegoat by parents. He held that more effort should be made by parents to view television with their children. In a 1963 interview with *The Toronto Daily Star*, Rainsberry said,

> Let us remember first of all that television is an artistic medium capable of providing right and significant social and aesthetic experience for children. Therefore, parents should monitor programs for children on a regular basis; they should share the experience of viewing television with their children. If we use television as a baby-sitter without frequent examination of the fare available on the screen, we must expect that negative influences on our children will pass unexamined and unchallenged.[38]

In the U.S., there was a concerted attempt to curb the amount of violence being shown on Saturday mornings by parent lobby groups petitioning the Federal Communications Commission and the United States Congress. A sustained period of media-driven panic followed, establishing the premise that television was desensitizing a generation of young people to violence.

The OECA had been planning from almost its outset to counter-program Saturday mornings with a block of high-quality children's shows that contained a mixture of adventure, comedy, and interaction. Neither CBC nor CFTO-TV had put up much of a fight for the Saturday-morning slots, both electing to show repeats of older U.S. series like *The Flintstones* and *The Partridge Family*, or in the case of the CBC, repeats of *Sesame Street*. For Channel 19, Saturday mornings were an opportunity to experiment with programming and prove they could hold their own against the glossy American series currently commanding young viewers' attention. The outcome was mixed, but the OECA's push into Saturday

A 1975 print ad for the Saturday Morning Supershow, TVOntario's valiant attempt to bring educational programs to the cartoon wastelands of Saturday morning programming for kids.

mornings ended up creating several vital series that advanced the careers of creatives like Clive VanderBurgh and Jeremy Pollock within the organization.

Debuting in January of 1975, OECA's long-in-development antidote to the violent and crass commercialism of Saturday mornings finally arrived. Entitled the Saturday Morning Supershow, it ran from 8:30 a.m. until 11:30 a.m. and comprised *Monkey Bars*, *CUCUMBER*, *The Adventures of Timothy Pilgrim*, *Tell Me a Story*, a thirty-minute quiz show called *Quiz-Bang*, and reruns of *Calling Captain Consumer* and *Polka Dot Door*. *The Globe and Mail*'s TV supplement *Broadcast Week* announced: "The educational station launches a Saturday-morning package of programs designed to lure kids from the cartoons."[39] The OECA's marketing for the block stressed its educational value:

> Give your child a head start in life with TV of value. A child's mind is a delicate, growing thing, fresh and receptive. The experiences of childhood shape our minds, leaving lasting effects on our ability to learn and develop. That's why it's important for parents to guide their youngsters' television viewing, to help them choose shows which are enriching as well as entertaining. We recommend Channel 19's Saturday Morning Supershow. A three-hour block of specially selected programs which help children learn as they laugh.[40]

44

Monkey Bars (1975)

CREATED BY VARIETY-SHOW MAVERICKS BILL HARTLEY AND Jack Humphrey (*The Tommy Hunter Show* [1970]), *Monkey Bars* was a sugary mash-up of variety show and sketch comedy, soundtracked by endless power-pop and dance sequences. (Music director Cliff Jones composed over sixty pop songs for the series, which were peppered throughout each show.) Clearly indebted to the Children Television Workshop's *The Electric Company* (1971), which taught basic phonetics and grammar concepts through live-action sketches and poppy songs, *Monkey Bars* was an all-singing, all-dancing assault on the senses.

The cast of *Monkey Bars* (Scott Fisher and John Kozak as Dingbat) and *CUCUMBER* (Nikki Tilroe as Beaver) celebrate the launch of the Saturday Morning Supershow (1975) with cake!

Pitched as a fifty-minute educational variety and magazine show for viewers aged seven to twelve, *Monkey Bars* featured the misadventures of a group of five child singers (called The Monkey Bars) who endlessly found themselves having to deal with two villainous cretins, Hassle B. DeMille (who described himself as "a theatrical impresario and junk dealer") and his thick-browed henchman, Dingbat. The kids were played by Scott Fisher, Catherine Kennedy, Jeanette Klopsch, Anthea Parascus, and Alan Park, and grown-ups included Patrick Rose, R.G. Brown (as Hassle B. DeMille), John Kozak (as Dingbat), and Julie Amato (who later provided the voice of Pretty on *Readalong* [1975]).

Monkey Bars introduced educational objectives such as fitness and creativity through play and dance. An animated segment starring Metric Man facilitated kids' understanding of metrication, and a segment called "Word Play" took a playful approach to basic grammar. There were even elements of media literacy with some sketches set in a television studio. Viewer participation was encouraged through a heady mix of sketch comedy (guess the punchline), slapstick (follow the moves), singing (sing along), and dancing (dance along), all soundtracked by really great pop music. If nothing else, *Monkey Bars* was an eclectic, Frankenstein's monster mix of many ambitious parts.

45
CUCUMBER (1975)

IF *MONKEY BARS* WAS THE SOUL OF THE OECA'S SATURDAY Morning Supershow, *CUCUMBER* was its heart. Developed by Clive VanderBurgh, *CUCUMBER* was another magazine-style approach to children's entertainment, in some ways harkening back to *Razzle Dazzle* with its interactive audience component soliciting letters, jokes, content, and ideas from young viewers. The series was targeted at six-to-eight-year-olds. The title *CUCUMBER* was an acronym spelled out in the raucous opening theme song both written and performed by VanderBurgh — "Children's Underground Club of United Moose and Beaver for Enthusiastic Reporters" — and was hosted by a moose and a beaver. Moose was played by *Uncle Bobby* regular and occasional *Polka Dot Door* host Alex Laurier, while the more thoughtful Beaver was performed by Nikki Tilroe of the Frog Print Theatre.

Moose and Beaver were independent journalists living in a remote treehouse, studying nature, science, history, music appreciation, and other contemporary issues about life in a forest, as well as more topical concerns such as the effects of television, advertising, and general safety. In addition to the theme song, VanderBurgh wrote all the music for the series. Moose explains the series raison d'être in the first episode: "Enthusiastic reporters are people who love to find out the answers to questions. They want to know who, what, where, when, why, and how." A recurrent feature of *CUCUMBER* was its attention to ecological issues, something that was rather uncommon in scripted children's television at the time; a decade later, it would become a focal point for series like *The Raccoons* (1985) and *OWL/TV* (1985). Moose and Beaver handled the more sensitive subjects such as species extinction and deforestation delicately, raising awareness while respecting their audience, thanks, no doubt, to the vision of creator Clive VanderBurgh and series director Susan Murgatroyd, a freelancer who also worked on *Polka Dot Door* and *Readalong*. VanderBurgh recalls the extensive amount of research that went into *CUCUMBER*:

> There was a time when you could know every children's show in North America; I went to New York and talked to the people who did *Captain Kangaroo*, to people at CBS and ABC. I was at *Sesame Street* talking to the research people there. That was one of the fundamental differences at TVOntario, there was a research department, and we did

CUCUMBER (1975) was an ecologically conscious series focused on Moose (Alex Laurier) and Beaver (Nikki Tilroe), a pair of reporters who uncover all aspects of life in the forest.

> background papers on what the show was about, the cognitive outcomes that were expected. It wasn't just, here's a children's performer and we'll put them in front of a camera.[41]

VanderBurgh knew from the response to *Report Metric* that call-outs for viewer mail could be effective. *CUCUMBER* went a step further with Moose and Beaver inviting viewers to not only send mail, but to join the Cucumber Club. Members would receive a button and glossy magazine that featured original stories, children's drawings, activities, jokes, recipes, pet tips, and much more. OECA's head of childhood education, Vera Novakowski, remembers the success of calling out for mail:

> It called for participation on the part of the children. Invited them to write in and to become members of a club

> that was for an older age group. It was an interesting meshing of entertainment. And it was not geared to any specific aspect of the curriculum. It was interdisciplinary in the sense that because it was magazine type, we touched on many topics which provided information but nevertheless tried to introduce an element of out of school activity, the club idea. And that was a very great success. The responses from the children became so heavy that it was difficult to cope with them. It was too time consuming and costly. And eventually we had to find ways of streamlining that involvement. It was very much a cross between entertainment and information.[42]

During its first few months on-air, *CUCUMBER* generated an impressive amount of viewer feedback, with over six thousand letters during the first thirteen weeks, 175 projects from classrooms across Ontario, and over seven thousand memberships for the Cucumber Club.[43] Although only two series of thirteen episodes were produced, *CUCUMBER* was continually rerun by the network well into the early 1990s. Viewer solicitations were never edited out of future repeats, resulting in mail and club requests continuing to arrive even a decade after production had ceased.

In retrospect, the calibre of *CUCUMBER*'s guest stars was remarkable, and can be attributed to the show's talent coordinator, George Bourne. John Candy appeared in his very first television role playing a superhero called Weatherman shortly before his varied performances on *Dr. Zonk and the Zunkins*. (The Weatherman shows hints of his future *SCTV* character Dr. Tongue.) VanderBurgh recalls Candy being nervous about singing when they recorded for the show at Manta Sound on Adelaide Street East in Toronto.[44] Other notable guest turns included Rosemary Radcliffe (another rising star in Toronto's Second City comedy troupe and star of CBC's *Coming Up Rosie*); Martin Short as Smokey the Hare and, in an earlier pilot, as a human co-host alongside Heather Conkie; and a dazzling nine-year-old Jeff Healey — who was blind — playing guitar.

46

The Adventures of Timothy Pilgrim (1975)

A PILOT FOR *CUCUMBER*, WRITTEN BY ROY MOORE (*BLACK Christmas* [1974]), featured a serialized science-fiction story — a show within a show — entitled "Zachariah Gibson's Magic Trunk." Novakowski and her replacement at the OECA, Ruth Vernon, felt the *CUCUMBER* concept was strong enough on its own. The concept was pulled and given to producer Jeremy Pollock for further development. Pollock and Moore expanded the core idea of "Zachariah Gibson's Magic Trunk" to create *The Adventures of Timothy Pilgrim*, the OECA's first full-blown narrative science-fiction series for children.

The Adventures of Timothy Pilgrim told the tale of Timothy (Joey Davidson), a young shoeshine boy who, when he stumbles upon a magic trunk while trying to escape bullies on King Street West in Toronto, is accidentally transported a hundred years into the past. In 1875, he encounters travelling snake oil salesman Zachariah Gibson (David Hemblen), and the two new friends zigzag back and forth in time to both the past and present. Serialized over ten episodes running at fifteen minutes each, *The Adventures of Timothy Pilgrim* created a template for future didactic science-fiction at the network, which Pollock returned to in *Read All About It!* (1979), *Read All About It! Part 2* (1980), and *Zardip's Search for Healthy Wellness* (1988).

Contrasting with the harsh overlit video look of most children's productions filmed in studios, *The Adventures of Timothy Pilgrim* was shot on 16mm film on location in both the gritty streets of downtown Toronto (representing the present), and the more pastoral Kleinburg and Rockton, Ontario (representing the past). Director of photography Michael Ellis introduced a cinematic quality to what would otherwise have been a routine videotape production. This filmic touch gave the series a much different look from its contemporaries, and it was easily sold to many PBS stations in the United States where it was often paired with repeats of the Jon Pertwee and Tom Baker episodes of *Doctor Who* (1963), which was also rooted in the concept of time travel.

47
Tell Me a Story (1975)

HARKENING BACK TO DODI ROBB AND PAT PATTERSON'S *Telestory Time* — the very first preschool series made in Toronto and broadcast by the CBC in 1953 — *Tell Me a Story* was a ten-minute celebration of the art of storytelling. Anchored by Susanna Friesen, the series featured contemporary and traditional children's literature, often presented with illustrations, mime, and music, and was narrated by a rotating group of storytellers. In total, twenty episodes running at fifteen minutes each were produced and regularly aired on the network until the mid-1980s.

Appearing on the program alongside Friesen were Dennis Lee (*Alligator Pie* and *Jelly Belly*), who would later become Toronto's inaugural poet laureate, Indigenous singer David Campbell, Alex Laurier, and the Patchwork Players — guitarist Martin Laba, author Marilyn Beker, and Marilyn's younger sister, mime Jeanne Beker. Beker had studied in Paris with pioneering mime Étienne Decroux; she would become an international broadcast personality best known for her work on Citytv's *The NewMusic* (1979) and *FashionTelevision* (1985). She was also the host of *Rockflash* on MuchMusic beginning in 1984.

48

The End of the Saturday Morning Supershow (1976)

BACK IN JANUARY 1975 WHEN THE SATURDAY MORNING Supershow first launched, *The Globe and Mail*'s television critic Blaik Kirby criticized the block as being too educational and not entertaining enough to lure young viewers away from cartoons:

> The essential problem is that to win this fight, Channel 19 has to produce shows that are entertaining. It seems, however, to have spent more energy on sheafs of field studies that say kids will like the Saturday Morning Supershow, than it has on making the show a delight. Channel 19's mission in life, which it can never ignore, is education — and in this case it has not been able to produce shows that are simultaneously educational and interesting.[45]

Noting that the development of the Saturday Morning Supershow had begun eighteen to twenty-four months before, Kirby went on to suggest that newly minted Channel 19 program director Jim Hanley would likely have created a different flow of programming than what was being offered: "I suspect that, under Hanley, these particular projects might have been launched very differently, and probably better. He is well aware of sugar-coating the educational pill by making his shows interesting."[46] Kirby's observation proved correct as the block was radically reworked and then finally cancelled in the spring of 1976.

Long before the launch of the Saturday Morning Supershow, Ran Ide and Jim Hanley faced the fact that Channel 19 was not reaching the important eighteen-to-twenty-four demographic. In his memoir *Transparent Blackboard*, Ran Ide noted:

> Our mandate was to serve citizens of all ages and we had been singularly unsuccessful in reaching the older teenagers and the young adults. To do so we had to respond to what interested them, and that was popular culture.[47]

Around this time, Hanley and popular CHUM-FM DJ Reiner Schwarz developed a counterculture music program entitled *Nightmusic*, hosted by Schwarz and airing every night on Channel 19 between 11:00 p.m. and midnight. The series was "part talk show, part lecture, part performance art, part concept — all very loosely structured"[48] and featured live performances from bands and artists such as Rough Trade and FM (featuring a pre-bandage Nash the Slash).

As trailblazing as *Nightmusic* was — predating MTV, MuchMusic, and even Citytv's prophetic *The NewMusic* — it was expensive to produce and, as budgets shifted, the Saturday Morning Supershow became its first casualty. The block had not performed to expectation, with other channels airing brand-new Saturday-morning cartoons such as *The Tom & Jerry Show* (1975) and *Return to the Planet of the Apes* (1975) more likely to garner playground credibility than the eat-your-greens shows that played all school week.

Both *CUCUMBER* and *Tell Me a Story* were renewed for one additional season each, while *Monkey Bars*, *The Adventures of Timothy Pilgrim*, and *Quiz-Bang* were cancelled. Most of the *Monkey Bars* production team, including Bill Hartley, eloped to Montreal to create a similar Saturday-morning song-and-dance variety show called *Kidstuff* (1975) for CTV affiliate CFCF-TV. The

Saturday Morning Supershow was reconstructed for the fall of 1975, and now featured a Saturday lineup of *Polka Dot Door*, *The Adventures of Jeremy* (the English dub of *Colargol*), *The Adventures of Timothy Pilgrim*, *CUCUMBER*, *Big Blue Marble*, *Monkey Bars*, *Calling Captain Consumer*, and *L'atelier des pissenlits*, and a Sunday lineup consisting of *Polka Dot Door*, *The Adventures of Jeremy*, *Fingerbobs*, *CUCUMBER*, *Monkey Bars*, *Tell Me a Story*, and *Colargol* (the original French-language version of *Jeremy*).

Only *CUCUMBER* and *Tell Me a Story* featured new episodes, while the rest were repeats and series purchased from independent producers. *Big Blue Marble* was an anthology series featuring stories from children around the world that was meant to encourage intercultural understanding. It came from the United States via public broadcasting producer International Telephone & Telegraph (ITT). *L'atelier des pissenlits* was a French-language puppet series, while *Fingerbobs* was an educational series that used finger puppets to explore geography. *Colargol* was a charming stop-motion series that charted the adventures of a bear named Colargol, in French, or Jeremy, in English. It was based on the books of French author Olga Pouchine and was broadcast in both its native French and in a dubbed English version. Although not educational content, screening both versions was an attempt by Channel 19 to encourage bilingualism.

While variations on this schedule remained in place until the late 1970s, the overarching aim of the Saturday Morning Supershow, a block constructed to challenge the dominance of cartoon programs on other networks, was viewed as a failure. However, it marked the first collaboration between Vernon and VanderBurgh and Pollock. These relationships would blossom for Channel 19 in the years that followed.

ENTER TVONTARIO

The Ontario Educational Communications Authority (OECA) had always been a confusing and overly complicated name for a television station, and simply "Channel 19" lacked the dynamism presented by their on-air programming. As its footprint expanded — 1975 saw the opening of its first high-power transmitter in Ottawa, as well as rebroadcast transmitters in Sudbury and Thunder Bay — the OECA sought a catchy and precise moniker for its exciting emerging television network.

In keeping with the channel's homespun spirit and no doubt to keep the costs low, the organization held an internal contest for all employees to submit new names for the channel. The submissions were duly entered and reviewed. The victorious entry was TVOntario, submitted by in-house movie maven Elwy Yost. (His prize was a book on the films of Marilyn Monroe.) The name was fitting: futuristic sounding but also a callback to the educational television days. In-house designer Dick Derhodge created a new logo that remained with the network for twenty years until a branding overhaul in 1994. Canada Modern, an archive of modernist Canadian graphic design, describes the Derhodge TVO logo:

Dick Derhodge's logo for the newly named TVOntario.

"With its bold, playful and geometric construction, the logo feels wonderfully appropriate for the audience. The glyph-like VO retains a human-centred feel akin to pictograms and iconography, further connecting it to education and interaction."[49]

49
Readalong (1975)

USING PUPPETS, CHILD ACTORS, SONGS, AND PUZZLES, *Readalong* was methodically engineered to teach the fundamentals of reading to a younger audience. It also became the flashpoint for a new style of children's television production at TVOntario, as the first to apply formative and summative research methods. Each episode ran ten minutes and was mostly presented by a joyful Boot (a talking boot), who along with his friends — Pretty (a pink shoe), Granny (an elderly lady), Hole (a hole), House (a haunted house), Word Vendor (a travelling salesman), Who Owl, the Explorer, Mister Bones, and the Thing (a monster) — helped illustrate new vocabulary to young viewers.

Readalong was the result of many years of work started by Ruth Vernon, a former schoolteacher from Scarborough who joined the OECA full-time in 1970 as a utilization officer. OECA's utilization office was devoted solely to consulting and organizing workshops and conferences to assist groups of educators using television in the classroom. When Vera Novakowski departed, Vernon was promoted to superintendent of children's programming. Vernon brought a strong awareness of primary and junior curriculum to the department with an emphasis on math and language. Working with former high-school principal Larry Al Fasan, Vernon had developed an ambitious five-year plan for children's programming that would mean allocating 80 percent of all OECA funds to reading, writing, and arithmetic, starting at grade 1 and going up to grade 6.[50]

Readalong was the first of her many great collaborative successes at TVO. Vernon believed in quality research, and lots of it, resulting in years-long incubation for programs that slowly moved from concept to screen. For example, in the case of *Readalong*, six different pilot episodes were created and then tested with students, parents, and teachers. Upon receiving a detailed analysis of each pilot, Vernon and her team would revise the show responding to a wide variety of reactive criteria.

At first, the sales team wanted the show to run for thirty minutes, but Vernon believed that from a "pedalogical and marketing standpoint"[51] ten-minute episodes would be more effective. Her belief was that ten minutes was the maximum amount of time they might successfully hold the attention of a child to the extent of picking up a new word and remembering it. *Readalong*'s writer Ken Sobol (*Inside/Out*, *Magic Shadows*) impressed Vernon with his suggestion that they use simple yet random and out-of-context visual objects like a boot or a skeleton to teach the basic tenets of reading.

The iconic star of *Readalong* (1977), Boot, was a puppet created by Noreen Young and voiced by Jack Duffy.

The first scripted pilot episode only featured the characters of Boot and Granny. Boot set up the central premise of the show by explaining how important it is to learn how to read and explaining the word "jump." "[Ken] liked the challenge, that kind of blending of humour and creativity and didactic learning,"[52] according to his son John Sobol. Once the basic outlines started to come together and the early scripts were being road-tested, the production began to look for a skilled puppet-maker who could carry these rough ideas and random totems into full-bodied characters. Sobol suggested Noreen Young, an Ottawa-area puppeteer who had created extraordinarily distinctive characters for CBC children's shows filmed in Ottawa like *Hi Diddle Day* (1969) and *What's New?* (1972).

Young's initial sketches for characters like Boot, Granny, and the Explorer were well received, and attention turned to casting a talent pool who could bring Noreen's remarkable puppets to life. Jack Duffy was the first hire, cast as the

Max Ferguson gave voice to the absent-minded Granny character on *Readalong* (1977), another wonderfully realized puppet by Noreen Young.

cordial star of the show, Boot. Duffy was at the time best known as "Captain Jack," his role as captain of the home team on CHCH-TV Hamilton's outrageous in-house charades game show *Party Game* (1970). Well-known CBC Radio satirist Max Ferguson was next on board as the absent-minded Granny, and finally Julie Amato was selected as Boot's sparring partner, Pretty the pink shoe. Duffy, Ferguson, and Amato then split the voices of the remaining characters. The puppets were operated by Young, Nina Keogh, and Bob Dermer, who had got his start at TVO a year earlier performing the puppet of Oswald the Owl on *Two Plus You* (1974).

Production began on an initial batch of thirty episodes in late 1975. Producer/director Peter McLean skillfully mixed footage of young children speaking directly to the camera with animation created by Joyce Cosby working under the supervision of TVO's in-house visual virtuoso Dick Derhodge. Some of the puppets were filmed in front of a green screen and then chroma-keyed into still images, while others appeared on constructed sets (such as Granny). Later episodes were more ambitious and paired children with the puppets, as well as mixing and matching the various characters for some segments. All this complex video editing was done by Brian Elston, who would later help give series such as *Math Patrol* and *Today's Special* their unique looks.

Readalong debuted at 9:20 a.m. on October 30, 1976, immediately following that day's instalment of *Report Metric*. This cunning scheduling ensured the program was more likely to be used in classrooms that were already screening *Report Metric* as part of their early-morning routine, seeing as the TV-on-a-media-cart was already set up and presumably emitting signals in front of the class. A second batch of thirty episodes was created in 1977, and a final thirty in 1979. Later directors included Susan Murgatroyd (*CUCUMBER*), Chris Homer, and Jeremy Pollock (*The Adventures of Timothy Pilgrim*). In 1979, TVOntario released a *Readalong* LP on vinyl and cassette as a supplement to in-class screenings of the series, featuring many of the songs used in the series (lyrics written by Greg Adams and Sobol, and music by Eric Robertson [*Read All About It!*]).

Readalong teachers' guides tied directly to the Ontario curriculum were created simultaneously with the writing and production of the show for all three series. The guides were written by educational supervisor Jennifer Harvey (who also worked in an advisory capacity on the series) and overseen by Vernon, and contained artwork by Noreen Young. This strategic approach became the default for all of Vernon's TVOntario series moving ahead. TVO's chief architect Ran Ide took great pride in recalling the genesis, manifestation, and ultimate success of *Readalong*: "To my mind, it was the finest and most widely used multimedia reading program ever devised."[53]

50
Homemade TV (1976)

IN 1976, CBC PRODUCER DON ELDER CONTINUED HIS ASsignment to recapture the after-school audience with a suitable comedy. Elder contracted a talented group of performers known as the Homemade Theatre

Company, composed of Fred and Larry Mollin, Barry Flatman, and Phil Savath. The company ran acting classes for children out of the Young People's Theatre on Front Street in Toronto and toured schools across Ontario, workshopping sketch comedy with students. Writer Jed MacKay was drafted to help transition the group's sketches into a television format, which was cleverly titled *Homemade TV*. MacKay devised a roster of fast-paced spoofs based on films, books, and other television series with themes that touched on childhood anxieties at home and at school. The program starred children from the Young People's Theatre program.

Homemade TV encouraged an open dialogue with its audience, who were invited to send in their own ideas for future parodies and segments. This type of viewer interactivity, which had also been fostered by *Razzle Dazzle* and *CUCUMBER*, proved incredibly popular. Due to budget cuts in 1978, *Homemade TV* was cancelled, as was the in-house development of any future comedy or variety shows for children.

This unfortunate decision derailed another series Elder had shot a pilot for called *Range Ryder & The Calgary Kid* (1977), featuring David Ferry as the Range Ryder and a young Scarborough native named Mike Myers as his sidekick, the Calgary Kid. Myers would later train at Second City in Toronto, before graduating to *Saturday Night Live* in 1989, where his signature character Wayne Campbell (first seen in Toronto on Citytv's *City Limits* in 1983) was spun off into the popular Hollywood franchise *Wayne's World* (1992). Written by *Homemade TV*'s Larry Mollin, Phil Savath, and MacKay, the show was an extended spoof on classic serialized Saturday-morning Westerns, such as Sid and Marty Krofft's gonzo *Land of the Lost* (1974). *Range Ryder & The Calgary Kid* (also known as *Adventure of the Dinosaur Badlands*) featured Ferry and Myers riding plastic horses in front of a chroma-keyed barren western vista where they come upon a valley of dinosaurs and set about taming them. While Myers had already had his first break on television as a guest star the previous year on *King of Kensington* (1975), one can only imagine what his career trajectory might have looked like had *Range Ryder & The Calgary Kid* gone to a full series.

51
Math Patrol (1977)

TVONTARIO PRODUCER CLIVE VANDERBURGH HAS DESCRIBED the network's head of children's programming, Ruth Vernon, as "a force of nature in terms of defending children and having a very strong view of how children should be talked to. And she was a great nurturer of production talent."[54] VanderBurgh's next major production for TVO after *CUCUMBER* was *Math Patrol*, the second chapter in TVOntario's vaunted math trilogy, following up 1974's *Two Plus You*. This outing, however, was a more complex and imaginative attempt to teach basic mathematical concepts using an ongoing narrative and creative characters.

Protagonist Sidney is the newest member of the Math Patrol, a clandestine agency that was established to solve global mathematical problems. Since the bumbling Sidney is the patrol's newest recruit, he must bear the shame of wearing a kangaroo disguise (the only disguise that would fit him). He longs for the day he can impress his boss, Mr. Big, so he can graduate to the plainclothes division. Sidney is assigned various missions by the shadowy unseen Mr. Big, along the way encountering a variety of oddball characters including Squiggles, Spot, and the Hand, all while solving math problems.

Animation, clay animation, stop-motion, and models were all used, creating a chaotic but enchanting visual patois that became VanderBurgh's signature. VanderBurgh also provided musical direction. As he says, "There aren't that many people who have written multiple songs about the commutative property of addition."[55]

Like *CUCUMBER*, the series showcased VanderBurgh's adeptness at staging educational subjects that lacked drama, making them much more palatable to children. Teachers loved to use *Math Patrol* in their classes. All the math content was closely scrutinized by Educational Services within TVOntario and followed the 1976/77 Ontario curriculum: "Everything from Sidney's predicaments to the successful completion of his missions were carefully planned and written."[56] In total, twenty episodes of *Math Patrol* were produced at a running time of fifteen minutes per episode.

Ever humble, VanderBurgh credits much of *Math Patrol*'s success to the assembled production team, including production assistant Jane Downey, writer Joanne Hauser, and editor Brian Elston, who provided much of the show's charm in post-production:

> I was able to bring a Canadian sensibility to an audience enamoured by American cartoons and American television shows. We did vast amounts of post-production, used techniques that hadn't been used in Canada — certainly hadn't been used in children's television — because TVOntario had the facilities. At CBC, you could have a studio and a big crew, but you had to shoot it live. TVOntario had a very small studio, no big crews, but lots of post-production capacity.[57]

Animation for *Math Patrol* was created by M.S. Art Services, and its beautiful opening credit sequence was devised by Dick Derhodge. John Kozak, who played the scenery-chewing dimwit Dingbat in TVOntario's earlier *Monkey Bars*, was cast as the lovable but totally inept Sidney; the booming voice of Carl Banas gave life to the seen-only-in-silhouette Mr. Big. Guest stars included Air Farce's Luba Goy; Canadian artist, mime, and mask-maker Naomi Tyrrell; and Nikki Tilroe (*The Uncle Bobby Show*, *The Waterville Gang*).

Math Patrol's finale, titled "Math – Who Needs It?," not only provided an overview of the series' central concepts but also dared to ask the existential question of why math was so important in life. VanderBurgh asked, "We use actors, puppets, stuffed animals, music, comedians, and an immense amount of research. If down the road the kid doesn't get anything out of it, what good is a program?"[58]

52
MathMakers (1978)

VANDERBURGH'S THEMATIC SEQUEL TO *MATH PATROL* CONtinued the noble quest to make Ontario curriculum mathematics more palatable to youngsters. Changing the formula slightly, this series was modelled after a situation comedy and added a postmodern element — a TV show about making a TV show — which undoubtedly made it just as interesting to teachers and parents as it did the target audience of grade 4 students.

The premise of *MathMakers* was based around the challenges of a television production crew headed up by Cal (Derek McGrath) and Laurie (Lyn Harvey) to create an educational television series that taught mathematics to grade 4 students. In the second series, Laurie was replaced by Cal's neighbour Kathy (Barbara Barsky). Many of the key creatives involved in *Math Patrol* also worked on *MathMakers*, including production assistant Jane Downey, writer Joanne Hauser, and editor Brian Elston. Also, like *Math Patrol*, there was extensive use of animation, clay animation, and puppets. *MathMakers* also deployed much more complex visual effects and continued to push the boundaries of what you could do with chroma-key in a small studio environment.

Derek McGrath brought an element of physical comedy to the role of Cal, who performed a number of different roles. McGrath had a natural knack for comedy, and he would go on to great success landing parts in U.S. sitcoms such as *AfterMASH* (1983), *Cheers* (1983), and *Growing Pains* (1985), and co-starring in CTV's *My Secret Identity* (1988). One of his first television roles had been in OECA's *The World of B.J. Vibes* (1973).

Notable guests on *MathMakers* included George Murray (*The Forest Rangers*), Doris Petrie (*King of Kensington*), and *SCTV*'s Tony Rosato and Joe Flaherty. Flaherty appeared as flamboyant quiz show host Ronnie Buck Rogers on the intergalactic show-within-a-show "Make Your Move." A total

of twenty-six episodes of *MathMakers* were produced, each with a running time of fifteen minutes. The series was often sold as a bumper package with *Math Patrol*.

Ruth Vernon's master plan had so far resulted in three extremely successful programs: *Readalong*, *Math Patrol*, and *MathMakers*. All had achieved curriculum goals and created hit shows that performed with audiences in both classrooms and at home; perhaps even more importantly, they sold well on the international market. They were about to be joined by an even more popular fourth series.

Joe Flaherty appeared as intergalactic quizmaster Ronnie Buck Rogers in *MathMakers* (1978), TVOntario's follow-up series to *Math Patrol* (1977) and *Two Plus You* (1974).

53
Write On! (1977)

A SNAPPY, FIVE-MINUTE GRAMMAR LESSON DISGUISED AS A sitcom for students of all ages, *Write On!* had a remarkable pedigree that helped secure its place in the TVOntario schedule for almost two decades. TVO's internal catalogue described *Write On!* as

> TVOntario's response to the complaint that some students can't express themselves well in writing because they have not learned basic grammar. The series tackles the problem with fast-paced situation comedy set in a smalltown newspaper office manned by a crusty, short-tempered editor and his two green reporters who act as his constant foil.[59]

Write On! tackled subjects such as punctuation and tenses, and turned them into set-ups for punchlines. Bumbling reporter Henry Kent (Paul Brown) is dragged into a variety of increasingly bizarre spots, while his fellow reporter Miss Newton (Diane Dewey) and grumpy boss Mr. R.H. Morton (Jack Creley) typically exacerbate the situation. The series was ostensibly aimed at young people, but was just as informative and useful to grown-ups, thanks to the clever scripts by Jed MacKay and Ken MacKay (no relation). Jed MacKay started at OECA in 1971 revamping a straightforward program aimed at teachers entitled *Chalk Dust* into one of the channel's earliest attempts to turn serious subjects into something more entertaining, which he retitled *P.L.O.* (Teachers used to write P.L.O., please leave on, on chalkboards so janitorial staff would not erase their work.) Jed MacKay would later write key episodes of *Today's Special* (1981) and *Calling All Safety Scouts* (1982), create *Join In!* (1989) and *Polka Dot Shorts* (1995), and take over the show running of *Polka Dot Door* when Ted Coneybeare retired.

Write On!'s catalogue of oddities featured homages to rock band KISS, Dracula, punch-drunk boxers, aliens, hostage situations, and, as the TVO 1980 Broadcast Guide noted, "tattooed ladies."[60] The rapid-fire delivery of the scripts by the three leads recalled Howard Hawks's *His Girl Friday* (1940), as did the inspired framing and camerawork courtesy of director Leo Orenstein. Orenstein was an artistic polymath who dabbled in live theatre, television, and film, as well as being an artist, playwright, producer, and teacher. He directed more than 150 episodes of television, including many one-off teleplays including adaptations of Anton Chekhov, George Bernard Shaw, and Eugène Ionesco, for the CBC.

Guest stars included Robin Duke (*SCTV*), Frank Ruffo (*Read All About It!*), and Maxine Miller (*The Howdy Doody Show*, *Misterogers*). *Write On!* producer

Paul Brown, Diane Dewey, and Jack Creley (from left to right) starred in *Write On!* (1977), a beautifully costumed and punchy five-minute-long grammar lesson that often appeared between other programs in the TVOntario schedule.

Philip Nixon was also responsible for TVOntario's effective-but-bonkers short film adaptation of Isaac Asimov's "The Ugly Little Boy," also in 1977, filmed entirely on location at the Ontario Science Centre. *Write On!*'s instantly recognizable instrumental opening and closing music was a piece of library music entitled "Laurel and Who!" by Brian Bennett, former drummer of U.K. band the Shadows. A total of sixty episodes of *Write On!* were produced and remained a mainstay of the TVO schedule, often running as interstitials in the evening if a film or series underran its allotted time slot.

54
Parlez-moi (1978)

PARLEZ-MOI WAS PRODUCED AT TVONTARIO TO TEACH Quebec French to English-speaking children through repetition and humour. It was memorably hosted by Marc Favreau, a well-known Quebec comedian, performing as his popular clown alter ego, Sol. The series combined learning with comedy sketches that were both physical and verbal. Each episode would begin with Favreau, as himself, introducing a few French terms or phrases in

Pirate Ayes: Sol the Clown (Marc Favreau, right) removes his eyepatch in a pirate-themed episode of TVOntario's *Parlez-moi* (1978).

English. Then a short sketch featuring Sol the Clown would follow, with dialogue in French and incorporating the newly introduced words and phrases. Roger Periard often guested as the victim of Sol's incompetence. The episode would break the sketch into segments, replaying the French terms on the screen with Favreau's voice pronouncing them. After repeating this process three times, the entire sketch would be shown uninterrupted. "And now, the complete sketch again," was Favreau's catchphrase.

One of the network's very first productions, *Le monde des petits* (1971), had been designed to teach colloquial conversational French to English-speaking viewers, and was described by Ran Ide as a cross between *Sesame Street* and *Polka Dot Door*.[61] Another, *The Sunrunners* (1971), was produced by Peggy Liptrott and used animation from Rainbow, the company started by Al Guest and Jean Mathieson and better known for shows like *The Toothbrush Family* (1977) and the Inuit special *Ukaliq* (1975). Neither of these French-as-a-second-language programs had been able to build a sustained audience. TVO also acquired and screened the BBC's *Suivez la piste* (1966), a French-language course presented as a noirish detective thriller. While this series proved to be more popular in the ratings, it was not supported in class by French teachers. Ide recalls, "We decided to make our own made-in-Ontario brand"[62] based on the success of the short-form format of *Write On!* and *Readalong*.

The husband-and-wife team of David Stansfield and Denise Boiteau wrote the *Parlez-moi* scripts, the first of their many collaborations with TVOntario that would later result in *Eureka!* (1980), *Bits & Bytes* (1983), and *How Do You Do?* (1988), all three starring Billy Van.

Regarding Favreau's portrayal of Sol, Stansfield told author Greg Oliver:

> He played really naive, almost like a newborn baby. He was perfect for teaching French, because everything had to be explained to him, as if to a baby, because he knew nothing, almost as if he came from another planet.[63]

In total, ninety episodes of *Parlez-moi* running at ten minutes each were produced. The popular series was aired on PBS in the United States and turned up on the TVO schedules well into the late 1980s. Many Ontario residents of a certain age will never forget they learned the fundamentals of speaking French from a downtrodden hobo-looking clown.

55
Read All About It! (1979)/ Read All About It! Part 2 (1981)

REFERRED TO AT TVONTARIO AS THE SON OF *READALONG*, *Read All About It!* was another reading program, this time aimed at grades 4 to 6 and with a pulpy science-fiction twist. It followed the adventures of three kids who uncover strange otherworldly events unfolding in their sleepy town and decide to publish their own newspaper while investigating. "We can't do much to get them away from *Kojak* or *Battlestar Galactica*, but what we can do is make our educational programming appealing on a different level,"[64] producer-director Jeremy Pollock told *TVO Plus* magazine in 1979.

Coming almost five years after the first strains of *Readalong* began development, *Read All About It!* was the next chapter of Ruth Vernon's master plan to transform the way in which curriculum-based educational programs were fashioned and received. Even with the great success of *Readalong*, there was nothing for the kids when they grew out of that show. Vernon was alarmed at the research coming back to TVOntario: "Teachers felt children were just not motivated to read. One of the chief things was to improve their vocabulary and get them to recognize that they could find out for themselves what words mean."[65]

In late 1977, an officer of TVO's office of project research, the aptly named Goody Teachman, surveyed over two hundred grade 4 children about their interests in a variety of subjects to help determine content for the *Readalong* follow-up series. For example, the children were asked to choose from a list of ten settings for a new television show, and a "haunted house" proved to be the most popular at 60 percent.[66] Pollock recalled in a 2002 interview:

> We did a lot of interviewing with the intended audience, and this was just after *Star Wars* came out. So, there was a tremendous interest in space travel and aliens, and it was something kids wanted to see in a show. There was a very strong impetus for us to involve space and some kind of time travel.[67]

Furnished with detailed research that broke down everything from their favourite age for characters on television (the same as them, at 57 percent), to how much television they watched (majority three to five hours per day), Vernon commissioned a group of writers to develop concepts using elements from these findings, such as outer space, time travel, haunted houses, and child protagonists.[68] Out of this field of potential authors, Clive Endersby emerged. His scripts for *Two Plus You* (1974) had been well received, and the feeling was if he could teach them math, he could teach them anything. Endersby revealed in 1979:

> The value I bring is to look at it from the point of view of pure entertainment. The people here know what they want to get across to kids and I know how to get it across in the most interesting manner. A drama series is more gripping than a magazine show and I'm the voice of drama.[69]

Endersby took the research and crafted a truly spooky opening that played more like an Italian *giallo* than an episode of children's television: Three kids investigate an old dilapidated Victorian coach house, which one of them has inherited. Invisible fingers scrawl a message pleading for "HELP" on a dusty window, while a menacing, black-gloved man lurks outside the house watching the children. Suddenly, two robots reveal themselves from within the coach house and warn the children of imminent danger. The doorknob twists slowly inward as the camera slowly zooms to blur and ominous music plays over the credits.

As with Pollock's earlier *Adventures of Timothy Pilgrim*, the serialized nature of the narrative kept kids interested and eager to find out what would happen next. *Read All About It!* took that approach one step further by ending each show on a zoom blur when something dramatic was about to happen. It is unlikely anyone who watched that first episode of *Read All About It!* in a classroom with their peers will ever forget the sheer terror of it all, especially the cliffhanger ending with no immediate resolution. Serialized cliffhanger television had been a popular format in the 1950s and early 1960s, but, other than soap operas, had mostly faded as a viable televisual storytelling format.

One exception was the U.K. import *Doctor Who* (1963), a science-fiction television series whose stories contained weekly cliffhangers, often placing the main characters in peril. (See p. 27 for the Toronto-based beginnings of *Doctor Who*.) Since 1976, *Doctor Who* had aired on TVO on Thursday and Saturday at 7:00 p.m., so many children in the province were accustomed to lingering unresolved images of terror. (It was also broadcast on the Buffalo PBS station WNED-TV Monday through Friday, meaning Toronto residents could see the show almost every day.) Since TVO's preschool block ran from 6:00 p.m. until 7:00 p.m., a thematic whiplash occurred as soon as *Doctor Who* began. Infamous U.K. media critic and moral crusader Mary Whitehouse often attacked *Doctor Who* precisely because of its cliffhanger endings, warning that children would be left in a state of trauma while the mental image of open-ended distress replayed in their minds.

Endersby recalls getting notes from some of TVOntario's in-house educators that some elements of *Read All About It!* were too frightening, including the series villain, the "big bad" alien Duneedon:

> Ruth came to me and said the educators are asking for a new villain because they don't like Duneedon. I said, he's the villain! He's not supposed to be liked! They looked at what some of the kids had written, and one of them had said Duneedon is really terrible, he's like J.R. [Ewing] in *Dallas*. I said to Ruth, you're never gonna get a better review.[70]

After six episodes were made to test in schools in 1978, production was put on hold while feedback and further research was conducted. Some teachers requested physical copies of *The Herbertville Chronicle*, the newspaper produced in the show by the children, so they could be shared in the classroom. This idea was worked into the supplemental packages prepared by the educational supervisors, including Jennifer Harvey who oversaw a team of specialists for the publication of the *Read All About It!* teachers' guide, which included in-depth information and suggested post-episode exercises for the class.

After testing was complete, an additional fourteen episodes were produced. This included location shooting that took the crew out of the studio and, like *The Adventures of Timothy Pilgrim*, was shot on 16mm film, contrasting with the bright video look of the studio sessions. Much of the outdoor filming was done in Brampton, Ontario.

In the final four episodes, the children travel to alien planets and space stations, and pilot spaceships, which perhaps seemed slightly outlandish to attempt on such a low-budget show. However, by this point extensive chroma-key work had been done on *MathMakers* and, combined with some excellent models, the result was certainly comparable to anything seen on *Doctor Who*.

Toronto special-effects guru Warren Keillor (*Black Christmas*) created the robots, Otto and Theta, as well as the space station. The inspired set design was by Chris Adeney, who had overseen TVO's notable but rare foray into science-fiction with the short *The Ugly Little Boy* (1977). Eric Robertson provided eerie incidental music and the memorable theme song. David Collard, Lydia Zajc, and Stacey Arnold were cast as the three young protagonists Chris, Lynne, and Samantha, while Sean Hewitt played the silver-faced evil alien overlord Duneedon with a menacing laugh that echoed through the entire series.

Upon completion of the first series, Teachman was again tasked with surveying Ontario students and teachers and creating a three-stage summative evaluation of the effectiveness of series one, before work could begin on series two. Teachman analyzed ten grade 4 and 5 classes, and six teachers, all from the Durham District School Board. She concluded that the series,

> with slight modifications, appears to be highly successful in meeting the needs of language arts teachers and students at the junior level. It is suitable for both grade 4 and grade 5 curricula as an instructional system and is also a highly desirable broadcast series for the target audience.[71]

Of note was her observation that "the teachers reported that their students particularly enjoyed the theme song and sang along with every program."[72]

In an unusual development for TVO, Endersby was asked to novelize the first season. Pollock recalls:

> The one thing TVO never got into, for political reasons, was getting into a cottage industry of spinoff merchandise. Certainly, PBS and their production affiliates have done remarkably well. The whole aspect of toys coming out of TV shows was still new at that point, but the interest here was to create a whole new level of reading.[73]

The book was published by Methuen with an initial print run of six thousand copies, most of which were sold to school libraries.

In addition to Pollock and Endersby, *Read All About It! Part 2* found most of the first series cast returning, although the character of Samantha (Stacey Arnold) was written out and replaced by newcomer Alex (Michael Dwyer).

Far more ambitious in scope than its predecessor, *Read All About It! Part 2* featured mini-arcs including a storyline that found the kids marooned in the past after being transported back in time to the War of 1812. These sequences were shot on location at Queenston Heights, Ontario, and featured the children interreacting with historical figures, such as General Brock.

Another arc observed the protagonists facing off against a new villain called The Book Destroyer, who was erasing important literary characters (the first series had featured appearances from the Queen of Hearts, Merlin the Magician, and Captain Hook). Like all good sequels, it was the return of the big bad from the first instalment that delivered the real drama. In the final arc, Duneedon returned and had to be defeated once again.

The striking cover of Clive Endersby's paperback adaptation of his *Read All About It!* (1979) scripts, a spooky reading-and-writing series aimed at children in grades 4 to 6.

Although *Read All About It!* had only been designed for two series, its popularity, especially on PBS in the United States where it was fast developing a cult following, resulted in a demand for a third series. "They wanted a third series. We had tremendous support: classes and teachers wrote letters from all across North America, telling us how important it was in their classroom," recalled Pollock in 2002.[74] Sadly, and despite the show's popularity and almost instant cult status, a third season was not produced.

Both series of *Read All About It!* remained perennial hallmarks of the TVO afternoon and weekend schedule where it was often paired with *The Adventures of Timothy Pilgrim* for a double dose of educational sci-fi adventure. Even after the series was no longer offered through TVO's school distribution network, it was discovered on-air by many children who had not been exposed to it in the classroom.

Left to right: Chris (David Collard) and Lynne (Lydia Zajc) welcomed Alex (Michael Dwyer) into the main cast of *Read All About It! Part 2* (1981), which found the kids time-travelling back to the War of 1812 and later battling the maniacal Book Destroyer.

The series ran for two seasons each containing twenty episodes running at fifteen minutes each. International sales were brisk, with many American PBS outlets airing the show alongside *Doctor Who* in their schedule. TVO's office of project research manager, Olga Kuplowska, reported that she had received a letter from a teacher in Greenville, Mississippi, saying:

> I have worked extensively with the *Read All About It!* series for the past 2 years. Next year I hope to do a more in-depth study using the series. We have been told that we will be able to receive Part 2. My students were very excited about seeing the next part.[75]

For many foreign broadcasters, *Read All About It!* was an attractive purchase thanks to Ruth Vernon's involvement. A buyer from the Eastern Educational Television Network, which covered the New England states, once told Ran Ide that "his network would buy anything produced under the aegis of Ruth Vernon, sight unseen."[76]

56
Camp TVO/ What If... (1979)

ONE OF THE MORE INTERESTING TVONTARIO EXPERIMENTS happening at the end of the 1970s was Camp TVO, brainchild of the ebullient Jack Livesley. Former teacher and English department head, Livesley had joined the OECA in 1970 as a utilization officer. As passionate about new media as he was about Chaucer and Shakespeare, Livesley was soon promoted to programming, and then replaced Al Fasan as head of utilization at the network. Between 1973 and 1978, TVOntario offered workshops for kids on how to operate videotape machines, cameras, and early editing equipment, working in tandem with Jim Moriarty from the Metropolitan Educational Television Association (META). Together, Livesley and Moriarty co-authored three handbooks — *The Third Eye*, *Behind the Third Eye*, and *Picture This: Behind the Third Eye* — which became invaluable resources for teachers and young TV and filmmakers.

Meanwhile, within the research department at TVOntario, the summer programming season had been identified as being particularly boring for kids (and their parents) for a host of reasons, one of which was the complete lack of original programming on television. Since the beginning of the medium, summer had always been a wasteland of repeats and non-essential viewing. Livesley proposed an ambitious concept, Camp TVO, for the summer of 1979. It would feature a weekly one-hour programming block on-air in which viewers could participate at home. TVOntario would also create a series of activities, booklets, and video technique workshops that Ontario librarians could use when hosting a screening of the one-hour Camp TVO block at their library branch.

To fill out the block, a repeat of the U.K. import *Tom Grattan's War* (1968) was selected, as each episode contained a five-minute post-credit interstitial featuring Andrea Martin (*SCTV*) analyzing segments of the show from a filmmaking perspective. An original TVOntario production titled *What If...* followed immediately after.

What If... was a rather low-budget affair, even by TVOntario standards. It featured a cast of five children, three boys (Gary Eisler, Allan Levson, and Paul Tough) and two girls (Debbie Morrshead and Kimberly Clarke), and was introduced and tailed by Mystery Man, played by the exceptional Billy Van. Van was coming off a decade of popular work that had made him a household name via multiple monstrous roles in *The Hilarious House of Frightenstein* (1970) and *Party Game* (1972), both produced by CHCH-TV in Hamilton, Ontario.

The loopy and loose plot involved young Gary (Eisler), inventor of a time-machine, who accidentally sends himself into various alternative universes. In one universe, everyone is sad, while in another, life is determined by ritual ceremony — there were six universes in total. Gary's friends spend the series in their tree fort attempting to bring him back home. The Mystery Man addresses the viewer throughout claiming to be omnipotent and in control of the situation.

The vague plot resolution was no doubt intended to influence play-acting within the library workshops and at home. The *What If...* leaders' handbook, made available to all participating libraries screening Camp TVO, stated that the show "creates a situation the children viewing can develop and resolve on their own."[77] The handbook suggests that after viewing the show children should take cues from the story and act out alternative endings (certainly a novel way of fixing any scripting issues).

Due to the fact that supplementary materials were required to follow what was happening within the show, *What If...* was never repeated on-air. Series director Ted Regan went on to helm episodes of *Today's Special* (1981), and the star, Eisler, joined the cast of *The Body Works* (1980).

57
The Littlest Hobo (1979)

IN 1979, CFTO-TV'S STATION BOSS DOUG BASSETT FORGED ahead on what was to become the network's first Canadian evening drama series, *The Littlest Hobo*. Based on a 1958 U.S. film and 1963 television series filmed in British Columbia of the same name, the show followed the adventures of Hobo, an itinerant German shepherd unencumbered by an owner.

Through CFTO-TV's production arm, Glen-Warren Productions, filming took place throughout the summer of 1979 on videotape (as opposed to film-stock to keep costs down) with location shoots across southern Ontario and in Toronto. It was budgeted at $150,000 per episode, but there were rumblings of production delays and trouble with keeping the dogs in line. CFTO-TV refused to screen the opening episode to the press, and Bassett told the *Toronto Star*, "There's no reason why the press should see it before anyone else."[78] When *The Littlest Hobo* premiered on October 11, media reviews were unanimously poor. Film and television critic Ron Base went so far as to suggest punishment for those involved in its creation:

> At the CBC, drama has achieved a sophistication it hasn't known for years. At CTV, we've got a dog. Brother, do we have a dog. CTV executives should be sent to bed without their suppers (I would suggest spankings, but I'm basically non-violent). Better still, they should be made to watch *Littlest Hobo* episodes until they begin to scream for mercy.[79]

The ratings, however, told a different story. With over 1.6 million viewers for the opening episode and 1.7 million over the following week, *The Littlest Hobo* became the highest-rated Canadian-made series on the entire CTV network. The dog never looked back. During its six years on-air, *The Littlest Hobo* stuck to a very simple formula with new characters and locations each week: The free-spirited Hobo wandered into a dramatic situation, helped resolve it, then moved on, just like Richard Kimble in *The Fugitive* (1963) and David Banner in *The Incredible Hulk* (1977). The numerous guest stars tended to fit one of three categories: emerging local talent like Megan Follows, Michael Ironside, and Mike Myers; Canadian television perennials like Billy Van, Al Waxman, Harvey Atkin, and Rex Hagon; and Hollywood legends in their twilight years like Abe Vigoda, DeForest Kelley, Keenan Wynn, Vic Morrow, Henry Gibson, and Ray Walston.

The series was filmed almost entirely in Durham Region and Scarborough, with weekly stops in small towns, farms, and forests where the serene settings complimented the slower-paced storytelling. Several episodes featured Toronto prominently: The Hobo visited Union Station, the Canadian National Exhibition, the Ontario Science Centre, Chinatown, Kensington Market, the Beaches, the Metropolitan Toronto Zoo, Casa Loma, the R.C. Harris Water Treatment Plant, and, in one very memorable episode, even rode the old red Gloucester subway cars at Queen and Wilson TTC stations. He also attended popular out-of-town theme parks like Canada's Wonderland and Cullen Gardens & Miniature Village in Whitby, Ontario.

Sometimes it was Toronto playing itself — the episode "Duddleman and the Diamond Ring" takes place almost entirely in the Beaches and features the El Pueblo townhouses, the Goof (a Chinese restaurant infamous for its broken neon sign that was meant to say "Good Food"), and the Fox Theatre. In other episodes, Toronto stood in for American cities with New York City–style yellow taxicabs or Chicago police cars, although the city remained easy to recognize. The most ridiculous example is during the spookily prophetic episode "The Day of the Fugitive." A ship full of Russian plague carriers arrives at an unnamed U.S. port, and as the U.S. customs agents warn the infected sailors to stay aboard the ship, the CN Tower can be seen in plain view behind them.

Series star Hobo was portrayed by a rotating cadre of dogs — starting out with Toro, and including Lance, Bo, Thorn, and the most famous of

Down the road, that's where they'll always be: the stars of *The Littlest Hobo* (1979) — London (centre), Bo, Lance, Toro, and Thorn. Between filming each new series, the dogs often visited schools and local fairs to meet their adoring fans.

the bunch, London — all trained by Charles "Chuck" Eisenmann, a former professional baseball player turned handler who also wrote many books on dog training. During the off-season, Eisenmann and the dogs toured schools, malls, and fairs to help educate children about the responsibilities of dog ownership. "Every dog has the capacity to learn. The problem is that most owners don't know how to teach them,"[80] Eisenmann told *Starweek* magazine in 1979.

The Littlest Hobo's theme, "Maybe Tomorrow," was written by John Crossen and performed by Terry Bush and is perhaps Canada's best known folk song. Bush had been chosen to create the opening based on his popular country-western-flavoured jingles, which included odes to the Eaton Centre, the Metropolitan Toronto Zoo, and Canada Dry ginger ale. The series producers originally passed on Bush's ditty, opting instead to use a slow jazz piece, before coming to their senses and reinserting "Maybe Tomorrow" before broadcast. "It just captured the whole essence of the show and the dog.… The music part is nice, but I think it's more the lyrics that carry it,"[81] Bush said in 2022.

58
Matt and Jenny on the Wilderness Trail (1979)

EXECUTIVE PRODUCER RALPH C. ELLIS AND WILLIAM Davidson (*Razzle Dazzle*, *The Forest Rangers*) created this family-friendly series that followed the adventures of Matt Tanner (Derrick Jones) and his sister, Jenny (Megan Follows), as they traverse the wilds of Canada circa 1850 in search of their uncle. Set in multiple Canadian locations but shot in rural Ontario (mostly at the Kleinburg studios that had accommodated the earlier *Adventures of Timothy Pilgrim*), the series was created for Global Television with an eye on the international market.

Although classified as a family series, *Matt and Jenny* (the title it aired under) was noted for being quite frightening for children, with many episodes set during the night and featuring marauding threats from the forest. Television titan and *All in the Family* (1971) creator Norman Lear was apparently so enamoured of the show he bought the format rights, but never did anything with them. Eventually *Matt and Jenny* found U.S. acclaim after airing on the Nickelodeon cable channel. Follows went on to become a star as Anne Shirley in CBC's adaptation of *Anne of Green Gables* (1985). In total, twenty-six episodes of *Matt and Jenny*, each running at thirty minutes in length, were produced.

59
Kids Corner (1979)

THE 1970S HAD STARTED OFF WELL ENOUGH FOR BOBBY ASH, star of CFTO-TV's weekday *The Uncle Bobby Show* (1963). Although his national CTV network series *Uncle Bobby and Friends* had been cancelled in 1969, he was still in high demand in Toronto. In collaboration with Ash, Simpsons department stores retailed a line of Uncle Bobby clothing, including branded jackets, sweaters, and even baby clothes, proving, if nothing else, that Ash was ahead of the commercial craze about to envelop children's television in the wake of *Sesame Street* (1969). Ash's popularity was such that he openly discussed his rate card in a 1972 interview. For ten dollars, Ash would attend your party and be "amusing." For fifty dollars, he'd perform magic tricks and/or a puppet show. But for $150, he'd do all that, and bring along his trademark red double-decker party bus.[82]

Uncle Bobby (Bobby Ash) and Officer "Big" Big John (John Patterson) on the set of CFTO-TV's long-running *The Uncle Bobby Show* on an unknown date in the early 1970s. Eagle-eyed readers may spot Elmer the Safety Elephant tucked away to the left of Ash.

The Uncle Bobby Show's 8:30 a.m. time slot on CFTO-TV did not have much direct competition, and the format of the show remained the same, although it was enlivened by the addition of new special guests and puppeteers including Alex Laurier, Nina Keogh, Len Carlson, Darlene Armstrong, and Nikki Tilroe's Frog Print Theatre, which, at the time, was filming *The Waterville Gang* in the same studios at Channel Nine Court in Agincourt. Tilroe performed as Alicia the Squirrel, while brothers Ron and Cy Leonard created new puppet segments with a sentient train and its elderly driver called "The Clickity-Clack Express." A new regular cast member appeared in the form of Toronto police officer Meredith Cutting, who sang and played an acoustic guitar live as the Singing Policeman. Cutting, for his part, was never fond of the title:

> I hated the term "The Singing Policeman," but it was Bobby Ash that coined the phrase. The first show I did, he said "I'd like to introduce you to the newest member of our cast — he's our singing policeman." Because I was sitting there in uniform doing this, the name stuck, and I was there for the next eight years.[83]

Elmer the Safety Elephant's traffic rules were still discussed regularly, and he now had a cohort who made frequent appearances on the show — Blinky the talking police car.

As much as these new friends injected change into the now decade-old Uncle Bobby formula, the show was looking tired and beginning to feel like a relic. The program was regularly attacked by *Toronto Star* columnist and child psychologist Michele Landsberg,[84] who reported on books, films, and television she deemed appropriate for young people. More troublingly, there were whispers behind the scenes about Ash's increasing inclination to perform under the influence.

No one in executive management at CFTO-TV particularly cared for *The Uncle Bobby Show*, but it continued to serve its primary purpose and deliver the mandated hours of children's content CFTO-TV was required to produce on condition of licence. It ticked a box many viewed as a distraction from the prestige productions and live shows sharing valuable studio space. In 1975, portions of Sidney Lumet's Academy Award–winning film *Network* (1976) were filmed at 9 Channel Nine Court studio, home of *The Uncle Bobby Show*. Wildlife illustrator Barry Kent MacKay recalls watching Peter Finch's infamous "I'm mad as hell and I'm not going to take it anymore!" newsroom meltdown as it was shot, with the rest of the Uncle Bobby cast in the wings.[85] (*Network* satirizes a broadcast channel so bereft of morals it allows a crazed alcoholic to be on the air because he gets good ratings.)

As budgets were cut, and the number of episodes produced per year declined, Ash surely saw the writing on the wall. Toward the end of the run, he was buying props, crafts, and magic accessories with his own money, bringing them to the tapings himself. After watching the success Ernie Coombs and his wife had with creating the Mr. Dressup-approved Butternut preschool, Ash followed suit and launched three nursery schools after taking a childhood education course at Seneca College in 1976. He named them Bimbo Centres, after his alter ego, and charged fifty dollars per child a week. To supplement his dwindling income, Ash took on a part-time job as a school bus driver in Durham Region and Scarborough, where he was repeatedly chastised by older students who recognized him from television. Ash would often try to curry favour with his passengers by handing out pens with small blades for opening mail, branded with the Bimbo logo of his nursery schools, predictably resulting in carved up seats and other acts of wanton vandalism on the buses.[86]

A paper advertisement for one of "Uncle" Bobby Ash's personal appearances in the 1970s, where he often arrived in his own personal London Routemaster double-decker bus.

Although *The Uncle Bobby Show* had been a hallmark of CFTO since 1963, first as a morning show and weekend program, then during the lunch hour, by 1979 the stage was set for its inglorious exit. The show was retooled for the fall 1979 season and retitled *Kids Corner*. Ash was reduced to a bit player, usurped by an R2-D2 rip-off called 2E. (The post–*Star Wars* craze could be felt across many children's productions at the time.) Perhaps the bluest legacy was what happened to Bimbo the Birthday Clown: "When the show was finished, somebody took him and put him in the garbage. It was a very sad end,"[87] Ash told the *National Post* in 1999.

In the years that followed, *The Uncle Bobby Show* was recalled by many as a strange fever dream of a broadcast. Those who caught it early in the run remember a compelling and thoughtful children's program full of energy and vigour, while those who watched the later era (it was rerun on CFTO-TV through the 1980s, and by YTV into the early 1990s) remember something closer to a real-life "Krusty the Clown Show" (*The Simpsons* [1989]).

BLINKY

In the late 1960s, Toronto police sergeant Roy Wilson approached local radio station CHUM-FM to sponsor his new creation — a humanized police car that could teach children of all ages about road safety without scaring them too much. The vehicle was christened Blinky, thus named because after imparting safety lessons he would wink, if not blink. Based on Wilson's sketches, a standard-issue Metro Police Plymouth Fury was modified to incorporate two large eyes and a long nose. Blinky's eyes moved back and forth and blinked through an adaptation of the regular windshield wiper system. The car was operated by a safety officer in a booth located nearby and linked with cables laid neatly across the floor. As the front windshield was covered, and visibility completely obscured by his "mask," Blinky could not be driven on roads (also, he didn't have an engine) and therefore was either towed around or remained stationary during his many visits to schools, shopping malls, and, most memorably, his annual appearance in Toronto's Santa Claus Parade.

The original Blinky was a yellow Plymouth Fury. However, in the late 1980s, when the entire fleet of Toronto Police cars were repainted, Blinky was reborn as a white Ford.

Blinky fever swept Toronto by the mid-1970s. Irwin Toy and Tonka engaged in a bidding war to win what they viewed as the lucrative Blinky licence allowing them to mass-produce toys, T-shirts, and collectibles (the offers were rejected by the police commission). In 1975, the *Toronto Star* spent $23,500 as a public service to create a ten-minute animated short called *Blinky: Traffic Safety*, which was shown on 16mm film in schools across Toronto by liaison officers, and often on *The Uncle Bobby Show*. The cartoon featured Len Carlson (best known in later years as Bert Raccoon from *The Raccoons*) as the voice of Blinky.

When visiting schools to discuss road safety, Blinky's modus operandi would change radically, depending on which grade he was visiting. So, while kindergarteners might be treated to Blinky singing a song or reciting a poem about pedestrian safety, eighth graders were treated to a frightening demonstration of Blinky slowly backing over a doll filled with red paint, graphically illustrating the result of what happens to children who don't properly observe their surroundings: blood-red asphalt.

60
The Canadian Children's Channel (1979)

AFTER FINISHING SCHOOL IN 1975, KEVIN SHEA JOINED Scarborough Cable 10, a local community-based cable channel owned by Conway Upper Canada (CUC) Broadcasting, a media company founded by Geoffrey Conway in 1968. Conway was a communications visionary, and through cable he foresaw the inevitability of niche broadcasting via specialty channels that would offer consumers limitless channels catering to every conceivable taste. CUC filed an application with the CRTC in the mid-1970s for the creation of three specialty networks in Canada: a consumer channel, a multicultural channel, and a children's channel.

At the time, the CRTC had no mechanism for granting specialty channel licences, as cable was a relatively new phenomenon. Home Box Office (HBO) in the United States began operating their specialty service in 1972, but it was only available to a small number of subscribers in Wilkes-Barre, Pennsylvania. With public demand growing for additional television options, the CRTC granted CUC an experimental broadcast licence that contained an enormous number of restrictions including the prohibition of any forms of advertising and the requirement of 100 percent Canadian content.

Operating out of Scarborough Cable 10, the Canadian Children's Channel was launched by Shea in February of 1979. "Our projections are that two or three years from now, there's going to be less children's programming available on conventional broadcast stations," Shea told CBC News. "We're trying to move the kid away from the set. We're worried about the fact that kids watch too much television."[88]

Owing to the intense regulatory restrictions, the channel was only able to create roughly four hours of content per day, which then needed to be bicycled across the country to CUC's other cable stations. After six months, the Canadian Children's Channel folded due to lack of proper funding.

Shea recalled an interesting event that took place after CBC News reported on the channel's arrival:

> Literally two days later we get a call from some executives at Warner Brothers in America saying, "Can we come up and visit?" Because the notion of a kids' cable channel was unheard of. And about two months later, they started Nickelodeon.[89]

Nickelodeon, the first dedicated children's network in North America, launched on April 1, 1979, and its early schedule featured many imports from Canada — most famously, *You Can't Do That on Television!* (1979), the Ottawa sketch-comedy show, which proved so popular the channel eventually expropriated the show's defining visual gag — slime — for its own branding.

Shea was soon hired by Rogers Cable, where he continued to work on a viable and sustainable channel dedicated to children's programming in Canada.

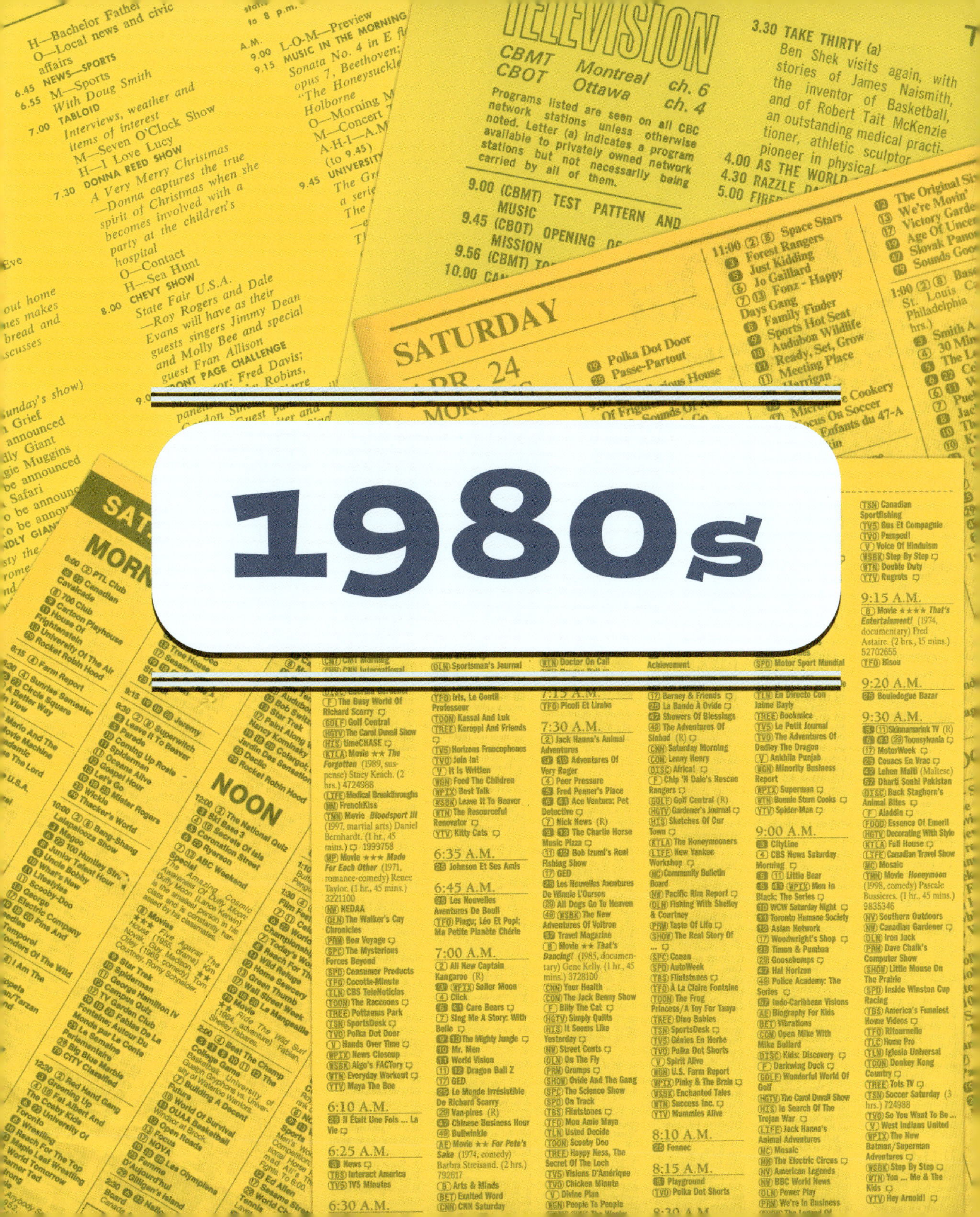

1980s

61

The Kids of Degrassi Street (1979/80)

IN THE MID-1970S AT EARL GREY SENIOR PUBLIC SCHOOL IN the east end of Toronto, teacher Linda Schuyler was instructing her grade 7 and 8 students a very early, non-curriculum-based version of media studies. Schuyler had worked briefly at TVOntario and was still involved in documentary filmmaking on the side. As media studies was still in its infancy, there was a lack of quality resource material on the subject. Earl Grey's librarian, Bruce Mackey, supported Schuyler by ordering a selection of books with "film" or "filmmaking" in their titles, hoping to aid in the students' understanding of this emerging academic stream. One of the books was *Ida Makes a Movie* (1974) by Kay Chorao. Mackey hadn't realized that it was an illustrated book for young children, featuring a kitten who wants to make a movie. Schuyler felt the story's core theme — persistence of a young female filmmaker — was powerful, but mostly lost on the preschool audience the book was aimed at. She started thinking about how the book could be turned into a film.

After determining that the market was awash in animated films for young children, Schuyler set about producing a live-action version featuring kids who were slightly older. Such a film could be used in classes as a filmmaking primer and as an exercise in social studies. Schuyler visited New York and purchased the film rights from Chorao for two hundred dollars. Schuyler and close friend Christopher "Kit" Hood had created a production company called Playing With Time, Inc., for some of Hood's commercial work, as well as for their first collaboration, a short documentary entitled *Jimmy: Playing with Time* (1979) about an elderly pianist trying to break his own world record for playing non-stop at the Canadian National Exhibition.

Ida Makes a Movie (1979) was their debut fiction film and featured many of the stylistic techniques they felt were missing from productions aimed at younger audiences. Director Hood was heavily influenced by the British kitchen-sink drama movement of the fifties and sixties, as well as by filmmakers, such as Ken Loach and Lindsay Anderson, whose work was characterized by gritty social realism and focused on working-class families. The effect of this movement was visible in *Ida Makes a Movie*, which was shot in an almost cinéma-vérité style with hand-held camerawork, naturalistic performances (non-actors played all roles), and on-location filming, including in Mackey's house at 98 De Grassi Street in the working-class neighbourhood of Leslieville. Elwy Yost was given a cameo role as himself, judge of the film festival where Ida's film causes a stir.

The head of children's television at the CBC, Nada Harcourt, took an interest in the film and Schulyer's Playing With Time production company. Harcourt had been elevated to department head as she held the promise of reinvention in a changing age, bringing some edge and an awareness of contemporary culture. She was inspired by the work of the Young People's Theatre and felt that dramatic one-off teleplays and short films were key to capturing a young audience, as opposed to daily serials. In a 1983 interview Harcourt said:

> If you can make a film that truly expresses the child's world with talent and genius, you are obviously going to have first class material. People … want to be reminded of the way they were, to expand the awe and wonder that a child has.[1]

The thirty-minute-long *Ida Makes a Movie* was well received on its CBC broadcast, airing with other short children's films under the umbrella title of Just Down the Street. Playing With Time followed it up with two more productions, *Cookie Goes to Hospital* (1980), addressing childhood anxiety about going to hospital, and *Irene Moves In* (1980), a look at inherent childhood racism.

In 1982, Harcourt encouraged Playing With Time to develop these short films into a series, which they titled *The Kids of Degrassi Street*, based on the location of the first film. Toronto's real De Grassi Street had been named after

Italian soldier Filippo De Grassi, who had been awarded four hundred acres of land in the Don Valley in 1833 after fighting for the British.[2] For the series, the name was intentionally stylized as one word — Degrassi.

A title sequence was created featuring a short maudlin piano piece overtop black-and-white stills of kids playing on a street in chilly-looking Leslieville. The show featured many young non-professional actors who would continue working with *Degrassi* on later series where they played different characters: Stacie Mistysyn, first as Lisa, then later as Caitlyn Ryan; Neil Hope as Griff, then Derek "Wheels" Wheeler; Christopher Charlesworth as Benjamin, then Scooter; Anais Granofsky as Karen, then Lucy Fernandez; Arlene Lott as Rachel, then Nancy Kramer; and Sarah Charlesworth as Casey, then Susie. Between 1979 and 1983, nine episodes were produced, initially in smaller batches (only one single new episode aired in 1983) until an eleven-episode season was ordered for the 1984/85 season, and aired in an afternoon slot.

Schuyler was inspired by the hit prime-time series *Hill Street Blues* (1981), which used overarching character stories within self-contained episodes, and used a similar storytelling device in later episodes of *The Kids of Degrassi Street*. The most obvious was seen in the blooming romance between Griff and Lisa, which was thrown into peril when Griff used a derogatory term he learned from his crass older brother Duke to describe an intellectually challenged crossing guard. (Duke was played by Dave James, who would later appear in *Degrassi Junior High* [1987] as Mike Nelson, the deadbeat birth father of Hope's character Wheels). The fall 1985 season comprising a final six episodes gained the subtitle *Yearbook* and was moved to CBC's more glamorous Sunday evening family block alongside *The Edison Twins* (1982), *Fraggle Rock* (1983), and *The Beachcombers* (1972).

As with *Inside/Out* (1973) before it, *The Kids of Degrassi Street* was hailed for being a realistic and non-condescending exposé of how real kids behaved, spoke to one another, and interacted with adults. It also perfectly captured working-class, multicultural Toronto in the early 1980s, a somewhat Martian atmosphere to viewers in the U.S. (on PBS), the U.K. (on BBC), and Australia (on public broadcaster ABC-TV). In 1985, the *Toronto Star*'s television critic Jim Bawden wrote,

> There's an emerging bittersweet character to *The Kids of Degrassi Street*, arguably the finest children's series ever to run on Canadian TV. By describing the sharp vignettes as kids' TV, I'm aware I'm already limiting it. As an adult, I've watched from the beginning without any feeling of condescension.[3]

The CBC's earliest head of children's television, pioneer Fred Rainsberry, was also a big fan of Schuyler's work on *The Kids of Degrassi Street*. In 1987, he cited the series as a model of good children's programming, stating that as a former teacher, Schuyler "knows the values that are respected in the educational community, and she is interested in relationships among children."[4]

The kids are all right: Some of the cast of *The Kids of Degrassi Street* (1979) pose in front of the De Grassi Grocery store, a key location in the series where drama often occurred. Clockwise from left: Neil Hope (Griff), John Ionnou (Pete), Sarah Charlesworth (Casey), Stacie Mistysyn (Lisa), Tyson Talbot (Billy), Danah Jean Brown (Connie), Arlene Lott (Rachel), Christopher Charlesworth (Benjamin), and, centre, Anais Granofsky (Karen).

By the time they were shooting the final block of episodes in 1985, Schuyler, Hood, and chief writer Yan Moore had already envisioned an even more serialized follow-up (with a continuous narrative), which would graduate the action to a junior high school covering grades 7 and 8. Although school had played a small part of the first Degrassi series, it was not the central setting; rather it was the east Toronto neighbourhood. CBC's then head of children's programming, Angela Bruce, who had succeeded Dodi Robb's caretaking of the role after Harcourt departed, invited representatives from WGBH Boston to meet with Schuyler. WGBH was one of PBS's flagship affiliates and, along with the

Children's Television Network in New York City and TVOntario in Toronto, produced the most respected children's educational content in North America. Senior executive Kate Taylor, an ex-teacher herself, told Schuyler, "You guys are just what we need. I want to bring your new show to the executives at WGBH. And to be clear, if we pull this off, we'll need a minimum of thirteen episodes next year."[5] The resulting series was *Degrassi Junior High* (1987), a co-production between the CBC and WGBH, taking the franchise both literally and figuratively into a more mature direction.

While the Degrassi empire expanded significantly each successive decade with more complex scripting and a torqued production engine, it never again quite captured the poignant melancholy of childhood with as much authenticity as *The Kids of Degrassi Street*. As a cultural Polaroid of early 1980s Toronto, there exists no equal, in any medium.

62
The Body Works (1980)

FOLLOWING TVO'S 1979 PROGRAM CAMP TVO, THE FORMAT was slightly tweaked in 1980 for Camp TVO 2, adding *The Body Works*, a new fitness series that "offered kids a chance to jump, dance, and run their way to a fitter future."[6] Each ten-minute episode of *The Body Works* featured repeated exercises for beginner and intermediate levels, as well as health tips and interviews with kids about nutritional habits and healthy lifestyles.

Gary Eisler, Angela Fletcher, Mike Kim, Jeff Walker, Tiffany Welch, and Helen Yu, who ranged from seven to fourteen years old, were the featured hosts. The series mascot was an animated hippopotamus called B.W., who

The Body Works (1980) on the cover of *School Broadcasts*, TVOntario's biannual catalogue that documented all series available to schools and teachers for grades K to 8.

commented on their reporting and occasionally joined in the exercising. A tie-in record featuring the show's catchy horn-led theme song and detailed exercise instructions was released in 1980 on the Apex label.

The series was directed by Milton van der Veen (*The Science Alliance*), and eighteen episodes were produced in total. Additional reruns in the Camp TVO 2 block included the U.K. import *Vision On* (1965), a fondly remembered series designed for children with hearing impairment that captivated all viewers with its inspired visual storytelling, and TVOntario's own *The Adventures of Timothy Pilgrim* and *Get It Together*, a five-minute crafting show for kids. While the Camp TVO format did not return, an additional series of *The Body Works* was created in Alberta with a new cast for the ACCESS network. Both seasons ran together on TVO for the remainder of the decade.

63
Galaxie (1980)

AFTER THE FAILURE OF THE CANADIAN CHILDREN'S CHANNEL, Kevin Shea joined Rogers Cable, which by 1979 had acquired multiple cable systems across Canada. Savvy to the economic possibilities of specialty channels, Rogers had been impressed by Shea's attempt to introduce the Canadian Children's Channel from the modest launchpad of a low-bandwidth, local community station. Shea had conducted comprehensive research in the late 1970s studying the effects of American children's programming on ABC, CBS, and NBC on Canadian viewers. Children were exposed to a steady diet of American culture through Saturday-morning cartoon blocks, as well as on weekday mornings and after school. The content was saturated in advertising and contained often questionable morals and rampant examples of sexism, racism, and violence. Shea was determined there was not only an economic advantage to a Canadian alternative, but a social one as well.

Frustratingly, although domestic satellite communications were invented in Canada, the nation was squandering its tremendous capacity. The Anik satellites that Canada had launched in the 1970s were intended to deliver television signals across North America, most importantly within Canada itself. Owing to the country's vast size and rugged geography, many people were outside of the range of tower VHF broadcasts, and while UHF helped the situation for those in cities, growing suburban communities were underserved. Yet the Anik-class satellites — powerful communication Goliaths — were simply being rented out to American specialty cable movie channels such as Home Box Office (HBO) and Showtime. Shea viewed this as a waste, "another crazy missed opportunity."[7]

Also during the 1970s, content carrier separation was mandated by the CRTC, which meant cable companies such as Rogers were forbidden from owning their own cable networks. Keen to assemble a variety of their own proprietary specialty channels, the company charged Shea with a division within the company called Cable Satellite Network (CSN).

In early 1980, CSN approached TVOntario with a proposal for a dedicated children's network. The programming would be composed solely of archive TVO content, while the venture would be owned fifty-fifty by both Rogers and TVO. This move would theoretically get around the thorny issue of content carrier separation. Shea and Rogers believed that TVO would be the best partner for this endeavour, thanks to its credibility with educators, parents, and, most importantly, children.

The initial plan was to bundle existing TVO programs such as *Polka Dot Door*, *Guess What?*, *CUCUMBER*, *The Adventures of Timothy Pilgrim*, *Readalong*, *Read All About It!*, *Math Patrol*, *MathMakers*, and others into a daily twelve-hour block that could then be offered as a specialty channel to cable subscribers across Canada. Rogers would provide TVO with additional funding to create new and stimulating programs that would air exclusively on this cable channel, which was christened "Galaxie." When the CRTC announced they were accepting proposals for specialty channels in Canada, Rogers and TVO filed applications for Galaxie, both in 1980 and 1984. Both times the licence was not granted, however it was not owing to the fifty-fifty ownership structure proposed by both parties. (Galaxie did briefly appear in 1983 in several Canadian markets for Rogers cable subscribers.)

The reason for the rejections was that CRTC had ultimately decided any dedicated children's network in Canada would require significant funding, and it did not believe Rogers and TVO were able to attain it. In its June 11, 1984, ruling, the CRTC stated:

> As is the case with almost every other area of programming, quality programming for young audiences is expensive to produce or acquire and distribution costs are high, especially on a national basis. Thus, the most critical factor in determining whether Canadians will be able to produce and deliver a suitable, high-quality programming service for young Canadians is the matter of funding. It seems unlikely that a viable national Canadian youth service can be developed until this question is resolved.[8]

Undeterred, Shea continued in his quest to formulate a dedicated Canadian specialty channel, which he would finally achieve before the decade was through (see p. 241).

64
Today's Special (1981)

WHEN TVONTARIO MAVERICK CLIVE VANDERBURGH WAS FIRST told of the Galaxie initiative during a meeting, it was also revealed to him an additional $1.3 million would be allocated to the development of five new series earmarked for the Rogers cable channel. Naturally, the leadership team at TVO turned to VanderBurgh based on his innovative programming run from *CUCUMBER* in 1974 through to *Math Patrol* and *MathMakers* in 1978. He was the network Midas. He was also viewed as financially disciplined, bringing his shows in on time and on budget. VanderBurgh remembers suggesting in the meeting that in lieu of doing five shows, why not take all that money and invest it in one single show? It would be a blockbuster children's program that could represent the culmination of everything the department had absorbed since inception. "A perfect example of saying something, walking out of a room, and then thinking, my God, what have I done?"[9] recalled VanderBurgh.

Ruth Vernon, head of the children's department at TVO, gave VanderBurgh her backing. She believed if anyone could, it was him. The two were sympatico on exhaustive research, extensive testing, and balancing the delivery of curriculum objectives with popular entertainment. They believed vehemently in the importance of creating educational shows that could stand alongside the bigger-budgeted and bombastic American content encroaching on Canadian culture more intensely than ever. In his pitch to Ruth Vernon titled "Pre-School Pilot Proposal," dated November 17, 1980, VanderBurgh wrote:

> What an Opportunity We Have!
> *Polka Dot Door* is the only new long-running pre-school project developed for a network in the last ten years. Even *Polka Dot Door* is an adaptation of a BBC production. The impact

> of *Sesame Street* developed 10 years ago is still with us, but the freshness and excitement of a promised new age of children's television programming is not obvious by scanning the wide variety of television signals available in any major market. What happened? The "pre-school pilot project" being developed by TVOntario is a concerted effort to add a new, original series for pre-school kids. It will capitalize on the experience of *Sesame Street* and bring new and fresh ideas forward and provide a stimulus for new discussion about children's programming while providing a model and also a challenge for others.[10]

The document outlined what VanderBurgh had identified as the five central pillars of this proposed show, which he suggested should be stories; poetry; social awareness; performance, including music and dance; and games.[11] Later he recommended the show engage in what he termed a "Questioning technique," asking questions that involve the viewer and inviting them to test out their ability in numerous cognitive areas:

> Children learn more from and are more interested in things they can actually experience, take part in, feel a part of. Needless to say, television with its present one-way only capabilities has traditionally been restricted to presenting material which allows children to vicariously watch a studio audience or eavesdrop on other people having fun. More and more, shows are attempting to speak to the child at home and involve him in the activities of the program. *Polka Dot Door*, *Mr. Dressup*, *Mr. Rogers' Neighbourhood* and *CUCUMBER* have acknowledged the presence of the viewer. TVOntario's *Readalong*, *Math Patrol*, *Read All About It!*, *The Body Works*, and *MathMakers* solicit active involvement from primary and junior kids as does CTW's *Sesame Street* and *Electric Company*.[12]

After months of research, which again took him to the Children's Television Workshop in New York City, the PBS affiliate WGBH in Boston, and the CBC in Toronto, VanderBurgh sketched out a basic premise, characters, setting, and format for a show he called *Today's Special*, a title he believed to be philosophical in perspective but, more importantly, sounded cool.[13]

Set in a Toronto department store's toy section after hours, *Today's Special* would focus on a tabula rasa character — a floor mannequin who magically comes alive when the store closes (and the words "hocus pocus alimagocus!" are spoken). Joining him was an anthropomorphic character, a young mouse, who would represent the point of view of a child. The matronly role would be filled by a woman who works at the department store, and, finally, an older night watchman would showcase wisdom with age. Each thirty-minute episode would have a distinctive theme identified by the single-word title: "Hats," "Snow," "Family," and so on. Additional program inserts would feature animation, music, mime, and educational content used to buttress the show's theme and weave a simple moral lesson.

In his pitch document, VanderBurgh emphasized the importance casting would play in the series:

> The show will include two adult performers and a variety of puppets who will play continuous roles as well as change character as the need arises. These continuous characters will give the program our identification and allow children to develop warm relationships with their television friends. As well as fulfilling dramatic purpose, these characters will have their expertise in dance and music. It is a goal of this program to provide performance in the arts at a very high level and consequently the selection of these people who will demonstrate their craft will be very important.[14]

Jeff Hyslop was given the part of the mannequin. A musical polymath, Hyslop was known for his astonishing ability to act, sing, dance, direct, and choreograph, often all at once. He had been atop VanderBurgh's wish list from the beginning, but no one had believed they could lure him away from musical theatre to the rigours of a television series. When Hyslop happily accepted the role, the mannequin character was named Jeff in honour of this casting coup.

Polka Dot Door host Nerene Virgin was chosen as the department store's employee, Jodie. Virgin had proven herself an absolute natural at communicating with children, both on television and in her live appearances on the *Polka Dot Door* stage show. Muffy the mouse was designed and built by Noreen Young, while Nina Keogh was cast as the puppet's voice and operator. Keogh was duly informed by VanderBurgh that her character would only speak in rhyme. The night-watchman puppet, named Sam Crenshaw, was built by Young and was voiced and operated by Bob Dermer. The puppet was reused from an earlier pilot VanderBurgh had created, *Music Inc.* (1978), an educational music show constructed around classical quintet the Canadian Brass.

Additional roles were filled with other familiar faces (and voices): The store's interactive computer system TXL Series 4 was voiced by Robyn Hayle (*Téléfrançais*); enthusiastic stockroom puppet Mrs. Pennypacker was operated and performed by Cheryl Wagner (*Big Comfy Couch*); Muffy's country cousin Mort was voiced by Bob Stutt (*Fraggle Rock*); the Mime Lady was Nikki Tilroe (*CUCUMBER*); and the magician who brings Jeff to life, Waldo the Magnificent, was Barry Baldaro (*Coming Up Rosie*).

The series was set (and filmed on occasion) at the Simpsons department store located in downtown Toronto at 184 Yonge Street. Incidentally, it was at this store that CBC's first head of children's programming, Fred Rainsberry, had encountered an exhibition featuring the marionettes of Violet Keogh, Nina's grandmother, prompting him to offer her a job that led to Nina's parents, John and Linda, working at the CBC.[15]

VanderBurgh said in his original pitch that if the *Today's Special* pilot was successful, he recommended commissioning the production of fifty episodes for the inaugural season, arguing that ten to fifteen shows were simply not enough to create an impact. He may have also sensed that there might not be further injections of Galaxie money. This ambitious suggestion was overruled. In the end, two pilot episodes were produced: "Hats," written by Joanne Hauser (*Math Patrol*), and "Snow," written by Clive Endersby (*Read All About It!*).

In the spring of 1981, both pilots were extensively tested, and the results were published in August of 1981 in an internal TVO document, "Today's Special: Formative Evaluation of Two Pilot Programs," compiled by a team of TVO research officers. It illustrated their findings through a collection of graphs and essays, and the results were voluminously disseminated with a collection of discussions and conclusions that guided the production of further episodes. Among many other surprising findings, VanderBurgh was shocked to discover that the quizzes, which he had begrudgingly included, were well received:

> We learned the most remarkable kinds of things. As an educational organization, we had included quizzes because we thought that was part of our mandate. We thought we'll sugar-coat it with all the rest of the programming. What we found out was quizzes attract the highest attention, much to our surprise. Kids wanted more quizzes. Kids want an opportunity to interact with the television.[16]

Hocus pocus alimagocus! Nina Keogh operating Muffy, the resident house mouse, on *Today's Special* (1981), who only spoke in rhyme, mostly all of the time. The Muffy puppet was created by Noreen Young.

Series writers VanderBurgh, Hauser, Endersby, Jed MacKay, Kate Lonsdale, Candice Bist, Juli Voyer, and Ian Ritchie used the study as a baseline for all future episodes, which were also reviewed and tested before broadcast. VanderBurgh was not exaggerating when he told Fred Rainsberry that *Today's Special* was "the most well researched, thoroughly thought-out children's program in the country."[17] After the production of forty episodes, *Today's Special* switched to a linear storytelling style as opposed to the earlier segmented magazine approach, based solely on the concurrent research.

For the 1984 season, MacKay penned the series' most infamous episode, "Butterflies," a stark treatise on death that follows Muffy's experiences

Shout it loud and clear! The heart and soul of *Today's Special* (1981) — Nerene Virgin as Jodie, Bob Dermer as Sam, Jeff Hyslop as Jeff, and Nina Keogh as Muffy. Puppets designed by Noreen Young.

after she befriends a doomed monarch butterfly. The 1983 *Sesame Street* episode concerning the death of series regular Will Lee (Mr. Hooper) and its effect on Big Bird is cited rightfully as a television milestone; however, the subject is covered only for a short but emotional part of the episode. "Butterflies" goes all out by having the central characters console a distraught Muffy before each confronts their own mortality. It might just be *the* defining episode of Canadian television for Generation X.

The following season, MacKay upped the ante with "Phil's Visit," another "very special episode" about alcoholism that concerned an old friend of Crenshaw's verbally abusing Muffy after drinking too much. It featured a pre-episode warning and an uncharacteristic cold opening with Nerene Virgin addressing the audience directly about alcohol abuse. While the series never lost its sense of joy, it was not afraid to go to dark places.

During its seven-year run, *Today's Special* attracted a wide range of guest stars such as ballet dancer Karen Kain; Canadian jazz legend Oscar Peterson; folksinger Bruce Cockburn; children's entertainers Sharon, Lois & Bram; and notable small-screen talent like John Stocker (*Dr. Zonk and the Zunkins*), Sheila McCarthy (*I've Heard the Mermaids Singing* [1987]), Gerard Parkes (*Fraggle Rock*), Charles Palmer (*Coming Up Rosie*), Kay Hawtrey (*Read All About It!*), George Buza (*Maniac Mansion*), and Jayne Eastwood (*The Littlest Hobo*).

Airing on Tuesday and Thursday evenings in the post–*Polka Dot Door* 6:30 p.m. time slot, *Today's Special* was watched by an estimated audience of over four hundred thousand viewers per week, making it one of TVO's most successful series. It was sold to Singapore, the Caribbean, and South Africa.[18] It was also one of Nickelodeon's top-rated shows alongside other Canadian exports like *You Can't Do That on Television!* (1979) and *The Elephant Show* (1984), leading many to consider it — erroneously — an American program.

TV ON TOUR

From the earliest days of Toronto broadcasting, stars of children's television were engaged to make public appearances. Uncle Chichimus greeted children at Eaton's in the 1950s, the Professor and Kiddo the Clown visited the Hospital for Sick Children at Christmas in the early 1960s, and Uncle Bobby famously attended picnics, fairs, and school soirees with his double-decker bus in the 1970s. However, it wasn't until the early 1980s that it became a very lucrative, organized commercial enterprise.

Polka Dot Door host Gairey Richardson was among the first to see a viable business model in touring children's television properties. After arranging a licence with producer Ted Coneybeare, Richardson put together a team composed of a few on-air hosts who would stage a one-hour show featuring songs and skits. Jim Parker, a local musician, was offered one hundred dollars per show to dress up and perform as the series' totemic Polkaroo, and his first show was with *Polka Dot Door* host Nerene Virgin at the Galleria Mall at Dufferin and Dupont in Toronto. By 1984, there were multiple teams touring Ontario attending local fairs, shopping centres, and concert venues like the Kingswood Music Theatre at Canada's Wonderland.

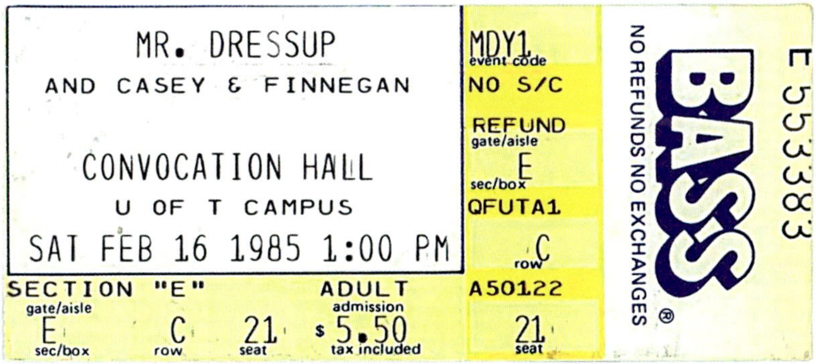

A ticket stub for a live *Mr. Dressup* event.

The *Polka Dot Door* live show incorporated popular elements from the television series, including Polkaroo (left), seen here with series hosts Gerry Mendicino (centre) and Cindy Cook.

In 1985, TVOntario staged three live performances of *Today's Special* in Toronto (Roy Thomson Hall), Ottawa (National Arts Centre) and Hamilton (Hamilton Place) featuring the main cast and guests. All three were filmed and edited into a sixty-minute episode titled "Live on Stage," which aired in 1985.

London, Ontario, concert promoter Don Jones was also attuned to the growing business of live children's entertainment, which at that point usually meant concerts headlined by Raffi or folk trio Sharon, Lois & Bram. Jones began to promote the *Polka Dot Door* shows, getting them into larger venues with ticketed seating. He later sought Mr. Dressup himself, Ernie Coombs, as another star attraction. Coombs had done live appearances, but they had been sporadic and unorganized. Jones offered to become his road manager and take *Mr. Dressup* on tour across Canada. Jim Parker joined the show as his warm-up act, then was promoted to puppet-handler when Casey and Finnegan were added to the tour. Casey and Finnegan puppeteer Judith Lawrence didn't join the road tour but recorded a tape to which Parker mimed the puppets. Coombs's tours became legendary and continued long after the series ended in 1996.

65
Kidsworld (1980)

AS THE DECADE BEGAN, THERE WAS A RENEWED INTEREST IN the news-for-kids-by-kids format that had been absent since CBC's *Through the Eyes of Tomorrow*. TVOntario's *Kidsworld* was a co-production with the Global Television Network and Astral Media, which had purchased the format rights (see p. 25) and title from the U.S. series of the same name. The concept was simple: Kids were invited to write or call in and request the stories they wanted to see, which a kid reporter would then follow up on. Aping the look of CBS's *60 Minutes* — each segment started with a close-up on a ticking stopwatch — most reports featured empowering stories about what kids were doing across the country (the TVO version would often include reports from the U.S. version). To be expected, there was a high demand for celebrity interviews. Famous Canadians like René Simard and American stars like Stevie Wonder and Henry "The Fonz" Winkler were interviewed by child reporters, who often asked more probing questions than their adult contemporaries, thanks to youthful indiscretion. TVO's *Kidsworld* ran for fifty-two episodes and was shown on both Channel 19 and the Global Television Network.

66
News from Zoos (1980)

ALMOST FROM THE VERY BEGINNING OF CHILDREN'S TELEvision, animals and wildlife have played a valuable part. Created by Michael Spivak (*Junior Roundup*), CBC's *News from Zoos* employed the novel format of a magazine show about zoo animals hosted by a talking chimpanzee. Charlie Chim the Chimp (voice by Carl Banas) and narrator Sandy Hoyt covered a wide variety of animal stories, including births, great escapes, and feeding routines. Footage was sourced from a consortium of zoos from across North America, including the Metropolitan Toronto Zoo, the San Francisco Zoo, and the Buffalo Zoo. Stock nature footage was used for stories about animals in the wild.

When Spivak was first creating the show, he was concerned after reviewing the assembled footage for his pilot episode that he did not have a catchy enough hook. His son, Jamie, said, "Look, if you can see the humour in it, why not have a monkey as the host?"[19]

67
Music Box (1981)

AFTER HOSTING *REPORT METRIC/REPORT CANADA* FOR ALmost a decade, Heather Conkie created her first show for TVOntario in 1981,

Music Box (1981) host Heather Conkie and guest Denis Simpson. Simpson was better known as a long-running co-host on *Polka Dot Door* and a member of the all-male vocal group The Nylons.

called *Music Box*. Conkie and Ruth Vernon felt that while there was a great variety of programs for children on reading and sciences, there was little being done for music education (beyond their attempt at spinning *Report Canada* off as *Report Music* in 1976).

Aimed at preschoolers, the thirteen-part series taught the fundamentals of music through a mixture of animation and live action. A *Starweek* profile said, "Pianist, conductor, singer and all-round musician Heather Conkie guides kids through a world of music that goes far beyond Raffi. Even kids who are tone deaf could enjoy this show, our panel felt, because it comes chockablock full of activities."[20] Conkie appeared as the chipper host who often debated musicianship with the titular domineering gramophone, a puppet operated by puppeteer Judy Anderson (*Lamb Chop's Play-Along* [1992]) and voiced by Canadian actor Elias Zarou (*Seeing Things* [1982]). The show featured guests, including children who performed a variety of instruments (including a young Dennis Martinez, who would later become known as DJ D-Scratch, 1995 Canadian DMC champion and member of the turntablist collective Turnstylez Crew); Conkie's fellow *Polka Dot Door* host and member of the vocal group The Nylons, Denis Simpson; and in one memorable episode, Rex Hagon (*The Forest Rangers*) as the Big Bad Wolf. Susan Murgatroyd (*CUCUMBER*, *Readalong*) directed all thirteen episodes, which were repeated frequently by TVOntario throughout the decade.

68

We Live Next Door (1981)

WE LIVE NEXT DOOR WAS THE FIRST FOLLOW-UP FROM THE TVO *Readalong* production team after they completed its third and final series. David Moore directed the series, which effectively used TVO's stylish mix of studio, stock footage, and chroma-key. Ten fifteen-minute episodes were broadcasted.

The show took place within a small community, Nutdale, located in the idyllic town of Rubyville. It featured a menagerie of bizarre, beautiful puppets crafted by Noreen Young based on characters created by writer Ken Sobol. The puppets were operated by Young and her brother Stephen Brathwaite. As with *Readalong*, there was a talking house and a scary monster, as well as random gabby objects including a pay phone and loaf of bread. The cult French pineapple from *Téléfrançais* (see p. 216), Ananas, actually made his debut on *We Live Next Door* but was called Philo and had a different face. *Write On!*'s Paul Brown appeared as the slightly aloof Ice Cream Man, who, along with the child actors, was the only human character. Billy Mae Richards, so beloved as the voice of Rudolph the Red-Nosed Reindeer in the 1964 Rankin/Bass stop-motion film, voiced several of the lead puppets, including the young boy Joey and Mayor Morris.

The chatty puppet character of the Nutdale Store from *We Live Next Door* (1981).

69
Calling All Safety Scouts (1982)

THE TVO PRODUCTION TEAM FROM *WE LIVE NEXT DOOR*, INcluding director David Moore, and puppeteers Noreen Young and Stephen Brathwaite, created *Calling All Safety Scouts*, a dramatically different six-part series using the same fifteen-minute format, characters, and puppets set in the ever-expanding universe of Rubyville and Nutdale. Scripts were written by Ricki Glinert and Jed MacKay, who also wrote many of the songs. Returning puppet characters from *We Live Next Door* included Squirrel, Kingsley Monster, Mayor Morris, Joey, T-Booth (the talking pay phone), and the Nutdale Store. A new character named Henrietta, designed by Young, was promoted to central protagonist.

The show was written up in *School Broadcasts*, TVOntario's programming guide for schools and teachers:

> Children who think ahead and think of others can become safety scouts like Henrietta, the main character in TVOntario's *Calling All Safety Scouts*. Safety Scouts prevent accidents, and Henrietta helps children to stay safe at home, in school, and in the neighborhood. In fast moving 15-minute programs, Henrietta adopts disguises to facilitate her search for people who deserve a safety scout badge.[21]

Each episode was designed around a theme and contained a specially composed song by MacKay. The six episodes were "Safety at School," "Safety at Home," "Safety in the Water," "Safety on Wheels," "Safety at Play," and "Safety in the Country." MacKay's song for the latter has been blamed for causing a generation to view poison ivy as an extreme danger.

Instructional safety lessons for children had been a benchmark of the genre since the earliest days of *The Howdy Doody Show* (1954), and characters such as Elmer the Safety Elephant became recurring segments in programs like *Kiddo the Clown* and *The Uncle Bobby Show*. However, since the early 1970s the domain of children's safety had often fallen to public service announcements on television, as well as industrial classroom films, often referred to as "scare films" for their propensity to engage in overly dramatic and often frightening scenarios to illustrate safety lessons. This practice reached its apex with a series of gory school-bus safety films (*Rain or Shine* [1970], … *And Then It Happened* [1972], and *Death Zones* [1975]) created by a United States Department of Defense contractor, Seven Oaks Productions, located in Ohio but widely screened in Ontario classrooms (many of these films were still being used well into the 1980s).

Calling All Safety Scouts was a response to the need for a more aspirational program that encouraged kids to be safety-conscious through membership in the Safety Scout club, like the Ontario Safety League's fostering of a communal school pride through the Elmer flag (see p. 69).

After production wrapped, some of the puppets, including Henrietta and the Monster (although not the same characters), were reused in *Mr. Finley's Pharmacy* (1982), a one-off anti-drug production for grades 2 to 4 created by Noreen Young for the Metropolitan Toronto Pharmacists Association. This fifteen-minute short was also repackaged in the late 1980s as part of the Canadian Association of Chiefs of Police's series of drug education videos, along with *Choose* (1988) and *Open Flame* (1987).

70
Kidsbeat (1982)

GLOBAL TV SERIES *KIDSBEAT* (1982) WAS CREATED BY FORmer *Razzle Dazzle* writer Ron Krantz and differentiated itself from *Kidsworld* with a postmodern flair and flashy editing style that looked more MTV than CBC. Krantz drew inspiration from Toronto's cult series *The All-Night Show* (1980), broadcast on CFMT-TV, Channel 47, which featured a hapless night watchman called Chuck the Security Guard taking over the studio in the middle of the night and playing B movies and old episodes of *The Twilight Zone*, which he jammed into the station's U-matic videotape machine. In *Kidsbeat*, the hosts would introduce a story and then hold up a videotape and manually insert it before cutting to the report for maximum McLuhan effect. In addition to reports about other children, *Kidsbeat* would cover pop culture, fashion, lifestyle, and even Fortean subject matter like UFO or Bigfoot sightings. Each episode also contained a music video at a time when they were new and novel, as well as the requisite celebrity interviews. The series evolved over the years and featured revolving hosts, including Kevin Newman and Nerene Virgin (*Today's Special*), until it was finally retired in 1998.

71
Going Great (1982)

GOING GREAT (1982) WAS CBC'S ATTEMPT AT THE VARIETY format, constructed around host Chris Makepeace, a young Montreal native and up-and-coming Hollywood star who had just struck box-office gold with his films *My Bodyguard* (1980) and *Meatballs* (1979). Based in Toronto, the show was a fast-paced look at the dynamic and extreme outdoor activities young people across Canada were engaging in, including BMXing, skateboarding, water-skiing, skydiving, and go-karting. Makepeace also visited bands and singers who would perform their latest hits in unusual places, including Toronto new-wavers Spoons belting out their hit "Nova Heart" in a nightclub during one frenetic episode. Keanu Reeves appeared as a segment reporter in his first television appearances outside of Kellogg's Corn Flakes and Coke commercials. CBC originally only produced thirteen episodes; however, U.S. children's cable network Nickelodeon was so impressed with the series that they ordered an additional twenty-six.

72
You Can Write Anything! (1983)

TVONTARIO'S CELEBRATION OF THE WRITTEN WORD THROUGH an appreciation of books and bookstores with a slight supernatural bent, *You Can Write Anything!*, mixed animation, real sets, and extensive chroma-keying. It represented another unique Ruth Vernon and Jennifer Harvey offering intended for the classroom. It joined *Report Canada* and *Readalong*, which were shown together in the afternoon to fit with school timetables.

Aimed at grades 1 to 4, the stories revolved around a busy children's bookstore where local kids visited to listen to stories, buy books, and learn about writing. At the conclusion of every episode, a painting of the bookstore's founder came alive and commented on some aspects of the story. Everything that took place outside of the bookstore set used chroma-key, a technique usually used extensively on TVO's puppet shows like *Readalong* and *Téléfrançais*, but more sparingly with human actors. Rex Hagon played a Toronto policeman with a suspect Scottish accent.

A bookstore like no other: behind the scenes of *You Can Write Anything!*

Most of the *Polka Dot Door* production team worked on *You Can Write Anything!*, including director David Moore and writer/lyricist Jed MacKay. Music was performed by Eric Robertson (*Read All About It!*). Each episode closed with an onscreen caption thanking the World's Biggest Bookstore, the Children's Bookstore, Tiddley Pom Books, Toronto Public Libraries, and Scholastic Books, presumably to foster an interest in book purchasing by young viewers.

HOME VIDEO LIMBO

When the home video boom began in the early 2000s with DVD releases of classic television series, TVO was often inundated with requests for many of its shows. Sadly, the contract structuring by TVO did not factor in home video releases or even repeats after a certain amount of time had elapsed. Series writer Clive Endersby explained to the popular Rick's TV website:

> Due to special "educational" arrangements (i.e., lower fees) that channels like TVOntario had with the various unions — writers, actors, directors, musicians — renewals of clearance rights and royalties had to be paid in advance for a set number of years — rather than an after-payment of a percentage of sales as is normal for commercial programs. They cannot afford to renew these clearances "up front," which would decimate their program budgets in any one year. Both TVO and the various union members would dearly love to switch these contracts to a "percentage of sales" system, but the law is the law and neither side can change an existing contract without agreement from all who signed it. In a series like *Today's Special*, for example, that means contacting 400 people, many who have either moved, some to other countries, or died.... DVDs did not exist in those days, there are no provisions for them. The task is just too overwhelming for networks and unions to take on. It's unfortunate because TVOntario has so many wonderful children's programs from that era which are now sitting on a shelf gathering dust because of an agreement which, at the time, allowed the shows to be produced — but hamper any use of them in the present day.[22]

73
Artscape (1983)

TVONTARIO EXPLORED THE WORLD OF ART APPRECIATION through paintings and galleries in 1983's *Artscape*, a little-seen but fondly remembered eight-part adventure serial complete with interdimensional conflict, cliffhanger endings, and complex art history and style. Youngsters Tracy (Priscilla Oxendine) and Craig (Chris Todman) are accidentally transported into another dimension known as Artscape during a class field trip to an unspecified gallery clearly meant to be Toronto's Art Gallery of Ontario (AGO). To survive and return home, they must learn about visual art and its properties from a variety of strange humans, aliens, and interdimensional beings.

Artscape was written by Clive Endersby, no doubt brought onto the project due to his sterling work on the earlier serialized pulp science-fiction adventure *Read All About It!*, which clearly influenced the show. Endersby recalls it being the moment he tried to drag TVO's archaic script formatting rules into the present:

> TVO scripts were very different. They were based on a BBC model, on one side was dialogue, on the other any action the camera people needed to know. I asked if we could write Artscape as a normal script, so I submitted one and Ruth Vernon hated it. She said, I can't understand what's going on. So, I redid it in the old way. I didn't change a single word. And she approved it.[23]

Special thanks were given at the end of each episode to artists whose work appeared, so Vincent Van Gogh and James McNeill Whistler got shout-outs, along with the location of the work (the Museum of Modern Art in New

York, and the Louvre in Paris, respectively). The guest cast featured Janelle Hutchison ("Today's Special: Live on Stage"), Diane Douglass, John Stocker (*Dr. Zonk and the Zunkins*), Judy Haladay (*The Science Alliance*), and CHUM-FM radio jock Tom Rivers as the voice of the electronic gallery guide. The series instrumental theme music by Bruce Ley (which sounds uncannily close to Whitney Houston's cover version of "Saving All My Love For You") overused a saxophone, sadly lessening the drama of each cliffhanger, unlike the spooky minimalism that had been so masterly employed by Eric Robertson in *Read All About It!* Sometimes, less is more.

74
Fragglе Rock (1983)

IN 1981, INFLUENTIAL CREATOR OF THE MUPPETS, JIM HENSON, told a room of writers and puppeteers from *The Muppet Show*, "I want to do a show that will change the world, and end war."[24] Over the course of the next few days, the group hatched the elevator pitch for a show called Woozle World — later to be rechristened *Fraggle Rock* — where three different species of Muppets learn to peacefully coexist:

> What the show [would really be about] is people getting along with other people and understanding the delicate balances of the natural world. We make the point that everything affects everything else, and that there is a beauty in harmony of life to be appreciated.[25]

At the time, Henson was about to embark on the production of feature-length film *The Dark Crystal* (1982), and he found himself returning to the worldbuilding of *Fraggle Rock* throughout *Dark Crystal*'s difficult shoot in the United Kingdom. The design of the show ended up much darker than anything he had previously produced and was much closer in spirit to *The Dark Crystal* than *The Muppet Show*. Michael Frith, *Fraggle Rock*'s conceptual designer, said, "*The Dark Crystal* was a 25 million dollar R&D project for *Fraggle Rock*, because all that stuff we invented for *Dark Crystal* I rolled right into *Fraggle Rock*."[26]

Since his first foray into children's television in 1968, Henson had learned much about the industry. He wanted to ensure *Fraggle Rock* was accessible to networks across the world and suggested a narrative wraparound that would allow foreign-market versioning to be baked into production from the beginning. Henson was keen to avoid the issues non-American broadcasters faced when trying to make their own versions of *Sesame Street* (see p. 101): "I've always felt it would be a lot more interesting, internationally, to start off with a show with that in mind; [to produce a show] that would have the ability to adapt, to change and shift."[27]

Henson and his team were so confident in their *Fraggle Rock* pitch that they took the extraordinary step of beginning pre-production without any broadcaster yet signed on. Toronto was chosen as the location for shooting: "Given the show's commitment to interdependence and a global consciousness, I can't imagine it being filmed anywhere else," said *Fraggle Rock* producer Lawrence Mirkin.[28] Henson had a history in the city, and three of his earlier Muppet specials had been filmed here — "Hey, Cinderella!" (1969); "The Muppet Musicians of Bremen" (1972); and "Emmet Otter's Jug-Band Christmas" (1977).

As the team began a massive casting call to find the crème de la crème of the puppeteering world, Henson's agent informed him that he had found the show not only one broadcaster, but three — the CBC in Canada, Television South (TVS) in the United Kingdom, and Home Box Office (HBO) in the United States. At the time, HBO was only a pay-TV movie channel, but it was keen to expand its footprint and subscriber base by producing original television series. HBO promised Henson much more creative freedom than ABC, CBS, or NBC would have. The CBC and TVS were simply happy to be working with the genius behind the massively successful *Muppet Show* and *Sesame Street*.

At the time, the CBC had figured out that they could increase viewer numbers by slotting non-children's programs into kids' prime viewing time; for example, *Three's Company* (1976), a light sitcom aimed at older viewers, aired after school and became a sustained ratings bonanza. For *Fraggle Rock*, the co-production was classified as family viewing as opposed to children's, which would allow commercial sponsorship because it fell under the auspices of the light entertainment division.[29]

Fraggle Rock followed three different species of Muppets — the Fraggles, Gorgs, and Doozers. The Fraggles and Doozers lived in a complex cave environment called Fraggle Rock, while the Gorgs lived above ground. Fraggles and Doozers were small, while Gorgs were giants. Another world, called Outer Space, was just a contemporary Earth. In the North American and German versions, the only entrance to the world of Fraggle Rock was through a small hole in the garage of an oddball handyman; in the British version, the access was in a lighthouse; and in the French, through a bakery. This allowed for unique wraparound segments to be filmed separately and contain the appropriate cultural references and language. Additionally, one Fraggle character named Traveling Matt appeared in film inserts each episode, adventuring around "Outer Space" and sending humorous postcards back to the Fraggles. Each country that broadcast *Fraggle Rock* featured Traveling Matt locations unique to its country (so, in the Canadian version, Traveling Matt went to the CN Tower and Canada's Wonderland).

The show's writing team was overseen by Jerry Juhl (a trusted Henson collaborator who penned the scripts for *The Muppet Movie* [1979] and *The Great Muppet Caper* [1981]), and included Sugith Varughese (a versatile writer/actor/director, probably best known for his role as Mr. Mehta in *Kim's Convenience* [2016]); Jocelyn Stevenson (later, head writer on *The Magic School Bus* [1994]); and noted Canadian poet bpNichol. As with all Henson productions, another important piece of the *Fraggle Rock* magic was the music, here written and performed by Toronto natives Philip Balsam and Dennis Lee, author of the classic children's poetry books *Alligator Pie* and *Jelly Belly*. The duo wrote over a hundred songs for the first season alone.[30]

Fraggle Rock premiered at 5:30 p.m. on the CBC on January 23, 1983, drawing 2,743,000 viewers — 44 percent of all televisions in Canada were tuned in. At the time, anything upwards of two million was considered a massive success. The second episode, on January 30, held strong at 2.2 million viewers.[31]

The series ran for five seasons, ending in 1987, and spawned two cartoons (*Fraggle Rock: The Animated Series* [1987] and *The Doozers* [2014]) and two spinoff series (*Fraggle Rock: Rock On!* [2020] and *Fraggle Rock: Back to the Rock* [2022]), along with tie-in books and comics, and an array of merchandise. In 1987, all of Henson's characters from *Fraggle Rock*, *The Muppets*, and *Sesame Street*, joined together for a one-off seasonal spectacular, "A Muppet Family Christmas," co-produced by ABC in the U.S. and the CBC in Canada. It was filmed at 9 Channel Nine Court, the studio for CFTO-TV in Agincourt, an area of northern Scarborough.

Perhaps *Fraggle Rock*'s most startling legacy was being the first Western children's show broadcast in the Soviet Union. On January 8, 1989, the state broadcaster aired an episode of *Fraggle Rock* to such substantial ratings that it added both *Fraggle Rock* and *The Muppet Show* to its schedule.[32] Just over one year later, on January 31, 1990, the very first McDonald's restaurant in Russia opened, the largest in the world, overseen by Torontonian and McDonald's Canada president George Cohon, who'd had success running the previous largest McDonald's in the world, at the Metropolitan Toronto Zoo in Scarborough.[33] American popular culture was thawing the Cold War and expediting the fall of the Soviet Union. It seems *Fraggle Rock* fulfilled Henson's promise, and the Fraggles, Doozers, and Gorgs helped us avert a third world war.

75
Téléfrançais (1984)

IN 1983, RUTH VERNON COMMISSIONED AN INFORMATIVE language series with a simple remit — *Readalong*, but for French. Naturally, the original production team behind *Readalong* was reunited to develop a concept, and the ensuing fruit was *Téléfrançais*. Ken Sobol and Noreen Young's successful partnership had not only borne out *Readalong*, but also *We Live Next Door*, another offbeat show blending humans and puppets then chroma-keying them onto wild and colourful backgrounds. Both shows had featured Sobol's trademark use of anthropomorphism through characters like Boot, Hole, a talking loaf of bread, and a demure pineapple.

It was the pineapple who became the breakout star of *Téléfrançais*, tweaked from his appearance as Philo on *We Live Next Door* and now canonized as Ananas, alongside two human children, Jacques and Sophie (later, Catherine), a puppet pilot called Pilote (who disappears after the fourth episode), and a cutaway skeleton rock band called Les Squelettes, distant relatives of *Readalong*'s Mr. Bones, no doubt. Once again, the puppets were operated by Noreen Young, Stephen Brathwaite, Nina Keogh, and Bob Dermer, while the amusing music of Les Squelettes was written by Bruce Ley and Jed MacKay.

How did Ken Sobol, the hardbitten Cleveland-by-way-of-Hollywood-and-New-York screenwriter and journalist, know enough about conversational Quebec French to write the scripts? According to his son John Sobol:

> He was interested in how you marry pedagogy and television. And there was a teaching consultant, and he was told repetition is really important in learning a language. And it doesn't matter what the first word is. You've just got to get started. So, what if we said that word five thousand times in the first

> episode? They'd say, that's crazy. But would it work? They'd say, yeah, it would. So, okay, let's do that.[34]

Since 1984, Ananas, a talking pineapple, has taught several generations how to speak conversational French, thanks to the series *Téléfrançais*.

Each episode followed a simple formula: The children and/or Ananas would uncover an event or location that became the topic of a song by Les Squelettes, along with a barrage of other comedic cutaways. The extensive use of video chroma-key, placing humans and puppets into stock footage and still images both real and animated, gave the series a colourful comic-book feel, something *Téléfrançais* leaned into with its use of comic panels and speech bubbles. As per John Sobol's observation, repetition played a central role in the writing, starting with the catchy theme song that just repeated a few key words: "Téléfrançais! Téléfrançais! Bonjour! Allô! Salut! Téléfrançais! Téléfrançais! Lisez! Parlez avec nous!"

In all, thirty episodes of *Téléfrançais* were produced, each with a running time of ten minutes. The program was still being used in schools as recently as 2024, a testament to its ability to introduce the basics of conversational French to new learners.

Eight years later, Sobol and Young collaborated on a follow-up to *Téléfrançais* — *Rigolecole* (1992), a slightly less fantastical take on learning conversational French. It took place at a school, and the kids and teachers were all human puppets plus an amphibian-looking character that appeared to be a fish. Supplementary materials included a teachers' guide, an audiocassette of featured songs, and a puppet-making kit.

Another great, albeit unrealized collaboration between Sobol and Young occurred in 1987 when they co-created a pilot for the CBC entitled *Bats*, concerning a group of puppet Bats that fly into Toronto and moonlight as a nocturnal heavy metal band. It again featured Young's distinctive creations, operated by Stephen Brathwaite, Bob Dermer, Nina Keogh, Trish Leeper, Bob Stutt, and Young herself, and voiced by Dermer, Stutt, Jayne Eastwood, Luba Goy, John Stocker, and Billy Van. Alas, the CBC elected not to take the pilot to a full series.

Young also created puppets for two further TVO series directed by David Moore in the late 1980s — *Tales from the Blue Crystal* (1986) and *Art's Place* (1989). *Tales from the Blue Crystal* featured fantastic stories and legends by Donia Blumenfeld Clenman, observed by a pair of puppet clamshells and seafaring pirates. As with Young's other TVO series, the puppets were chroma-keyed overtop of animation and underwater footage. *Art's Place* featured a more traditional TVO setting — a house — where young students were taught the basics of painting by humans and puppets including a squirrel, a talking bush, and an ancient mirror. It incorporated short educational films alongside animation and still drawings.

76
The Edison Twins (1984)

IN THE LATE 1970S AND EARLY 1980S, THE CBC CHILDREN'S department was once again grappling with an after-school schedule dominated by cartoons based on toy properties (such as *He-Man and the Masters of the Universe* [1983] and *The Smurfs* [1981]) and reruns of action-oriented prime-time U.S. network series (including *Charlie's Angels* [1976] and *CHiPs* [1977]). While the CBC had themselves found great ratings in lazy late-afternoon reruns of *Three's Company* (1976), the head of children's programming, Dodi Robb, had been quietly building a tranche of quality counter-programming for the afternoon. Robb was promoted out of the children's department in 1981 and was succeeded by Nada Harcourt, who continued to refine work on the 4:30 p.m. period in the schedule. This block had so far included *The Kids of Degrassi Street* (1979), music-and-sports variety show *Going Great* (1982), and an assortment of short one-off teleplays, including *Jen's Place* (1982) with Megan Follows. There was also a vehicle for children's folksinging group Sharon, Lois & Bram in the development pipeline.

Added to this mix was *The Edison Twins*, a quirky live-action-adventure show made by Canada's leading animation house Nelvana and co-produced with the Disney Channel in the United States. Disney's partnership with the CBC dated back to the mid-1950s when *Junior Magazine*'s acquisition of film titles led to a more formal relationship. Nelvana was started by Micheal Hirsh, Patrick Loubert, and Clive Smith. Based on the financial success of the U.S. network Nickelodeon, launched in 1979 as the first cable channel for children, Disney had followed suit in 1983 with the launch of the Disney Channel. In addition to its vast film and television library, it was actively seeking co-production ventures worldwide.

The Edison Twins was pitched as the Hardy Boys with modern science, featuring a squabbling pair of supersmart teens (and their annoying little brother) applying brainpower to resolve their weekly misadventures. An animated science lesson based on the plot concluded every episode. The series was shot on location in Toronto and the suburbs of Etobicoke, including Weston, where the Edison's family home was located. Andrew Sabiston (*Polka Dot Shorts*) and Marnie McPail starred as twins Tom and Annie Edison, while Sunny Besen Thrasher was little brother Paul. Corey Haim (*Lucas* [1986] and *The Lost Boys* [1989]) appeared as a semi-regular before his Hollywood career took off in 1985.

The Edison Twins ran for seventy-eight episodes over six seasons. Its catchy theme song was written and performed by Los Angeles transplant Bob Segarini, a Q107 disc jockey and founding member of the cult rock band

The Wackers. An old friend of Clive Smith, Segarini was called in at the last minute to guest as an aging rock star in an early episode when the original actor didn't show up. While on set, Segarini overheard production whispers that no one liked the theme song, so he offered up his services and, in the process, delivered one of the all-time greatest Canadian TV theme tunes.[35]

77
The Elephant Show/ Sharon, Lois & Bram's Elephant Show (1984)

THE POPULAR CHILDREN'S FOLKSINGING TRIO OF SHARON Hampson, Lois Lilienstein, and Bram Morrison first crossed paths at the Mariposa in the Schools project, which had grown out of the Mariposa Folk Festival, based in Orillia, Ontario, and started in 1961. By 1978 they had recorded a self-financed debut LP entitled *One Elephant, Deux Elephants*, distributed by A&M Records, an independent label founded by Herb Alpert and Jerry Moss in 1962. The album became a sensation in Canada, owing to the trio's unconventional mix of folk with other musical styles including rock and calypso. Their television debut came the following year, in 1979, when they performed a live concert featuring many of the songs from *One Elephant, Deux Elephants*, which was broadcast by the CTV network on a Saturday.

Not long afterward, Sharon, Lois, and Bram were introduced to CBC's head of children's programming, Dodi Robb, at an in-store concert at the Children's Bookstore on Avenue Road (the store later located a short distance away to Mirvish Village on Markham Street), a popular hub for children's entertainers. Impressed with their ability to engage the young audience, Robb asked, "Would you like to do some television? I would like to do some television with you."[36] Their first collaboration with the CBC was a one-off special called "Downtown," which aired on October 6, 1979, and featured them performing and interacting with children from the Kensington Community School on location in Kensington Market, in downtown Toronto.

A studio-bound follow-up entitled "Jungle Jam" aired on March 1, 1980. "Jungle Jam" featured a similar flow to "Downtown," but it made use of animation and chroma-key, as well as a variety of exotic animal costumes, including John Kozak (Sidney from *Math Patrol*) in a gorilla suit. This special featured children from the Daystrom Public School interacting with Sharon, Lois, and Bram on a colourful soundstage designed to look like a jungle. Both "Downtown" and "Jungle Jam" were written by Pat Patterson (*Telestory Time*) and produced by *Mr. Dressup*'s Shirley Greenfield. Both featured music direction from Bill Usher and included Judith Ann Miller in an elephant costume appearing as the Friendly Elephant. Sharon Hampson recalls that Robb, a veteran of children's programming, suggested they include "crumbs for mums":

> That was so clever! And we did that. Over the years, we learned to throw in little tidbits, the kids wouldn't be disadvantaged in any way, but the grown-ups might get a kick out of them.[37]

While both "Downtown" and "Jungle Jam" had been well received productions, Sharon, Lois, and Bram were focused on their subsequent albums *Smorgasbord* (1979), *Singing 'n' Swinging* (1980), and *In the Schoolyard* (1981), as well as their live performances and tours, which took them across Canada and into the United States. During this period, the trio co-hosted CBC's coverage of the Toronto Santa Claus Parade with *Sesame Street*'s Oscar the Grouch (Carol Spinney) in 1981, 1982, and 1983. They would walk the parade route performing live before the parade began and then rush to the control booth to provide live commentary with Spinney. Bram remembered Spinney as

> a lovely, lovely man. We really enjoyed working with him. We were surprised as anything to find out that he was both the puppet animator and the voice of both Big Bird and Oscar the Grouch. You would never see them twice in the same scene. The characters were so different — Big Bird was the innocent and Oscar the Grouch was the opposite, and he did them both.[38]

In 1982, Sharon, Lois & Bram appeared in a specially filmed segment for the Canadian version of *Sesame Street*, and they guest starred in an episode of TVOntario's *Today's Special* in 1983. While neither of these programs influenced their decision to craft an original television series based on their own output, Sharon recalls it was all happening simultaneously:

> They were good shows. It's hard to remember but I think that what happened was we had two producers that were motivated to make something, and a writer. And we sat around talking. We knew that our show was going to be based on music. And initially, there wasn't really a storyline. We knew that we wanted to play ourselves, not characters. What we were going to do — we were about music, and we wanted to do a show about the three of us and music, and kids![39]

The September 24, 1984, edition of the *Toronto Star* described this period as a "hurricane of activity"[40] for the group, with the launch of a new album (*Mainly Mother Goose*), a book with games and pictures (*Elephant Jam*), a tour and concert at Roy Thomson Hall, and a new thirteen-part television series for the CBC called *The Elephant Show*. "It's truly a magical moment for all of us,"[41] remarked Lois Lilienstein.

Each episode of *The Elephant Show* focused on a different musical instrument, introduced by fellow children's performer Eric Nagler. In addition to musical numbers and cutaways to live performances, the show explored the day-to-day lives of twelve "real" children, drawn from a pool of "professionals from agencies, friends, and street-kids."[42] There was an emphasis on family, curiosity, learning, exercise, and, of course, the healing power of music. Each episode concluded with their signature "Skinnamarink" song. The show was never heavy-handed and continued the approach taken in their music, which was to speak to children as peers and avoid condescension. Hampson maintains, "We applied the same principle to the music that we created for those shows."[43] Retitled as *Sharon, Lois & Bram's Elephant Show* for its next four seasons, the series attracted an impressive array of guest stars, including Jan Rubeš (*Guess What?*); singer-songwriter, painter, and activist Mendelson Joe; actor Louis Del Grande; *SCTV* comedian Andrea Martin; prolific film actor Maury Chaykin; and folk singer-songwriter Murray McLauchlan.

Much of the series was filmed on location outside of the studio, showcasing many Toronto landmarks including Centreville Amusement Park on the Toronto Islands, High Park, Young People's Theatre, Kensington Market, and buildings such as the CN Tower and the Gooderham "Flatiron" Building at Front and Church. Morrison remembers:

> It was a conscious decision to spotlight a lot of Toronto locations on the show, and that's because Toronto had so many different spots that were visually very appealing and gave room for us to move and do music and dance and have guests.[44]

In total, sixty-five episodes were produced, running at thirty minutes per episode. The series was co-produced by TVOntario, which aired episodes a

Above: Children's folk trio Sharon Hampson, Lois Lilienstein, and Bram Morrison, a.k.a. Sharon, Lois & Bram, had their debut television appearance together in 1979 on CTV's *One Elephant, Deux Elephants*.

Below: Sharon Hampson, Lois Lilienstein, Bram Morrison, and their elephant friend pose for a promotional shot for *The Elephant Show* (1984).

few weeks after their initial appearance on the CBC (similar to the *Sesame Street* arrangement). In 1985, an important foreign sale was made to the children's specialty cable network Nickelodeon. Along with fellow Canadian shows *Today's Special* from TVO and *You Can't Do That on Television!* (1979) from Ottawa's CJOH-TV, *Sharon, Lois & Bram's Elephant Show* became one of Nickelodeon's top-rated programs.

What was it about these Toronto-produced shows that resonated so much with young viewers in the United States, and made them stand uniquely apart from other children's programming from around the world? "Perhaps because there were small budgets, it forced the shows to be more real. It started before us and continued after us," Hampson said in 2024. Bram Morrison agreed, and further suggested, "It has to be the imagination and talent of the people who were involved in the series that existed before ours ever did."[45]

78
The End of the Friendly Giant (1984)

ON DECEMBER 11, 1984, CBC PRESIDENT PIERRE JUNEAU ANnounced $75 million in cuts were being implemented to the service, eliminating 1,150 positions and severing 750 employees. One of them was Bob Homme. After twenty-six years on-air, *The Friendly Giant* was unfortunately seen by some as a relic from a bygone era. Not only its fifteen-minute format, which had long since given way to thirty- and sixty-minute models, but its very essence. The casual pacing and laidback banter of *The Friendly Giant* had been considered old-fashioned as far back as 1970, when *Sesame Street* exploded the entire genre of children's television and executives began to favour faster-paced storytelling and editing.

Also factored into the executive mindset was the fact that, since the beginning, Homme had resisted public appearances, feeling that viewers (especially children) believed he was an actual giant. To see him in real life as merely Bob Homme, a man pretending to be a giant on television, would destroy the illusion and bond with the audience he had worked so hard to foster. Public appearances by children's television hosts had been encouraged as far back as the 1960s, but by the 1980s it was a profit-generating business. TVOntario had successfully created a live *Polka Dot Door* experience, and *Today's Special* was gearing up for blockbuster live shows in Toronto and Hamilton. Ernie Coombs was mobbed at public appearances, and popular live children's entertainers like Sharon, Lois & Bram and Fred Penner were selling out shows across Canada. Homme's reluctance to appear in public as his famous character was seen as honourable to the craft but resulted in the production missing out on new lines of revenue. Homme was sixty-four years old.

The Friendly Giant had already been slashed to only forty new episodes for the 1984/85 season, and Homme's contract with the CBC had expired in early December. In perhaps the most unfriendly outcome possible, Homme learned of the series cancellation by reading about it in the newspaper. He later told the *Toronto Star* that he'd suspected something was awry after noticing the uptick in repeats of his older shows: "When they repeat an episode for the fifth time, then it becomes very serious. I've served three generations. Mothers aged twenty-five make sure their tots catch the show. It's very gratifying."[46] After twenty-six years of service, no one from the CBC executive or production branches contacted him to formally let him know the show was dead. He did, however, receive a call from CBC Radio asking for a quote on the show's cancellation.[47] An ignoble fate for both Homme, and the gentle Friendly.

When the story broke, there was an immediate public outcry. Heart-broken letters to the editor swamped the *Toronto Star* in the final weeks of 1984, and a "Save Friendly!" letter-writing campaign was directed toward the office of Denis Harvey, vice-president of English TV at the CBC. Questions were asked on the floor of Parliament Hill. CBC's head of children's programming, Dodi

A publicity photo for *The Friendly Giant*, which aired on the CBC from 1958 until 1985, at which time it became a casualty of massive network cuts and television executives who felt the series was too slow for 1980s viewers.

Robb, offered Homme a consulting role on a future show (which he declined), and two seasonal specials ("Friendly Summertime," which aired in 1985, and "Friendly Springtime," which aired in March of 1986), in which Homme would have the chance to say goodbye to his audience.

Music and music appreciation had been the backbone of *The Friendly Giant* since the very beginning, so it was fitting that the final episode guest starred Homme's real-life son Richard "Rick" Homme, who played a synthesizer on-air — a miniature synthesizer was also created for Rusty and Jerome to examine. "I wanted to do something with a synthesizer just to examine this problem that there is now with synthesizers replacing musicians,"[48] said Homme.

When the CBC announced that popular children's entertainer Fred Penner was getting his own series in the old *Friendly Giant* daily time slot, some in the media unfairly labelled him "The Giant Killer," a label Penner despised. Dodi Robb had approached Penner to create his own series, eventually titled *Fred Penner's Place*, in 1984. Incredibly, it was the first new in-house CBC children's production since *Mr. Dressup* in 1967 (the bulk of the CBC children's shows had been co-productions up to this point). *Fred Penner's Place* was produced by CBC Winnipeg, and later in Vancouver, and ran until 1997. In the wake of these schedule changes, CBC's two-hour morning block of children's programming was branded Hodge Podge Lodge starting in 1987 and featured the commercial-free lineup of *Fred Penner's Place*, *Mr. Dressup*, and *Sesame Street* with animated interstitials airing between the shows.

79
It's Mainly Music (1984)

IT'S MAINLY MUSIC, HEATHER CONKIE'S FOLLOW-UP TO *Music Box* (1981), was aimed at an older audience and dispensed with all of the fantastical elements from the preschoolers' show. It was shot entirely on location and was modelled after a sitcom. The series-long narrative followed three young musicians (Justin Kadis, Nicholas Kindler, and Kimberley Temple) and their music tutor, played by Conkie, as they mastered their instruments and discovered more about the craft in time for a jamboree. A comedic element was added by having Conkie play dual roles: She also appeared as her own landlady, the mysterious and opinionated Agnes Peabody. The character of Peabody proved popular enough to warrant her own series, entitled *Dear Aunt Agnes* (1986), although it focused on family dynamics as opposed to musical application.

It's Mainly Music was directed by Jeremy Pollock (*The Adventures of Timothy Pilgrim*) and ran for one series of ten episodes, running fifteen minutes each. The scripts were written mostly by Conkie and Clive Endersby (*Read All About It!*). Conkie provided original music for the series as well as its theme song, which she also performed.

80
The KangaZoo Club (1984)

THE KANGAZOO CLUB WAS PRODUCED BY QUADRAMEDIA Management Inc. for the Global Television Network in Toronto, and was hosted by a pair of young animal lovers, Russell Chong (*YTV Rocks*) and Melissa Glavota, alongside KangaZoo, a costumed kangaroo character voiced by Julianne Rice. Along with exciting animal footage provided by the Metropolitan Toronto Zoo, African Lion Safari, and Marineland, the show featured Chong, Glavota, and KangaZoo interviewing animal experts, zoo workers, and handlers. They also sang songs with a studio audience of young children and encouraged viewers to send in short stories, artwork, and photographs of their favourite animals.

81
OWL/TV (1985)

OWL MAGAZINE WAS FOUNDED IN 1976 BY FORMER SCHOOL-teacher Annabel Slaight and Mary-Anne Brinkmann, who conceived it as an imaginative publication to help children aged eight to twelve better appreciate the delicate balance of nature — OWL stood for "Outdoors and Wildlife." Their Young Naturalist Foundation had been spun out of the Federation of

Ontario Naturalists (FON) as a non-profit organization; the FON was happy to support Canada's very first nationwide nature magazine for children. The magazine ascended quickly through word of mouth, and by 1979 it had a circulation of a hundred thousand copies per issue, putting it in the top tier of most-read magazines in Canada. It was praised and supported by teachers, parents, and librarians, and year-long subscriptions were a popular Christmas present for grandchildren.

In 1979, a second title, *Chickadee*, aimed at six-to-eight-year-old readers, was released. It was estimated that by the early 1980s both titles had a combined circulation of almost two hundred thousand, reaching 10 percent of Canada's preteen demographic. A television program was the next logical step in the magazines' evolution.

Eventually premiering in November 1985 on the CBC, *OWL/TV* was devised by Slaight and Paulle Clark, and co-produced with the National Audubon Society. Along with *Fred Penner's Place* (1985), *Wonderstruck* (1986), and *The Elephant Show* (1984), *OWL/TV* was among the last programs commissioned by Dodi Robb, the outgoing head of CBC's children's department. Robb had returned to the children's department as a temporary caretaker after Nada Harcourt departed and was shortly replaced by Angela Bruce. Like *The Elephant Show, OWL/TV* used real kids, not professional actors, "to achieve the maximum degree of identity between the show and the young viewers,"[49] in a segment unsurprisingly called "Real Kids." The Real Kids were seen organizing others to help clean up their neighbourhood or run a yard sale to raise money for World Wildlife's Save the Pandas fund. Slaight told *Starweek* magazine the series was not just an extension of the magazine, but an alternative way of thinking about what the natural environment for a child actually is: "That environment might be his or her bedroom, backyard, clubhouse, fort, classroom, or (city) block."[50]

Each episode presented a variety of segments that included animation, puzzles and games, and, of course, animal footage, but also covered heavier subjects such as deforestation, pollution, and overpopulation. One regular segment titled "You and Your Body" featured a wisecracking skeleton with glowing eyes called Boneparte who helped viewers learn about their bodies.

Boneparte was voiced and operated by Michael Lennick, a visual-effects guru who got his start doing experimental video work on CFMT-TV's anarchic *The All-Night Show* (see p. 207) and worked on several David Cronenberg films including *Videodrome* (1983) and *The Dead Zone* (1984). In another segment, "Mighty Mites," kids were chroma-keyed into nature footage to make it appear they had been reduced in size and placed into a thrilling adventure with insects, *Honey, I Shrunk the Kids* (1989) style.

A punchy theme song composed by Jonathan Goldsmith and performed by Cree Summer Francks helped make the entire *OWL/TV* package one of the great success stories of the 1985 season. A PBS network representative attending that year's Festival of Festivals in Toronto let slip that 25 percent of their educational children's television was made in Ontario.[51]

The first series of *OWL/TV* received high ratings, however Slaight felt its weekday 4:30 p.m. slot kept it from gaining an even larger audience. For the second series, it was moved to 5:00 p.m. on Sunday evening. Complications arose when PBS backed out of its $250,000 commitment to a second season.[52] Thankfully, an injection from TVOntario (which began airing the series in repeats in September of 1986) and Telefilm Canada kept the series alive until 1990, when CTV took it over, producing new episodes until 1994.

82

Spirit Bay (1985)

SPIRIT BAY WAS AN UNCONVENTIONAL ENSEMBLE FAMILY show set in the fictional northern Ontario Ojibwe community of Spirit Bay. It detailed the effects of modern life on a reservation from the perspective of the community's young people. The series' many characters struggled to maintain traditional connections to Ojibwe culture as Westernized society became more pervasive. The series was spun out of the stand-alone drama *A Time to Be Brave* (1982), which had caught the attention of CBC's head of children's programming, Nada Harcourt. Harcourt professed that the CBC itself had wrestled with "the accessibility of television to native children, and [wanting] them to see a reflection of their life as authentically as possible,"[53] and she'd urged the production team to develop a series based on the community featured in the film. Like *The Kids of Degrassi Street*, it played into Harcourt's desire to see more anthology storytelling featuring children on the CBC. Producer Paul Stevens said:

> We looked at a lot of films and found that native society in Canada was portrayed in a few ways only — the noble savage or the social documentaries on tough times. We want to portray people with lives and contemporary values and concerns that we can learn from right now. It's a vibrant society; it's not all in the past.[54]

As Canada's first major television series focused on an Indigenous community, it provided a tremendous opportunity for the cast and crew, who included Trevor "Tre" Smith as Rabbit, Graham Greene as Pete "Baba" Green, Tom Jackson as Will Littlebear, Tantoo Cardinal as Annie, Gary Farmer as Cheemo, and Margo Kane as Mrs. Walker. Greene told *The Globe and Mail*, "There are other programs dealing with other realities. We've dealt with (social issues) on a community level, without making them news-style 'problems.'"[55]

A total of thirteen episodes with a running time of thirty minutes each were produced of the CBC/TVO co-production, which were repeated often by CBC, TVO, and later the Aboriginal Peoples Television Network (APTN).

83
Wonderstruck (1986)

ONE OF A SLATE OF SUCCESSFUL, ORIGINAL SHOWS COMmissioned by head of the CBC children's department, Dodi Robb, *Wonderstruck* was a science program, aimed at eight-to-fourteen-year-olds, hosted by Bob McDonald (now best known for the CBC Radio show *Quirks & Quarks*).

Educational science programs for children had proven extremely challenging, and although there had been a few noble attempts, no one had really cracked the subgenre. The first attempt was in 1953 with Percy Saltzman's *How About That?* Saltzman was a calm and plain-spoken host who demonstrated science experiments, but his show was more demonstrative than involving.

In 1982, TVOntario created a ten-part series called *The Science Alliance*, which featured hosts Rex Hagon and Judy Haladay and a group of children conducting re-creations of famous scientific discoveries in a variety of locations (including Ontario Place and the Ontario Science Centre). The program employed graphic overlays and animation to help explain some of the more complex concepts. A bonus episode featuring prolific Canadian actor Lawrence Dane (*Scanners* [1981]) in place of Hagon was also filmed.

It took until Bob McDonald's *Wonderstruck* hit the air, however, to prove that a science show could not only be entertaining but exhilarating. Eschewing jargon and complex mathematical formulas, the dynamic McDonald instead focused on was fun. "We are an after-school program," he told *Starweek* magazine. "We do want to inform, but we also want to entertain, because those viewers who come home from a hard day at school don't really want another lecture."[56]

Coming from a teaching role at the Ontario Science Centre, McDonald knew how to communicate with children without patronizing or speaking down to them. The subject matter was also eclectic — in the first episode he demonstrated various uses of dry ice, fed pandas at the Metropolitan Toronto Zoo, and showed how old black-and-white Laurel and Hardy films were being colourized in film laboratories. The CBC released several *Wonderstruck* books filled with experiments kids could do at home, as well as accompanying science kits. The show also made a point of asking viewers to write in with questions and experiments they would like to see McDonald do in future episodes. *Wonderstruck* wrapped up in 1992, just as the genre exploded with U.S.-produced programs like *Beakman's World* (1992), *The Mr. Science Show* (1992), and *Bill Nye the Science Guy* (1994).

84

Dear Aunt Agnes (1986)

IN THE MID-1980S, TVONTARIO RESEARCHERS DISCOVERED through conversations with teachers that increased numbers of children in their classrooms were experiencing upheaval at home due to divorce and families separating. Further research indicated that other than prime-time dramas aimed at adults, there were no children's shows exploring this complex new reality. Ruth Vernon and Heather Conkie considered how a program might address the issue and settled on a dramatic show with a sitcom setting anchored by the Agnes Peabody character from *It's Mainly Music* (1984). Although Agnes had played a minor role in the earlier series, she'd proved popular with both children and adults due to her sage, offbeat personality. She was old-school and charming, but iron-willed and relatable. Most people knew someone like Agnes Peabody.

Dear Aunt Agnes told the story of a family affected by divorce living in Toronto's affluent Rosedale neighbourhood. Twelve-year-old Andrew and his fourteen-year-old sister, Alex, whose father lives in Vancouver, are left in the lurch when their mother takes an urgent diplomatic job in Senegal. A university student named Gary is boarding in their lavish home (Conkie's actual residence at time of filming). Aunt Agnes agrees to become their minder, and the stage is set for generational conflict, merry misunderstandings, and comic calamity. Vernon was also keen to explore how rapidly values were changing in the 1980s. She told *The Globe and Mail*:

> *Dear Aunt Agnes* was developed not to teach values — that belongs in the home — but rather to provoke thought and discussion between children and parents on moral dilemmas faced by children. It's particularly important now because it's so much harder for kids and parents. When I was growing up, it was much easier. There was this all pervasive, middle-class environment where everyone shared the same values and beliefs. It was a world of moral absolutes and certainties.[57]

Both Vernon and Conkie were adamant the series take a pensive approach rather than become preachy or degenerate into lectures about right and wrong. Episodes often found the characters at odds with one another and the audience was left to decide. Things were grey, rather than black and white. Conkie said, "Some people believe that educational television should concentrate on teaching the tangible, like music, reading, science. But without a solid core of values, children are not going to make the best use of everything they learn."[58]

Two series of thirteen episodes running at thirty minutes each were commissioned in 1985, with scripts from Conkie, Jeremy Pollock, Clive Endersby, Ken Sobol, and Jim Henshaw, based on input from the TVO research team on what issues were topical and relevant to kids. Early episodes deftly mixed drama and comedy and explored jealously, honesty, money management, anger issues, politics, and peer pressure. There was even room for a horror-themed

The classic opening sequence for *Dear Aunt Agnes* (1986) featured an idyllic Rosedale location, a TTC bus, catchy lyrics sung by Heather Conkie, and a powerful synth stab that threatened to blow out modest television speakers.

episode ("In a Fog") that found Andrew and Alex home alone during a blackout, a minimal and spooky two-hander (i.e., a "bottle" episode involving only two characters) written like a stage play and expertly penned by Clive Endersby (*Read All About It!*). The series' catchy theme song, written and performed by Conkie, with its jump-cut title sequence featuring a TTC bus dropping Agnes off in Rosedale, remains one of TVO's most iconic show openings.

Dear Aunt Agnes became a genuine TVO hit, attracting upwards of two hundred thousand viewers twice a week. Surprising to Conkie was not so much its popularity amongst children but that adults clearly liked it as well. Unfortunately, its success could not have come at a worse time — budget cuts reduced TVO's provincial grants from $55 million to $49 million, causing the cancellation of not only *Dear Aunt Agnes* but *Today's Special* as well. "We can survive with what we're doing now, but we have no one to develop next year's programming department," warned Ruth Vernon.[59]

Today's Special had already racked up seven seasons and 122 episodes, while *Dear Aunt Agnes* was just getting started. Viewer frustration regarding the decision was sharp. The *Toronto Star* reported that some threatened to withhold their pledge donations during one of TVO's drives until the series was resurrected.[60] After TVO's 1987/88 season restructuring, *Dear Aunt Agnes* was commissioned for one final order comprising thirteen episodes at thirty minutes in length, but by this point the actors playing Alex and Andrew were noticeably older. The final season was significantly darker than the previous two, with a more serialized form of storytelling that included episodes about abuse, alcoholism, and eating disorders. The change in tone was hardly surprising, seeing as it was produced in the wake of *Degrassi Junior High* (1987), an internationally acclaimed teen drama where no controversial topic was off the table. A sombre sixty-minute Christmas special, "Christmas at Loon Lake," was also produced, filmed on location in Ontario's Muskoka region. Television critic Greg Quill called *Dear Aunt Agnes* "one of Canadian TV's most undervalued little gems" and described the Christmas special as "an absorbing piece of whimsical family entertainment strengthened by some fundamental human truths."[61]

85

Degrassi Junior High (1987)

ARRIVING ON THE AIR THE FIRST MONTH OF 1987, *DEGRASSI Junior High* built upon the promise shown by independent production company Playing With Time with their seminal work on *The Kids of Degrassi Street* (1979), with a thematic continuation aimed at slightly older children. The stakes were higher for everyone: Besides graduating the kids to a junior high school (shot at Daisy Avenue Public School, now Vincent Massey Junior School), the show was now a co-production between the CBC, Telefilm Canada, and PBS outlet WGBH Boston. Content would be monitored by more conservative U.S. eyeballs that might not understand what a "broom-head" was. The same warts-and-all approach adopted by *The Kids of Degrassi Street* gave the show instant credibility, once again playing out more like a gritty documentary than a kids' show, although the soap opera elements were more pronounced. Creators Kit Hood and Linda Schuyler were avid fans of U.S. television writers like Steven Bochco (*Hill Street Blues*) and liked to bleed character storylines from one episode to the next. Many of the actors and crew from *The Kids of Degrassi Street* stayed on (returning faces played slightly different characters, see p. 187), and the cast ballooned to over a hundred speaking roles, with roughly half of those making up the series regulars. Important new additions included Pat Mastroianni as jovial rogue Joey Jeremiah, Stefan Brogren as Archie "Snake" Simpson, Maureen and Angela Deiseach as the Farrell twins (Heather and Erica), Duncan Waugh as Arthur Kobalewscuy, Siluck Saysanasy as Yick Yu, Amanda Stepto as Christine "Spike" Nelson, and Dan Woods as the firm but endearing homeroom teacher Mr. Raditch.

Playing With Time acted like a repertory company that afforded equal status to all of its players. The young non-union cast was encouraged to share real-life experiences that might be incorporated into scripts, from benign (getting prescription glasses) to profound (dealing with an alcoholic parent). Legendary Canadian sex educator Sue Johanson even appeared as herself in several episodes when it was discovered the kids all listened to her radio program *Sunday Night Sex Show* on Q107. "I had this burning passion about the things I wanted to say to the children of Canada," Schuyler told *Starweek* magazine. "We were starting to see the burgeoning sexuality of all the kids whom we were working with, and what happens when a kid moves into that horrible middle ground when you're half child and half adult."[62]

Schuyler promised the show would tackle "meaty" issues like drug abuse, homosexuality, and, in their most celebrated early storyline, teenage pregnancy, but stressed the series was informing as opposed to advising. Like its spiritual predecessor *Inside/Out* (1973), episodes often ended on an unresolved freeze-frame, leaving viewers to decide the ultimate outcome.

Wendy Watson and Lewis Manne composed the opening theme song, which perfectly captured the mixture of sheer joy and existential dread awaiting kids every day at school. Within the show, Jeremiah's garage band The Zit Remedy (later shortened to The Zits) crafted a legitimate Canadian pop anthem with their one-hit wonder "Everybody Wants Something."

After its debut season aired in *The Kids of Degrassi Street*'s old Sunday 5:00 p.m. slot, it was moved to Monday nights at 7:30 p.m., and then ultimately 8:30 p.m. in prime time, where it faced off against glossy U.S. sitcoms like *Valerie's Family: The Hogans* (1986) and *Designing Women* (1986). International sales via WGBH were brisk and, by 1988, the show was airing in over forty countries around the world. In some countries, the more controversial episodes were either skipped or aired in later time slots.

The uniqueness of *Degrassi Junior High*'s production — using age-appropriate, non-union actors as protagonists, extensive location filming, and realistic scenarios based on real-life cast experiences — contributed to its enduring popularity. To this day, a rumour persists that actress Tori Spelling was so enamoured with the show she lobbied her Hollywood television mogul father, Aaron Spelling, to create an Americanized version following a similar formula, resulting in *Beverly Hills, 90210* (1990).

In 1989, the series was slightly retooled and retitled *Degrassi High*, owing to the increasing age of the central cast and the production's heightened ambition. While it followed the same basic template as *Degrassi Junior High*, its meatiest topics expanded to include suicide, cancer, and HIV/AIDS, while it continued to explore the evergreen drama that stems from bullying, drug abuse, sexual situations, and parental and teacher relationships. As tempting as it may have been to keep recycling these issues, by 1991 Playing With Time felt the series had run its course and sought an exit to avoid diluting the important work they had created over the previous five seasons.

A special feature-length series finale titled "Degrassi High: School's Out" aired in January 1992, tying up many loose ends, but also adding new dimensions of boundary-pushing with frank portrayals of sexual situations, Mastroianni's bare bum, and multiple uses of the word "fuck," uttered by both Brogren and original *The Kids of Degrassi Street* player Stacie Mistysyn. While the telefilm was seen by 2.3 million viewers across Canada, it ended the franchise on somewhat of a depressing note (although it could be argued

Come give us a try at *Degrassi Junior High* (1987): The impressive second chapter of the Degrassi saga arrived in 1987 with a fresh new crop of Toronto kids. From left: Anais Granofsky (Lucy), Duncan Waugh (Arthur), Siluck Saysanasy (Yick), Amanda Stepto (Christine a.k.a. "Spike"), Nicole Stoffman (Stephanie), and Pat Mastroianni (Joey).

that that itself was on-brand). Also in 1992, Playing With Time produced a six-part documentary series called *Degrassi Talks*, in which the series stars Rebecca Haines, Neil Hope, Mastroianni, Mistysyn, Saysanasy, and Stepto travelled across Canada and spoke candidly with teenagers about issues raised through the program.

The seismic fallout from the Degrassi series cannot be understated. It not only created the most successful television franchise in Canada, but helped export Toronto as a thrilling and exotic destination around the world. Fans of the series can still be found sleuthing old filming locations in Leslieville, hoping to uncover the Shoppers Drug Mart where Jeremiah first bought condoms, or the dusty video store where Yu and Kobalewscuy rented the pornographic VHS tape *Swamp Sex Robots*.

The franchise returned to television on CTV in 2001's *Degrassi: The Next Generation*, running until 2015, and launching the international careers of a new crop of kids including Shenae Grimes-Beech, Cassie Steele, and Aubrey Graham (better known as Drake). It was followed by *Degrassi: Next Class* in 2016, while a long-rumoured HBO version fell victim to the Hollywood writers' strike in 2023.

86
My Secret Identity (1988)

ALTHOUGH UBIQUITOUS NOW, LIVE-ACTION SUPERHEROES were still a rarity on television in the 1980s, helping make 1988's *My Secret Identity* an instant hit with young viewers. It followed the misadventures of an accidental superhero, dorky fourteen-year-old Andrew Clements (Jerry O'Connell), who attained his powers after getting blasted by a photon beam in the laboratory of his neighbour, the absent-minded Dr. Benjamin Jeffcoate (*MathMakers*' Derek McGrath). As a fan of comic books, Clements relished his newfound purpose and, after taking on the identity of Ultraman, set about using his powers for good. After a real-life cease-and-desist letter from the Japanese Tsuburaya Productions, owners of *Ultraman* (1966), the moniker disappeared as fast as a speeding bullet.

My Secret Identity was launched with much fanfare alongside a tie-in paperback from Scholastic (written by Jovial Bob Stine, a.k.a. R.L. Stine, later of *Goosebumps* fame), helping spread the word in schoolgrounds across North America. The series was a co-production between book publisher Scholastic, Crown corporation Telefilm Canada, and American production company Universal Television, and aired on the CTV network in Canada. More of a comedy than an adventure series, it was filmed on location in Toronto, although set in the fictitious suburb of Briarwood. At the time of release, O'Connell was best known as the rotund kid from the 1986 drama *Stand by Me*, but as the series progressed and he grew into a teen heartthrob, *My Secret Identity* focused more on his high-school life than on the comic-book stylings of the early seasons.

87
Ramona (1988)

EIGHT-YEAR-OLD RAMONA STRUGGLES THROUGH A TUMULtuous existence where no one understands her, and she is constantly at odds with her older sister, Beezus. Based on the bestselling Ramona books by Beverly Cleary and adored by children, this Toronto production from Atlantis Films Ltd., starring Sarah Polley as Ramona in her breakthrough role, aired on Hamilton's CHCH-TV before winning accolades on PBS in the U.S. The real mystery was why production ceased after only ten episodes, although Polley had much greater luck with her next series, *Road to Avonlea* (1990).

88
YTV (1988)

AFTER BOTH OF HIS ATTEMPTS TO ESTABLISH A DEDICATED children's channel collapsed at the unyielding hands of Canada's federal broadcast regulator, the CRTC, Toronto communications guru Kevin Shea found his third attempt was the charm. His first foray had been with Scarborough Cable in 1979 (see p. 180), and several years later he tried again with the TVOntario–Rogers Cable gambit Galaxie (p. 190). Shea subsequently built a strong coalition of partners, including Rogers Broadcasting Ltd., CUC

Broadcasting (Scarborough Cable), and independent producer Rob Burton (from CJOH Ottawa), and successfully garnered a broadcast licence in 1988 for Canada's very first cable service for children, YTV (presumed to stand for Youth Television, but that has never been confirmed by the network).

Also in 1988, pay-television company Allarcom and Astral Media joined forces to broadcast exclusive Disney content to Canada via the Family Channel, a formidable competitor just as the nascent YTV was launching. As it turned out, the commercial-free Family Channel seemed exorbitant at $9.95 a month, while YTV was free on basic cable. The Family Channel's programming also skewed toward an older audience, with shows like black-and-white reruns of *The Adventures of Rin-Tin-Tin* (1954), *The Mickey Mouse Club* (1955), and Shirley Temple film festivals.

In August 1988, shortly before YTV's inaugural broadcast, Shea — now YTV president — told the *Toronto Star*, "We want to put a network together that kids will really want to watch — and not because its 'good' for them.… We truly intend to be an entertainment network, and not an educational network."[63]

YTV divided its program schedule into three categories: preschool, teens, and family. Preschool content would air commercial-free in the morning, teen series in the afternoon, and family in the evening. The bulk of programming in its first year was a mixture of older Canadian, American, and British reruns, most of which had not been repeated since the programs originally aired.

Canadian series included *You Can't Do That on Television!* (1979), *The Forest Rangers* (1963), *Kids Corner* (1980), *The Friendly Giant* (1958), *George* (1972), *Sidestreet* (1975), *Willy & Floyd* (1966), *Harrigan* (1969), *Just Like Mom* (1980), and *The Trouble with Tracy* (1970); U.K. series included a glut of titles from the Incorporated Television Company (ITC) archive such as *The Muppet Show* (1976, often erroneously thought to be an American series), *The Tomorrow People* (1973), *The Adventures of Robin Hood* (1955), *Black Beauty* (1972), and *Boy Dominic* (1974); and U.S. cartoons such as *He-Man and the Masters of the Universe* (1983), *Ghostbusters* (1986), *BraveStarr* (1987), and *She-Ra: Princess of Power* (1985), although the live-action western *Bonanza* (1959) aired in prime time. New episodes of the Australian soap opera *Home and Away* (1988) ran in the late evening, as did a collection of golden-age Hollywood films under the banner "YTV at the Movies." Shea described YTV's initial original production *YTV Rocks* as "*Entertainment Tonight* for kids. We'll handle all the issues for teens, and we're going to go through a lot of experimentation. We'll respond to feedback. We want to be seen as a Canadian network."[64] Initial print ads for YTV's launch, which ran in TV guides across Canada, made the network's intentions clear:

> Finally, TV gives your kids what they've never had. A real choice. Because now, Canada's kids have a TV network devoted entirely to them. YTV — Canada's first network for kids, teens and families — brings you 18 hours each day of the best in young entertainment. From classic series like *Robin Hood* and *Bonanza* to the outrageous comedy show *You Can't Do That on Television*, to YTV's own daily entertainment special, *YTV Rocks*. Chances are, you already get YTV on your basic cable service. If you have a converter, you'll get our full feast of amazing entertainment automatically. So now you can do something to amaze your kids and reassure yourself. You can turn the TV back on.

YTV was initially available in more than four million homes across the country, and kicked off on September 1, 1988, with a feature-length opening-night special called "First Night," hosted by John Candy. An avowed fan of children's television, Candy volunteered to host free of charge, and considered kids' shows such as *Dr. Zonk and the Zunkins* (1974) and *CUCUMBER* (1975) as his first career breakthroughs. The special featured a performance from Toronto band Blue Rodeo, clips from many of the scheduled shows, and the memorable image of Candy getting a bucket of slime dumped on his head, à la *You Can't Do That on Television!*

With the daily teen-focused music magazine *YTV Rocks*, hosted by Laurie Hibberd and Michael "Q" Quast, and the later evening program *YTV Hits* (1988) with Ron Oliver, the channel was soon attracting the ire of Canada's

Check your local listings for channel position: a print ad announcing the launch of YTV in September 1988.

mighty cable music station, MuchMusic. According to Shea, "They were furious at the licensing of YTV. And in our first year, I think we had three different complaints from them to the CRTC about the kind of content we were carrying, which were taken very seriously at the time."[65] This led to a bizarre incident concerning the age of a fictional character from a decades-old American western. One of the CRTC's very specific conditions of YTV's licence was that, in all dramatic series, the major protagonist must be under the age of eighteen. This rule effectively prevented YTV from airing popular shows such as *Three's Company* (1976), the sitcom that had completely upended children's programming when it entered syndication and was added to numerous networks' after-school slots, including the CBC's, in the late 1970s. After numerous complaints to the CRTC regarding the airing of *Bonanza*, YTV was forced to send a representative to collect evidence in Los Angeles that the lead role, Joe Cartwright (played by Michael Landon), was intended to be seventeen at the time of filming. Despite meeting the CRTC's requirements, YTV exiled the hoary *Bonanza* anyway. It then turned its attention to creating a roster of original, in-house productions.

In 1989, YTV began its annual YTV Achievement Awards, a gala telecast honouring children across the country in fifteen separate categories that would continue as a symbol of the channel's commitment to Canadian youth until 2000. Initially hosted by Jim Carrey, the YTV Achievement Awards gave early recognition to Scarborough's Barenaked Ladies (1990 winners for best musical group, ahead of their infamous appearance on Citytv's *Speakers Corner*), actress Emily Perkins (*Ginger Snaps*), scientist Rachel Zimmerman, and environmentalist Marc Kielburger (co-founder of the WE Charity).

In December of that year, YTV found enormous success with "Santa Calls" (1989), a week-long live phone-in for kids featuring Jan Rubeš (see p. 117) as Santa Claus taking calls from across Canada in the original YTV studio at 545 Lake Shore Boulevard West. In addition to crashing the BC Tel service switchboard in British Columbia, Bell Telephone logged four hundred thousand incoming calls on the first night alone. As the decade ended, a vindicated Shea told the *Prince George Citizen*, "Kids have just as much right to be entertained as adults."[66]

89

Zardip's Search for Healthy Wellness (1988)

TVONTARIO DIRECTOR JEREMY POLLOCK, ACCLAIMED FOR his ability to seamlessly blend educational content with pulpy science-fiction storylines in the 1979 series *Read All About It!*, was enlisted by Ruth Vernon to helm a similar twenty-part serial in 1988; however, the subject of this series was health instead of literacy. Featuring scripts by Ken Sobol, *Zardip's Search for Healthy Wellness* told the tale of a robot (Zardip from the title, played by Keram Malicki-Sánchez) who had been sent to Earth by a dying breed of aliens hoping to unlock the secrets of health so they might restore their crumbling empire. Zardip befriended a group of young people who became his test subjects, and he reported back to his leader, Highship (voiced by Billy Van).

As with *Read All About It!* and *What If…* (1979), the kids spent their time in a fort (the Healthy Hideaway), and slowly began to suspect that there was more to Zardip than met the eye. The series mixed animation, clay animation, and live action to educate viewers on healthy lifestyles, including exercise and nutrition. The high concept elevated it from being just another lecturing program about eating your greens and allowed Sobol an opportunity to flex his B-movie storytelling techniques.

90
Join In! (1989)

AFTER *TODAY'S SPECIAL* HAD CONCLUDED IN 1987, THERE was a gaping department-store-sized hole in TVOntario's weekday early-evening schedule. For almost the entirety of the decade, 6:00–7:00 p.m. had been a power-hour of *Polka Dot Door* and *Today's Special*, at least on Tuesdays and Thursdays. *Polka Dot Door* was the preschool lead-in aimed at two-to-five-year-olds, but the later program needed to be slightly more complex, to expand the audience to older siblings and, possibly, parents.

Join In! creator Jed MacKay recalls a discussion with Ruth Vernon during which she lamented the end of in-house production. The mentality at

TVO was starting to shift toward licensing independent productions to fill out its schedule, and Vernon observed that the glory days of prolific production of original programs was drawing to a close.[67] Having proved his mettle as showrunner of *Polka Dot Door*, MacKay was eager to construct something entirely original that would retain the quality of *Today's Special* and keep TVO's Tuesday/Thursday 6:00 to 7:00 p.m. time slot competitive.

From left to right: Kia (Mishu Vellani), Jacob (Rudy Webb), and Zack (Marty Brier) invited young viewers to *Join In!* (1989), if only to see the enviable juice train in action.

During a brainstorm with writers Clive Endersby and Lori Howard, MacKay zeroed in on the growing concern over the so-called couch potato generation, and the perception that children's television was becoming far too passive; the number of viewing hours was increasing, while the number of hours spent playing or reading was decreasing. The three saw great value in a program that had interaction baked into its central premise, where viewers would be constantly encouraged to join in. MacKay was also keen to create a show that fully embraced the changing demographics of the city; a show that not only cast diverse performers but explored diverse musical styles as well. "I didn't feel shows musically reflected what kids were now listening to, the diversity of what little kids hear, particularly from their parents, or their older brothers and sisters," recalls MacKay.[68]

Taking a cue from the *Sesame Street* of the 1970s, which featured everything from funk-fuelled jams composed by Stevie Wonder to hard bop jazz played by Wynton Marsalis, MacKay decided to include numerous genres typically not heard on kids' shows, like reggae, blues, and harder rock 'n' roll. Bruce Ley served as music director for the show, while MacKay again composed.

Join In! promoted social skills, co-operation, and interaction and starred Rudy Webb as Jacob, Marty Brier as Zack, and Pamela Sinha as Nikki. Sinha departed after the second season and was replaced by *Polka Dot Door* host Mishu Vellani as Kia.

The three friends lived and worked together in a kitted-out studio loft in Lindsay, Ontario, that included a kitchen-to-living-room miniature juice and snack train. The series broke the fourth wall by having its characters directly address viewers and invite them to "join in" — clap, sing, play games, read stories, or solve puzzles. Real-life drama was incorporated into the scripts (such as close friends moving away, when a performer left the series). Frequent TVO guest star Billy Van voiced Abra the dog, who appeared in short stop-motion segments throughout the series.

91
The Magic Library (1989)/ Bookmice (1991)

ONE YEAR AFTER CRAFTING SCIENCE-FICTION-FLAVOURED *Zardip's Search for Healthy Wellness* (1988), Ken Sobol was invited to write for *The Magic Library* (1989), a more conventional series greenlit by Ruth Vernon to promote literacy. It was hoped that children's interest in books might be activated by an array of exotic human and animal puppets bringing classic stories to life. The puppets were created by Nina Keogh and operated by Keogh, Stephen Brathwaite, Trish Leeper, Karen Valleau, and Cheryl Wagner. Voices were provided by Billy Van, Steven Andrade, Malika Mendez, Marsha Moreau, and Noam Zylberman.

From left to right: Zazi (Trish Leeper), Norbert (Nina Keogh), and Leon (Karen Valleau) were the Bookmice, well-read rodents who promoted literacy in *The Magic Library* (1989) and *Bookmice* (1991).

Like a distant relative of TVO's earlier *Tell Me a Story* (1975), *The Magic Library* was recognized for highlighting a mix of authors, from classic to contemporary, featuring many Indigenous stories, as well as perennial favourites like Robert Munsch's *The Paper Bag Princess*. All twenty episodes were directed by Susan Murgatroyd (*CUCUMBER*, *Polka Dot Door*). It was followed a year later by *Return to the Magic Library* (1989), which dispensed with the other puppet characters and instead focused on three mice — Norbert, Leon, and Zazi — as central storytellers.

Owing to the continued popularity of the three mice, the series was overhauled again and rebooted in 1991 as *Bookmice*, directed by Jeremy Pollock. Norbert, Leon, and Zazi now resided in the walls of a far more expansive library. Taking a cue from *Today's Special* (1981), the action started when the library closed and the mice snuck out to read their favourite stories at night, while avoiding the library's roaming cat, Exit (voiced by Dan Hennessey, Keogh's co-star from *Dr. Zonk and the Zunkins* [1976]). *Bookmice* built upon the transnational premise of the earlier *Magic Library* shows by often including experimental and animated and stop-motion films from Eastern Europe, such as *Jak Ťuk a Bzuk putovali za sluníčkem* (1978), a Czechoslovakian series about two bumblebees. The mice read a wide variety of stories, new and old, from titles like *The Little Red Hen* by Mary Mapes Dodge to *Miss Nelson is Missing!* by Harry Allard. Many young performers guest starred as library patrons in the series, some of whom were portrayed as late readers. Vernon told the *Toronto Star*'s Jim Bawden this was done intentionally based on their research:

> Teachers must deal with many families where book reading is not part of the daily activities. Students enter kindergarten and they've never been read to — it's unfortunately happening more and more.... Some parents are illiterate themselves and can't read to their kids. Others just don't care.[69]

In total, thirty episodes of *Bookmice* were produced, and, along with *Join In!* (1989), it found fame stateside airing on the U.S. cable network The Learning Channel (TLC) in a preschool block called "Ready Set Learn!" *Bookmice* also marked the end of a long and successful line of educational children's programs produced by TVO under the guidance of Vernon, who retired from the network in 1993.

1990s

92
Road to Avonlea (1990)

IN 1985, THE CBC AND PBS CO-PRODUCED A TWO-PART made-for-television miniseries adaptation of Lucy Maud Montgomery's *Anne of Green Gables*, starring relative newcomer Megan Follows as the titular Anne alongside Hollywood luminaries such as Colleen Dewhurst (*Annie Hall* [1977]) and Richard Farnsworth (*The Grey Fox* [1982]). The atmospheric period adaptation was shot on location in Prince Edward Island and Ontario and stayed remarkably true to the source material, thanks to the vision of writer/director Kevin Sullivan. This was quickly followed up in 1987 with another miniseries, *Anne of Green Gables: The Sequel* (a.k.a. *Anne of Avonlea*), again starring Follows and featuring most of the first miniseries cast.

After the phenomenal international success of both miniseries, CBC kicked off the 1990s with *Road to Avonlea*, a lush weekly series set within the universe of Lucy Maud Montgomery's books. In the beginning, the series drew loose inspiration from Montgomery's Sara Stanley novels, including *The Golden Road* and *The Story Girl*, and starred Sarah Polley as Stanley, a capricious ten-year-old Montrealer forced to adapt to life in the tranquil town of Avonlea, Prince Edward Island (with Ontario locations in Uxbridge, Rockton, and Coppin's Corners standing in for the province).

Road to Avonlea was a CBC co-production with the Disney Channel in the U.S. where it aired under the title *Avonlea*. In Canada, *Road to Avonlea* was broadcast on Sunday evenings in the CBC Family Hour slot that typically aired stand-alone dramas or made-for-television movies.

Set within the same world as *Anne of Green Gables*, *Road to Avonlea* achieved continuity by featuring several crossover characters portrayed by the same actors as had appeared previously, including Marilyn Lightstone as Muriel Stacey, Patricia Hamilton as Rachel Lynde, and Colleen Dewhurst as

Marilla Cuthbert. The character of Anne Shirley was mentioned by others but never appeared onscreen. As the series progressed, it became much more of a soapy Avonlea anthology powered by a rich ensemble cast including Jackie Burroughs, Mag Ruffman, Cedric Smith, R.H. Thomson, Frances Hyland, and Michael Mahonen. Polley departed the series in 1994, returning for occasional spots.

Guest stars included Christopher Lloyd (*Back to the Future* [1985]), Diana Rigg (*The Avengers* [1965]), Michael York (*Logan's Run* [1976]), Madeline Kahn (*Clue* [1985]), Christopher Reeve (*Superman* [1978]), Stockard Channing (*Grease* [1978]), and a young Ryan Gosling (*Barbie* [2023]). The *Toronto Star*'s Sid Adilman said of *Road to Avonlea* that "no other Canadian series has been populated by such excellent irregular players."[1] Kudos to the series casting director Anne Tait.

Road to Avonlea was regularly hailed as compelling, wholesome family entertainment, and it won a total of eighteen Gemini Awards. When it concluded in 1996, Toronto-based production house Sullivan Films followed up with *Wind at My Back* (1996), based on Max Braithwaite's books set in depression-era 1930s Ontario. There was an additional seasonal special, "An Avonlea Christmas," which aired in 1998.

93
streetNOISE (1990)

EVER SINCE ITS INAUGURAL BROADCAST IN THE FALL OF 1988, Canada's first national specialty channel for children, YTV, had found early success with families and preschoolers. The teenage demographic, however, was proving difficult to capture. "They're elusive as gazelles. They're the toughest audience to reach, because they have so many options, interests and activities. We wanted to build a show that wouldn't give them time to graze."[2] YTV's vice-president of programming and production, Dale Taylor, teased in 1990.

Catering to perceived curt attention spans raised on diets of *Sesame Street* and music videos, YTV commissioned *streetNOISE*, a truly novel series whose mission statement was to "outzap the zappers."[3] Modelled after a general-interest magazine show — but on amphetamines — *streetNOISE* employed rapid-fire editing, dissolves, cutaways, speed adjustments, zooms, colour and grading changes, Dutch angles, audio manipulation, and segments that exploded onscreen with no context or resolution. "When you stop and think about it, it's really very complicated. So, we try not to stop and think about it," conceded post-production supervisor David Beatty.[4]

With topics as eclectic as its presentation style — graffiti, skinheads, LGBTQ, fast food, tattoos, child soldiers, rap music, etc. — *streetNOISE* often felt as if it were transmitting from another universe entirely. It acquired an immediate cult following and interest from both Canada's MuchMusic and MTV in the U.S. In a gushing review, *The Penguin Guide to Children's TV and Video* said:

> *streetNOISE* may have seemed superficial, loud, and trite to some adults, but it dealt with questions of importance to young people and accepted their answers without embellishment or prompting. It approached issues in a way that addressed the visual and auditory world of the teenager and took that world very seriously.[5]

A planned international version sponsored by Pepsi kyboshed the original YTV edition before it had a chance to really break through to the mainstream, and MTV stole the concept and style, wholesale, for their own take called *Buzz* (1990). But for a short time at the beginning of a tumultuous programming decade, YTV had momentarily outzapped the zappers.

94
Maniac Mansion (1990)

CREATED BY EUGENE LEVY (*SCTV, SCHITT'S CREEK*), BASED on a 1987 Lucasfilm computer game, and filmed entirely on location in Toronto, *Maniac Mansion* had a pedigree as odd as the eccentric Edison family it was centred on. Atlantis Films acquired the rights to the video game and brought Levy in to develop it into a series, envisioning a modern take on classic monster-themed family sitcoms like *The Munsters* (1964) and *The Addams Family* (1964). Levy instead refocused it as a postmodern situational comedy satire starring Joe Flaherty (*MathMakers*) as Edison family patriarch Fred, a stereotypical mad scientist who lives with his bizarre family in the titular mansion.

Many of the cast and crew of *Maniac Mansion* came from Toronto's elite Second City comedy troupe and its television spinoff *Second City Television,* a.k.a. *SCTV* (1976). Levy, Martin Short, Dave Thomas, and Andrea Martin contributed cameo appearances, while series regular Flaherty was one of Second City's founders. *Maniac Mansion* co-stars John Hemphill, Mary-Charlotte Wilcox, and George Buza all appeared on *SCTV.* Its theme song was co-written by Mary Margaret O'Hara, the sister of Catherine O'Hara (*Coming Up Rosie*). Owing no doubt to the contributions of revered Second City writers Michael Short, Paul Flaherty, David Flaherty, and director Jamie Paul Rock, the show often broke the fourth wall and contained extended parodic sequences, including the very first episode, which was presented as if it were the tenth-anniversary series special.

Maniac Mansion ran for three seasons, airing on YTV in Canada and Family Channel in the U.S., producing a total of sixty-six episodes running at thirty minutes in length.

95
The Afterschool Zone (1991)

ON MONDAY, SEPTEMBER 2, 1991 — LABOUR DAY — YTV launched a new afternoon programming block called "The Afterschool Zone" featuring an on-air host, or in the parlance of YTV, a program jockey (PJ). Gord the PJ Man (Gordon Michael Woolvett) invited viewers to stay with him as he introduced an episode of *Teenage Mutant Ninja Turtles* (1990) and he promised to stick around, popping up between shows from 4:00 p.m. until 6:00 p.m. to talk about life, TV, and everything in between.

The concept of using program jockeys as hosts for the network had come from YTV's first programming guru Merv Stone, a former CBC programmer, and, like many great ideas in television, was born out of economic necessity rather than artistic flourish. At the time YTV was limited to eight minutes of commercial time and most of the series aired contained twelve-minute commercial slots, created that way for the U.S. market. There was an omnipresent four-minute lag, which had been exhausted in YTV's first few years by its on-air running (and rerunning) of public service announcements, short National Film Board interstitials, and looped station promos. Stone suggested using young hosts *as* the interstitials, which would not only count toward original Canadian content (a.k.a. CanCon, a condition of the channel's broadcast licence), but could help keep audiences engaged, transitioning them from one program into the next by providing meaningful interaction with the young viewers. Even better, this structure gave the channel a televisual star system — a testing ground for new hosts and on-air talent — much in the same fashion as Ted Coneybeare had constructed the revolving host model on *Polka Dot Door* (1971) at TVOntario.

In Canada, specialty cable channel MuchMusic had been using video jockeys (VJs) to not only introduce music videos and interview celebrities but also to travel across the country and represent the channel as brand ambassadors since 1984. MTV in the U.S. technically set the precedent in 1981, however their VJs pre-recorded on weekends, and lacked the spontaneity and real-time anarchic folly the Much VJs brought. MuchMusic was also guided by creator Moses Znaimer's groundbreaking "Studioless Streetfront Television Operating System" — an approach that encouraged participatory and interactive elements at all levels of production — which made for great live television and kept audiences tuning in just to see what would happen next.

YTV had made a play for the music-video crowd from the very start with its first in-house productions *YTV Rocks*, with hosts Michael "Q" Quast and Laurie Hibberd, and *YTV Hits*, with Ron Oliver. In 1989, late-night *Rec Room* with Steven Birch and Janis Mackey was added to the schedule. These hosts worked within the context of music, but Stone and YTV president Kevin Shea saw a much larger play with the creation of the program jockeys.

After *Rec Room* ended in 1990, Mackey was recruited to become the very first program jockey for YTV. "The personality of the network was to speak to each child on a one-to-one basis with good eye contact and personalized to a certain degree so as to engage them into our PJ environment,"[6] recalls YTV's then VP of programming and production, Dale Taylor, who succeeded Stone. Reintroduced to viewers as PJ Jazzy Jan, Mackey appeared in the early afternoon between repeats of older series such as *Paul Hann and Friends* (1982), *Marie-Soleil* (1987), and *The Waterville Gang* (1972). The Afterschool Zone featured YTV's most in-demand series at the time, illustrating an irresistible eclecticism through a mixture of old and new, including *Teenage Mutant Ninja Turtles* at 4:00 p.m., *Count Duckula* (1988) at 4:30 p.m., *The Adventures of Rocky and Bullwinkle and Friends* (1959) at 5:00 p.m., and *Get Smart* (1965) at 5:30 p.m., spiced up with PJ appearances between shows.

The program-jockey format proved popular, and a variety of young people were cast as PJs with rotating shifts threading morning, afternoon, and weekend programming blocks on YTV. The first ensemble of PJs rolled out as PJ Jazzy Jan, Gord the PJ Man, PJ Robb (Rob Stefaniuk), PJ Rockin' Chan (Chandra Galasso), and PJ "Phresh/Fresh" Phil, better known as Phil Guerrero.

Guerrero had gotten his first break in television through friend Russell Chong (*The KangaZoo Club*), a field reporter for *YTV Rocks* who introduced

A postcard from 1992 featuring YTV's on-air PJs and Grogs, sent out to kids who submitted their artwork to be shown on The Afterschool Zone.

him to the production team. After shooting a few news stories for *YTV Rocks*, including one on the best places to buy jeans in Toronto, Guerrero was now armed with a demo tape. His easygoing persona and panache impressed the network so much he was hired and on the air almost immediately. He took the moniker PJ "Phresh/Fresh" Phil, in deference to the Scarborough hip-hop architect Maestro Fresh Wes. "They are the hot media stars for a new generation of kids — and they're changing the way young people watch television," *Starweek* magazine reported breathlessly. "The network host is a new species of TV animal; someone who appears at the 'top' and 'bottom' of the hour to 'welcome you back' after a program, read your letters, get you to try a craft or enter a contest — and, of course, ask you to stay tuned to the next show."[7]

Having been a host of The Afternoon Zone for just a few months, Gord the PJ Man was the first PJ to graduate when he became host of YTV's new show *Video & Arcade Top 10* (1991), a unique game show where contestants played games on Nintendo or Sega systems for prizes. The series also included news items on upcoming video game releases and behind-the-scenes looks at how games were made. Later seasons featured CFNY radio jock Nicholas Picholas as host, with notable talent such as Lexa Doig and Liza Fromer co-hosting. An almost bulletproof format, *Video & Arcade Top 10* aired until 2006.

96
The Grogs (1992)

IN 1992, A MANIACAL GROUP OF PUPPETS BEGAN TO APPEAR on YTV's Afterschool Zone. The puppets were created and operated by two twenty-year-old Toronto puppeteers and graduates of North York's Claude Watson School for the Arts, Jamie Shannon and Jason Hopley. They called themselves and their troupe of exotic puppet characters "The Grogs." Inspired as a child by Jim Henson's infinite menagerie of Muppets, Shannon was fascinated by European street performers he had seen while travelling and their creative use of puppets. Joined by his friend Hopley, the two set about constructing puppets and billing themselves as entertainers who would make appearances at birthday parties. They also happened to be friends with Stefaniuk, aka PJ Robb, who invited them to appear on YTV.

The greatest challenge for PJs was filling four minutes of time between shows. There were no scripts, just improvisation and gags gleaned from whatever episode of *Count Duckula* (1992) or *Batman* (1966) had just aired. The Grogs finally gave the PJs something to bounce off. Shannon and Hopley's imaginative character designs and boundless energy captured the eye of Dale Taylor, who had wanted to add a new dimension to the evolving world of PJs. "I had envisioned them as being our in-house incubators of non-live programming concepts. They were fun, creative, and pushed the envelope."[8] After many popular appearances in late 1991 and early 1992, the Grogs became full-time co-hosts in March of 1992, appearing daily in The Afterschool Zone and scattered throughout the YTV schedules. "We started going on with Rob for free, just having fun. And then YTV was like, oh we want to hire you, so we both ended up in university and being full-time PJs with the puppets,"[9] remembers Shannon.

The Grog gang included Gidian, a slightly neurotic purple dinosaur; Sorbet, a sweet innocent; Warren Chester, a scheming but ultimately benign green grumpster; Cupcake, a Yeti-like giant musical creature; Filth, an unclean dog-like animal; plus many others with wild personalities and names like Jasper, Iffer, and Rosencrantz. The Grogs were an immediate sensation with viewers, soon receiving more fan mail than their human co-hosts. In addition to their daily regimen, Grogs started to appear in other YTV productions, on YTV sales tapes, even in staff training videos. Along with *YTV's Hit List*'s Tarzan Dan and *Rock 'N Talk*'s Laurie Hibberd, the PJs and Grogs were cemented as mascots for the YTV network.

The Grogs, Jamie Shannon and Jason Hopley — a pair of budding puppeteers with enormous vision — were given the opportunity to run wild with their creations on YTV, so they took it.

With much of their dialogue improvised, Shannon and Hopley thought a lot about the Grogs' various personalities and were keen to explore emotions not usually seen in puppets on television. Grog Gidian's backstory was that his parents were divorced, and he was living with his mom. He understood his parents had issues getting along, but none of it made much sense to him. Fairly heavy subject matter for four minutes of screen time between cartoons.

That summer, the Grogs hosted the televised charity concert "Festival of Friends" along with PJs Jazzy Jan, Phil, Robb, and Rockin' Chan. Filmed on location at Canada's Wonderland with a running subplot involving the Grogs and PJs, the program featured popular children's entertainers Sandra Beech, Paul Hann, Kideo, Bob Schneider and the Rainbow Kids, Marie-Soleil, and Shari Lewis and Lamb Chop. YTV's very first blockbuster shot at Canada's Wonderland, the festival raised money for Kids Help Phone, and was co-sponsored by Jumbo Video, which sold and rented VHS tapes of the concert. Later in 1992, Stefaniuk departed the network to pursue a career in acting (*Catwalk*) and stand-up comedy. Jennifer Beech, daughter of children's entertainer Sandra Beech, was selected as his replacement, "PJ Jenn." YTV's relationship with Canada's Wonderland blossomed over the decade, culminating in the late-1990s Psyko Blast series of concerts where acts such as Hanson, The Moffatts, and Christina Aguilera performed with YTV PJs.

In December 1992, YTV's invitation to film and later broadcast the Santa Claus Parade in Cambridge, Ontario, was used to develop a more complex production featuring Grogs and PJs beyond their usual daily ad libbed appearances. The result was "The Grogs' First Santa Claus Parade" (1993), intended to test both the production team and performers outside of the relative comfort of The Afterschool Zone. The sixty-minute special went even further than *Festival of Friends* in scope and demonstrated that a scripted series with the Grogs was viable. However, the special was filmed in December 1992 and not broadcast until December 1993, by which time the relationship between Shannon and Hopley, the Grogs' creators, and YTV had dramatically changed.

97
The Big Comfy Couch (1992)

FRAGGLE ROCK ALUM CHERYL WAGNER STARTED HER CAREER in Halifax as a travelling puppeteer and clown in the Merrytime Clown and Puppet Company, visiting schools, hospitals, malls, and fairs to perform sketches about health and the human body. In 1982, the casting call for *Fraggle Rock* brought Wagner to Toronto, where she nabbed the roles of Ma Gorg, Lou Fraggle, and Bonehead Fraggle. She also voiced and operated Mrs.

Pennypacker in *Today's Special* starting in 1984, performed in the Canadian *Sesame Street* Christmas Special "Basil Hears a Noise" (1990), wrote an episode of *Under the Umbrella Tree* (1989), and had occasional spots on *Mr. Dressup.*

When *Fraggle Rock* concluded in 1987, Wagner developed a preschool series based partly on her experiences in the Merrytime Clown and Puppet Company. She was motivated by alarming reports of lethargy among children watching too much television. She partnered with fellow *Fraggle Rock* alum Rob Mills who had his own Toronto-based production company, Radical Sheep Productions, and who instinctively got the concept. *The Big Comfy Couch*'s ethos was anti–couch potato: Don't just sit there being passive, participate! Anchored by young female clown Loonette — a portmanteau of "loony" and *lunettes*, the French word for large glasses — who sat on a comically oversized couch, the show was physical but realistic. It acknowledged the presence of immersive screens and comfortable couches in the lives of children, but encouraged movement so they might enjoy the best of both worlds. Mills told the *Toronto Star*, "We wanted to be visually striking. It's movement-based, not an exercise show, but sort of body awareness for kids. Everything is geared toward making it an imaginary physical show."[10]

Each episode had a unique theme, but there were recurrent segments, including the "clock stretch" when viewers were encouraged to lie on their backs and mimic the movement of clock arms as a form of exercise, and the "ten-second clean-up" when a mess was tidied in ten seconds or less.

Wagner had worked with a talented young actress and opera singer named Alyson Court on *Mr. Dressup* and suggested her for the part of Loonette. "I made Loonette very energetic," Court later recalled. "At first I worried about taking things too far, but she's a clown and you can go far with that."[11] The show also featured a cast of regulars, including the fan favourite Molly, Loonette's rag doll, who communicated only by way of onscreen thought bubbles.

Although Wagner and Mills began work on the series in 1989, it did not appear on television until 1992, when YTV picked it up as part of its commercial-free morning block of preschool series, where it aired after the popular *Shining Time Station* (1989).

The series was seen as risky, and its budget was piecemealed through the MacLean-Hunter Fund (a Canadian telecommunications company eventually taken over by Rogers in 1994), *OWL/TV*, Telefilm, and YTV. In January 1995, *The Big Comfy Couch* began airing on PBS. Later that year, it won a Gemini Award for best children's series and had become the centrepiece of YTV's morning block "The Treehouse." In 1997, it moved full-time to the Treehouse TV network in Canada, where it remained a hallmark of the schedule until its seventh and final season in 2006, when the role of Loonette was played by Ramona Gilmour-Darling.

98
Catwalk (1992)

ONE OF THE MANY GRITTY YOUTH DRAMAS THAT FOLLOWED in the backwash of *Degrassi*, *Catwalk* was a YTV co-production filmed in Toronto that also aired on MTV in the U.S. and is best remembered as Guelph native and later Hollywood star Neve Campbell's first major television series. It followed the exploits of a metal/rap band (called Catwalk), and its relational dynamics in the struggle to land a record deal. Catwalk comprised Johnnie Camden (played by *Zardip's Search for Healthy Wellness'* Keram Malicki-Sánchez), Daisy (Campbell), Mary (Kelli Taylor), and Jesse (Paul Popowich).

In the second season, Rob Stefaniuk (YTV's PJ Robb) appeared as guitarist Benny Doulon, replacing Johnnie when Malicki-Sánchez left the series. *Polka Dot Door* host Johnie Chase appeared in a minor role, as did future *Murdoch Mysteries* (2008) star Yannick Bisson. Paul Hoffert of the prog rock band Lighthouse and *The World of B.J. Vibes*, along with his brother David, provided the musical score.

Catwalk revelled in typical dramatic tropes but distinguished itself by being set in a slightly apocalyptic future that was never fully explained onscreen, leaving viewers to postulate on why the landscape was ruinous and spotted with oil drum fires. The series became mired in legal issues concerning ownership and was dramatically overhauled for its second and final season, during which Catwalk became more of a classic rock band.

99
Ready or Not (1993)

MUCH CLOSER TO *DEGRASSI*'S TONE AND SPIRIT WAS 1993's *Ready or Not*, a coming-of-age drama about two best friends, Amanda Zimm (Laura Bertram) and Elizabeth "Busy" Ramone (Lani Billard), growing up in suburban Toronto (it was shot on location in West Hill, Scarborough, but not identified as such). Billed as "a refreshingly honest look at young female adolescents facing womanhood,"[12] the occasionally comic series strived to realistically depict the sometimes-awkward lives of its two leads (the opening episode concerned the girls' search for a properly fitted bra) but avoided the exploitative route taken by many of its contemporaries. Creator Alyse Rosenberg modelled the program on her own personal experiences, and adapted the series out of her short film *Thirty-Two Double A*. She told *Maclean's* magazine, "Television has a huge effect on teens, especially on girls, who can be made to feel completely inadequate. We are trying to offer alternative ways to navigate the rocky road of adolescence, without being cutesy."[13]

Ready or Not was produced by local independent Insight, and aired on Global Television in Ontario. When looking for a U.S. broadcaster, an episode concerning Busy's first menstrual period and another about wet dreams caused a minor uproar, but the series was eventually picked up by the Showtime cable network just in time for episodes about voyeurism, masturbation, and sexual fetishes. "I think it's a disservice to this huge section of the population to not represent adolescence for what it is — which is good, bad, and ugly," Rosenberg said in 1994.[14]

Regardless of all the press-baiting risqué sex stuff, the show was really about the friendship of Amanda and Busy as they navigated grades 6 through 9 and was hailed for its realistic portrayal from the overlooked perspective of teenaged girls. Like *Degrassi*, location filming in and across Toronto, Scarborough, Mississauga, Etobicoke, and Oakville gave the show a unique visual personality that greatly contrasted with the polished settings of comparable U.S. teen shows like *Beverly Hills, 90210* (1990) and *My So-Called Life* (1994).

Ready or Not aired until 1997, amassing sixty-five episodes over five seasons, and winning a Gemini Award in 1996 for best youth series. It also featured notable early appearances from Ryan Gosling (*Barbie* [2023]) and Tamara Podemski (*Reservation Dogs* [2021]).

DON'T PUT IT IN YOUR MOUTH!

Public service announcements (PSAs) aimed at kids were common in the 1970s and '80s, and usually focused on positive lifestyle messages (don't smoke, don't do drugs, don't drink and drive) and bicycle and traffic safety (some featuring Elmer the Safety Elephant, see p. 69). Some included graphic warnings about hitchhiking or talking to strangers. PSAs had existed since the advent of television and were usually reserved for government announcements and safety messaging. They typically ran on television stations during commercial airtime that went unsold.

In the 1990s, a Toronto-based non-profit organization called Concerned Children's Advertisers (CCA, later Companies Committed to Kids) transformed the PSA industry by creating edgy and memorable campaigns targeting children eight to twelve years of age, devised by its board, which was composed of influential advertisers from across Canada. Members of CCA included the Canadian branches of McDonald's, Mattel, Disney, PepsiCo, Coca-Cola, Hasbro, and Kellogg's, as well as broadcasters such as Teletoon, Corus Entertainment, Bell Canada, Canwest, and CTV.

Between 1990 and 2017, CCA produced over thirty spots featuring topics like bullying, conformity, media consumption, self-esteem, and drug abuse, which aired daily on all Canadian stations, and were in especially heavy rotation on YTV, Teletoon, and CFTO-TV. Some of CCA's best remembered PSAs include the "House Hippo" (1999), a faux documentary spot warning about the dangers of believing everything you see on TV; "Don't Put It in Your Mouth!" (1992), in which a couple of blue puppets sing about the dangers of ingesting unknown substances; and "Hip Choice" (1993), a truly nightmarish short featuring puppets created by Jamie Shannon and Jason Hopley (The Grogs) who are startled by a drug pusher with scarred, rotting-flesh eyes. Hip Choice received so many complaints from parents that the CCA was forced to amend the short so it faded out before the dealer's eyes were revealed.

100
The Adventures of Dudley the Dragon (1993)

AS YOUNG PEOPLE TOOK A GREATER INTEREST IN ENVIRONmental issues, there was a lag in television series that reflected it back to them. *The Forest Rangers* (1963), *CUCUMBER* (1975), and *OWL/TV* (1985) may have been among the first ecologically minded kids' shows, but it was the success of *Fraggle Rock* (1983) that really inspired the 1990s wave. *The Adventures of Dudley the Dragon* (1993) featured an eight-foot-tall dragon who awakens to a strange new world after over-hibernating a few centuries. Dudley's young friends help him navigate this unfamiliar world, learning more about the environment in the context of a modern-day fairy tale.

The character of Dudley first appeared in a 1982 touring theatrical production *The Conserving Kingdom*, sponsored by the Ontario Ministry of Energy. The property was purchased by Toronto's Breakthrough Films, which turned the play first into a television special in 1984 and then later into a full series. This fact was referenced frequently as the series was accused of copying *Barney & Friends* (1992), a colossal PBS success that featured a large purple dinosaur. (Both series were heavily merchandized with plush stuffies for their lead characters.)

For the 1993 edition, most of the action took place in a fantastically designed studio forest modelled after the Caycuse Valley in southwestern British Columbia. Series co-creator and writer Alex Galatis played the part of Dudley, as he had in the 1984 version. "It's not so much a series about the environment as it is modern-day fairy tales that help children discover the world around them," Galatis told *Starweek*.[15] Notable guest stars included Graham Greene as Mr. Crabby Tree, a grouchy apple tree who complains when people pick his fruit, and Jackie Richardson as Mother Earth. The series was produced in English and French languages simultaneously, a Canadian first at the time.

French version *Les Adventures d'Arthur le Dragon* aired on TVOntario's French-language network, La Chaîne française (launched in 1987), while the English-language version appeared on TVO and later YTV. It ran for five seasons, and sixty-five episodes were produced in total.

101
TVO Grows Up (1992)

TVONTARIO EXPERIENCED A WATERSHED YEAR IN 1992 WHEN Peter Herrndorf replaced Bernard Ostry as chief executive officer and dramatically reshaped the network. Herrndorf came from the CBC, where he been a vice-president and general manager, and was best known for his work modernizing news and current-affairs programming as far back as 1967 on *The Way It Is*. He had since developed raw and edgy new series like *The Fifth Estate* and *The Journal*. At CBC, and later *Toronto Life* magazine, where he was publisher from 1983 to 1992, Herrndorf was viewed as an agent of change. His arrival at TVO marked the beginning of an epochal transformation, a complete top-to-bottom overhaul involving everything from philosophy to programming to branding. While news and current affairs had been a central tenet at the network from the beginning, they began to take on even more prominence and became the network's defining feature. Former CBC anchor Steve Paikin joined TVO in 1992 as a host of *Between the Lines* and the provincial political talk show *Fourth Reading*. In the coming years, Paikin would gradually replace Polkaroo and Elwy Yost as the channel's most identifiable idol.

A print ad highlighting TVOntario's continued commitment to broadcasting quality educational content, featuring its newly designed logo (1992).

In 1992, after-school slots were dominated by U.S. fare like *Teenage Mutant Ninja Turtles* (1987), *Batman: The Animated Series* (1992), and *X-Men: The Animated Series* (1992), while on the Canadian side of the dial the network was losing its audience to YTV, CFTO-TV, and even Global Television. To some, TVO looked, and felt, old-fashioned. In the 1970s and 1980s, the network had been a vanguard of innovation in the children's space, especially in its ability to stretch limited production dollars. It produced strong, compelling educational content, as palatable to young audiences as the crassly commercial output surrounding it. Now they appeared browbeaten, unable to match the deep pockets of their competition thanks to continued financial cutbacks by the province. Adding to the malaise were a glut of older TVO programs from previous decades that still aired in heavy rotation, including *Polka Dot Door* (1971), *Read All About It!* (1978), and even imports like *Fables of the Green Forest* (*Yama Nezumi Rokkī Chakku*, a Japanese animated series made in the early 1970s and dubbed into English in 1978). In an article about the precarious state of the network, *Toronto Star* reporter Antonia Zerbisias described TVO's traditional kids programming as "tired, stale, and unable to hold audiences."[16]

In June 1993, Ruth Vernon retired from TVO. A former teacher from Scarborough, Vernon had joined the network in the OECA days and spearheaded its hugely successful curriculum-based series, starting with *Readalong* (1975), and continued with the shepherding of everything from *Math Patrol* to *Dear Aunt Agnes*. She told the *Toronto Star*,

> Public Television has suffered enormous budget cuts, and programmers at private networks don't seem to care enough. So, the kids suffer.... Our department and the youth

> department next door contribute 82 percent of TVO's programming sales. Usually that money goes back to TVO as a whole and not to us, which would be nicer. I remember trying to peddle *Today's Special* to the big U.S. networks, who were not interested in any kids' series that did not come equipped with instant merchandise.[17]

Her departure marked the end of an era, not only in personnel but in production. The days of in-house TVO productions dominating the schedule were over, and their substitution with independently produced and foreign acquisitions was underway. Vernon didn't hide her indignation; she considered network television not just benign but damaging. She sounded the alarm on the way out: "You know there are five-year-olds out there watching *Married… with Children* (1987). How can TVO attract them?"[18]

By 1994, TVO was virtually unrecognizable from its earlier incarnation. A new minimalist logo designed by an outside agency replaced Dick Derhodge's iconic version across all network branding, and Derhodge and his in-house design team were let go. New promotional spots underlined these changes and the channel opted for a cooler, hipper vibe, abandoning the cozy homespun appearance of old. The long-running "voices of TVO," John DeLazzer and Susan Mitchell, no longer voiced the station's on-air promos. To streamline resources and address declining government funding and public pledge donations, TVO had been fully restructured, combining departments and handing out contract buyouts, layoffs, and position eliminations.

In July 1995, Alberta's public broadcasting channel, ACCESS, was sold with approval by the CRTC to a private confederation of CHUM Ltd., Moses Znaimer, and Ron Keast, marking the first privately owned educational television service in Canada. In June 1995, Mike Harris, leader of the Progressive Conservative Party of Ontario, won a landslide victory with his Common Sense Revolution promising to liquidate what they deemed wasteful provincial assets, including services such as TVO. The reality that the network could be sold off to private entities became the source of much alarm within Ontario and at TVOntario itself.

102
The Zone (1993)

FROM ITS INCEPTION, YTV MADE A VALIANT ATTEMPT TO APpeal broadly to many demographics including preschool, children, teenagers, and families. But in 1993, extensive research identified that the bulk of YTV's current audience were "tweens," a twee '90s-era moniker used to describe the commercially attractive eight-to-twelve-year-old demographic that existed in the chasm between children and teenagers. Leaning into this, YTV engaged the services of poppy U.S. design studio Big Blue Dot to create a visually imaginative rebranding. The Watertown, Massachusetts, agency produced a cluster of memorable variants of the YTV logo, until then a flat and ordinary affair. The rebranding placed the logo onto couches, robots, sneakers, blenders, spinning globes, dinosaurs, and a green skull. "We were looking at exploring the logo and to push it a little bit, based on the MTV approach. At the time, MTV had a million logos," remembers Nicolas Kadima, an OCAD graduate who ended up in YTV's art department after an internship.[19]

In September 1993, YTV broke its daily schedule into pieces and introduced the concept of "day parts." Nine a.m. until noon, Monday through Friday, was the commercial-free preschool block now called "The Treehouse" based on a suggestion by Dale Taylor: "It sounds nice and is both inspirational and aspirational, elevating in both thought and spirit. It was to be a destination and a 'safe haven' for kids and their growing, exploring minds."[20] To keep it short and sweet, "Afterschool" was dropped from the title of the afternoon block and it became simply "The Zone," while weekends 7:30 a.m. through noon remained "The Alley." Aashna Patel soon joined the roster as PJ Aashna, taking over The Treehouse and starting the broadcast day with her heartfelt rendition of "O Canada" every morning when the channel signed on.

A collection of YTV logos from 1993, when the network took inspiration from MTV's gallery of colourful branding.

The Zone was extended, now starting at 3:30 p.m., running a full three hours every weekday. Programs aired were an eclectic mix of new and old like *Batman* (1966), *Mighty Morphin Power Rangers* (1993), *Dennis the Menace* (1959), and *The Bots Master* (1993). Speaking about the impromptu nature of The Zone, Guerrero recalled:

> The Zone was not so much watched by producers. They just kind of let us do our thing. There were so many days where it's like, counting down, and we're about to go on live for like three minutes and it'd be like ten … nine … And I'd ask whoever's puppeteering, what are we talking about? Uh, movies? Oh, yeah. All right, we're back. You could not do that anymore. You just couldn't.[21]

PJ Phil had become the channel's breakout star through his unique charm and ability to connect with young viewers. Playing his acoustic guitar, or chatting about his favourite action movies, Phil spoke to the audience as his peers, and they responded in kind. "Phil was great, and he reflected the network's aspiration of being inclusive, multi-ethnic, hip, and sincerely pro-active in developing young talent with potential. Phil was a terrific ambassador for us on all levels," recalls Taylor.[22]

On October 31, 1993, the YTV PJs graced the network's prime time as hosts of "Dark Night" — a Halloween marathon of *Are You Afraid of the Dark?*, *Rugrats*, and *Garfield* episodes that also saw PJs Phil, Aashna, and Jenn share scary ghost stories on the candlelit set of The Zone. Dark Night would later become one of the network's annual tentpole events for the fall season. Guerrero recalled some of the controversy that followed Dark Night as it amplified the scare factor:

> It was such a funny, touchy subject, though, because you got to remember back then when this stuff started, there was always some fucking controversy going on with everything we were showing. And if it wasn't kids gambling POGs and Beyblades, it was the horror stuff that was too much for them. Or the Power Rangers. Those guys were beating each other up in the school yards. So Dark Night was a funny one. Every time we did it, it was like this little controversy. Oh, too scary! It's too much! There's a lot we got away with. There's a lot I got away with. I thought that was really funny. You just couldn't do that anymore.[23]

103
YTV News (1993)

A CO-PRODUCTION WITH CTV, *YTV NEWS* WAS KIND OF A 1990s updating of Perry Rosemond's *Through the Eyes of Tomorrow* (1966) with its integration of teenagers and youth at all levels of production. It was also a shrewd attempt by YTV to get into classrooms. Teachers' kits — which, for advertisers, were effective Trojan Horses — were prepared with lesson plans and accompanying videotapes of the show that contained company logos and references to sponsorship (the ubiquitous "brought to you by …").

When *YTV News* began in September of 1993, PJ Jazzy Jan — Janis Mackey — bid adieu to her PJ roots and was ported over to co-host. Dale Taylor remained enthusiastic about the show: "[*YTV News* was] another great initiative that gave us some credibility in terms of social advocacy, outreach, media literacy, and industry buzz. A great coup for a young fledgling network."[24] One early episode featured a story about a Northern Secondary School student named Jesse Brown who was publishing his own underground student newspaper. Brown would go on to found infamous journalistic digital media company and podcast network Canadaland in 2013.

104

YTV Jr. Jays TV Magazine (1993)

YTV JR. JAYS TV MAGAZINE WAS A SPORTS AND LIFESTYLE magazine–style show built around the then majestic Toronto Blue Jays, who had won Major League Baseball's World Series in 1992 and were about to do it again in 1993. Using the established Toronto-based print magazine *Junior Jays Magazine & Kids' Club* (1993) as a source of content and framing à la *OWL/TV* (1985), the *TV Magazine* featured PJ Phil, PJ Aashna, and PJ Jenn interviewing popular Blue Jays players like Joe Carter and Paul Molitor, visiting the SkyDome (now the Rogers Centre) and spring training in Dunedin, Florida, and speaking with kids who play baseball. Disc jockey "Tarzan Dan" appeared in cooking segments, while the show was hosted by the time-travelling character of Dr. Jay, star of the science-fiction comic that ran in the print magazine.

105

Warren TV (1994)

FILMED IN DECEMBER OF 1992, "THE GROGS'S FIRST SANTA Claus Parade" finally aired on December 23, 1993. During the ensuing year, the relationship between the puppeteers, Shannon and Hopley, and YTV had been strained by a dispute over ownership of the Grogs. Keen to capitalize on their popularity, YTV hoped to acquire ownership of the Grogs as intellectual property and create lines of Grog plushies, clothing, toys, etc. Shannon and Hopley were not satisfied with the offer, and in turn their contracts, set to expire on January 1, 1994, were not renewed. Despite any misgivings, an idea was hatched to both give the Grogs a dignified exit and provide YTV with an almighty programming stunt to kick off 1994.

YTV News

Volume 6, Number 2, Winter 1993

YTV Goes On "GREEN GROG ALERT" On New Year's Day

YTV Special Investigations Report
Grogville Detachment

NAME OF SUSPECT: WARREN CHESTER GROG
DESCRIPTION: Male Grog, Green
AGE: Unknown
HEIGHT: 1 ft. 6 in.
WEIGHT: Won't say
DISTINGUISHING FEATURES: Furry, sphere-like body. Googly, somewhat shifty eyes. Major attitude.

YTV Special Investigations Report
Grogville Detachment

Sources here have uncovered a plot by suspect (Warren) to stage a takeover of his current place of employment, one **YTV Canada, Inc.** on **Saturday, January 1, 1994 (New Year's Day).**

Sources say suspect intends to inform viewers (secretly) of his planned coup on upcoming segments of ***PJs, The Zone*** and ***The Alley***. We've been warned he is planning an **'all-request holiday'** and is urging kids to send in their requests of favourite YTV shows. His intention? To custom-tailor his **WARREN TELEVISION NETWORK** schedule according to viewers' requests.

Can the opinionated orb be stopped?

Will YTV become "WTV" (WARREN TELEVISION) on New Year's Day?

Or will YTV be under the grumpy Grog's rule forever?

YTV's Grogville detectives are on the case.

1

The cover of YTV's Winter 1993 newsletter heralding the Green Grog Alert for New Year's Day, 1994, which found the irascible Warren Grog hijacking YTV's broadcast signal and rebranding the network as WTV.

January 1, 1994, saw YTV hijacked by Warren Grog, who had ostensibly turned evil (first hinted at in the Christmas special). After disposing of the other Grogs by locking them out, Warren and his cohort Filth began to air the programs "they wanted to see," which included a random assortment of cartoons and episodes of *Batman* (1966), *Teenage Mutant Ninja Turtles* (1989), and even *YTV's Jr. Jays TV Magazine* aired out of order and occasionally interrupted by Warren's demented demands for respect and approval from viewers and Canadian television executives. In the lead-up to his takeover, YTV had aired promos that were hijacked by Warren as well. Throughout the day, footage aired of PJ Phil, PJ Jenn, and the "good" Grogs attempting to break into the YTV studios (now broadcasting as Warren TV, or WTV) and foil Warren's plan. Thanks to Filth switching sides, the incident culminated in a showdown that saw Warren apprehended and YTV returned to its rightful owners. Previously both MTV and MuchMusic had programmed full-day stunts with satirist "Weird Al" Yankovic in which he took over the curation of their networks and played only the music videos and interviews he desired (and called it AL-TV), but no children's network had ever executed something as spectacularly haywire as this. One can only imagine what viewers channel surfing through YTV on New Year's Day must have made of it all.

After this monumental farewell programming gimmick, the Grogs were never seen or mentioned on-air again. Starting Monday, January 3, 1994, PJ Phil hosted The Zone alone, while PJ Jenn took over The Alley, and PJ Aashna remained in the morning. As YTV plotted out a Grog-less schedule, the last remaining in-house puppeteer, Marty Stelnick, recalls going on-air with leftovers. "I started working with Jamie Shannon and Jason Hopley just before they left. Initially, I was using some old, non-Grog puppets that they had left behind."[25]

106
Snit (1994)

IN 1994, YTV ART DIRECTOR NICOLAS KADIMA OVERSAW A complete redesign of The Zone's set, including the creation of a new non-human character that would become PJ Phil's co-host — a mutated supercomputer called Snit. Kadima revealed the origins of Snit:

> Snit was based on a movie I love called *The Thing* [1982]. It was the idea that a kid stuck a piece of gum under a computer, and overnight it all kind of merged together. And there was a computer virus, if I recall, that kind of affected the computer, but because the gum was there, it kind of integrated it in its making. So, it was like a mutation.[26]

YTV's vibes ambassador PJ Phil and Snit, a mutated computer puppet-video hybrid designed by Nicolas Kadima and operated by Atul N. Rao.

Puppeteer Marty Stelnick had been creating a new gang of puppets called the Fuzzpaws as co-hosts for the station's commercial-free morning block, The Treehouse, when the Grogs had departed, leaving him YTV's sole puppeteer. He was duly assigned Snit duty. Stelnick operated Snit by speaking into a voice modulator and moving a set of false teeth that were filmed and broadcast on the creature's monitor. However, only two days into production, Stelnick fell ill and was hastily replaced by local puppeteer Atul N. Rao, who recalled:

> Phil was not interested in having another puppet in there, so it was very tense. But he came around and we got along. He started to see that it was less confrontational than Warren Grog. We were buddies. Our on-air personas were the same as our relationship. What you saw on The Zone was usually a continuation of what we were talking about off camera.[27]

The addition of frankly odd Snit and the radical redesign of The Zone set were further nods toward the tween demographic that continued to drive YTV's creative and commercial goals. The humble Kadima remembers: "With a tiny budget we literally rebuilt the set. It's like, it was blue and red. You should never do that on TV, in retrospect. Because it just vibrates like crazy. But we did a cooler set."[28] Guerrero recalled the new colour scheme with much the same feeling: "Everything was blue, red, and yellow. The nineties were weird."[29]

107
Squawk Box (1994)/ It's Alive (1994)

FROM THE EARLIEST DAYS OF TORONTO CHILDREN'S TELEvision, innovative sketch comedy was a prominent feature, starting with *Uncle Chichimus* in 1952 and carrying through *Razzle Dazzle* (1961) and *Kiddo the Clown* (1962) to Don Elder's and Trevor Evans's mid-1970s attempts to fashion a star system out of Toronto's Second City players in *Dr. Zonk and the Zunkins* (1974) and *Coming Up Rosie* (1975). However, it was not until 1979's *You Can't Do That on Television!*, an Ottawa-area sketch-comedy series for children produced at CTV affiliate CJOH-TV, that the Canadian spin on the format really broke through to an international audience. Created by U.K. expat Roger Price, *You Can't Do That on Television!* featured a large cast of children pushing the do-do envelope with fast-paced skits laced with gross-out imagery. The show's signature gag involved a bucket of slime dousing any cast member who uttered the line "I don't know."

The series was among the first offerings screened in the U.S. by the nascent children's cable channel Nickelodeon, where it became a ratings sensation and eventually informed the entire network's branding (more slime). In its wake, sketch comedy became a desirable format for low-budget children's shows and a host of imitators followed suit. Repeats and new episodes of *You Can't Do That on Television!* littered the early schedule of YTV, where it was hoped the show might help define "Canada's Nickelodeon."

Josh Morris, staff writer on *You Can't Do That on Television!*, got an early break when he was recruited by ex-CJOH news producer Rob Burton, who was YTV's first general manager. The two had met at CFTO-TV in Agincourt while filming *Turkey Television* (1985), a comedy program constructed of short interstitials for Nickelodeon based on the popularity of *You Can't Do That on Television!* and using some of that show's production team.

Morris first worked on *YTV Hits* (1988) with host Ron Oliver, who had once hosted CHEX-TV's morning children's show *The Silver Basketball* (1982) in Peterborough, Ontario. *YTV Hits* showed a variety of music videos, threaded together by skits involving Oliver and Morris. One episode found Oliver travelling around Toronto on the TTC asking random people trivia about television western series *Bonanza* (1959). Morris also voiced and operated a crude hand puppet called Ralph the Happy Contest Goose.

Also in 1989, Morris and Oliver devised *Rec Room*, a weeknight talk show for teens set in a creaky 1970s-inspired veneer-panelled basement with gaudy couches and an oversized wooden-framed television set. Hosted by Steven Birch and Janis Mackey, *Rec Room* attracted popular guests, such as Pat Mastroianni and Amanda Stepto from *Degrassi* and rocker Kim Mitchell; showed new music videos; and performed outlandish skits penned by and often featuring Morris. It once even presented an impromptu concert by hugely successful Mississauga hard rock band Triumph. Although it only lasted one year on-air, *Rec Room* served as an incubator of sorts: Mackey became YTV's very first program jockey (PJ), while managing producer Dale Taylor graduated to vice-president of programming and production. Taylor recalls, "[*Rec Room*'s] saving grace was CanCon numbers, as it was a pure volume play. It was twisted, funnily irksome, and a bit ahead of its time."[30]

With YTV's in-house production partners GRC, Morris was then drafted to develop *YTV's Hit List* (1991), a music-video program built around the

The cast of *It's Alive!* (1994), an attempt by showrunner Josh Morris to reinvent the anarchic spirit of *Saturday Night Live* (1975) for a younger demographic.

magnetic personality of popular radio jock "Tarzan Dan" Freeman. Morris had noted Canada's music channel MuchMusic was not playing much of the "cheesy" music young people were interested in. He recalls:

> MuchMusic was very snobby about music. They wouldn't play groups like the Backstreet Boys and Paula Abdul and that kind of thing initially; it was too juvenile for them. So YTV stepped up and we really made something out of things that thirteen-year-olds really wanted to hear at the time. MuchMusic wouldn't play those kinds of songs. So, it ended up creating very good ratings and a niche for itself.[31]

A more prestigious assignment for Morris arrived in 1992 with *Borderline High*, a one-hour look at high-school dropouts hosted by Alanis Morrisette. She was an old acquittance of Morris from her days on *You Can't Do That on Television!* and in 1995 would release her seminal album, *Jagged Little Pill*.

Produced with a grant from the federal Stay-in-School initiative, *Borderline High* dramatized the dropout phenomena with a cast that included "PJ" Phil Guerrero as Eduardo, a shady pool-hall hustler contemplating an early exit from his school. At the show's conclusion, Morrisette performed her breakthrough hit "Too Hot."

Two new local comedy series arrived on YTV in 1994, both promising to be *Saturday Night Live* for the *Sesame Street* generation. Premiering in late summer, *Squawk Box* was a thirty-minute group sketch series produced by Atlantis Films Ltd. As its title suggests — "squawk box" is an old derogatory term for console vacuum-tube radios — the series mimicked channel surfing, serving up a rapid-fire mix of spoofs presented in both black and white and colour. *Starweek*'s Louise Brown was less than impressed, saying,

> *Squawk Box* is openly Canadian in its references to places from Manitoba to Richmond Hill. And by its nature, it follows a strong Canadian tradition of ensemble sketch comedy. It's just that the humour is a bit juvenile — but then, I guess that's precisely the point.[32]

Morris returned to his sketch-comedy roots with a much more interesting reconfiguration of the genre, *It's Alive!* (1994). He described it to *Playback* magazine as a combination of "*Saturday Night Live*, [David] Letterman and *Beat the Clock* (1950)."[33] *It's Alive!* mixed Morris's peculiar brand of entertainment with interviews, puppets (operated by Grog masters Jamie Shannon and Jason Hopley, evoking Jim Henson's regular, if little-remembered, appearances in *SNL*'s first season), musical performances, obstacle courses, and game shows, all done in studio with a live audience (recalling the peanut gallery from *The Howdy Doody Show* and *Razzle Dazzle*). With a mammoth running time of ninety minutes per episode, the format also wrapped around YTV's Saturday repeats of series like *Mighty Morphin Power Rangers* (1993), *Are You Afraid of the Dark?* (1992), and the Gerry Anderson marionette puppet series *Captain Scarlet and the Mysterons* (1967). It also attempted to circumvent the CRTC regulations limiting commercial time by using live advertising via product placement within the show featuring brands like Canada Games and Nabisco.

For the second season of *It's Alive!*, the wraparound format was dropped and running time curtailed to sixty minutes, then it was reduced further to just thirty minutes in its fourth and last season. This came during an experimental time at YTV when multiple formats were tested and tweaked with rotating hosts and producers. YTV's later game show *Uh Oh!*, another slime-based affair with an S&M-outfitted character called The Punisher, began as a segment within *It's Alive!* before spinning off into its own series in 1997, barely held together under the weight of its own mayhem by Scott Yaphe as caricatured game-show host Wink Yahoo. *Uh Oh!* also featured comedian Shaun Majumder, who had started at YTV as a co-host of the Saturday-morning kids' block "The Brainwash" (1995) and announcer for YTV's other frenzied game show, *Clips* (1995).

108
Groundling Marsh (1994)

1994'S *GROUNDLING MARSH* WAS ADMITTEDLY AN EXTENDED homage to the works of Jim Henson, a hero to series creators Lisa Olfman, Joy Rosen, and John Delmage. Set in a bizarre-looking magical swamp "just past the edge of town," *Groundling Marsh* featured the mutated elf-like Groundlings, who were an equal mix of human, plant, and animal. Puppeteers for the series included Nina Keogh (as Crystal), Stephen Brathwaite (Mud), James Rankin (Eco), Patricia Leeper (Maggie), and Gord Robertson (Galileo). *Groundling Marsh* premiered on YTV in Canada, and the Disney Channel in the U.S., ultimately airing in ninety-four territories worldwide.

109
TVOKids – The Crawlspace (1994)

AT TVONTARIO, BBC PRODUCER ADRIAN MILLS WAS APPOINTed by newly installed CEO Peter Herrndorf to completely revamp the children's department, shedding the old curriculum-based ideology of the Ruth Vernon era for a new-spangled approach closer to ratings juggernaut YTV. Back in the U.K., Mills had directed and produced edgy British series like *Record Breakers* and *The Really Wild Show*; he even refurbished TVO's original muse, *Play School*. He also held a master's degree in education and child psychology. Mills lured Josh Morris, the prodigal YTV writer/producer who helped mint the network's approach with series like *YTV's Hit List* (1991) and *It's Alive!* (1994), to oversee the transformation of TVO's children's output, which included a major overhaul of *Polka Dot Door*. Morris told *Playback* magazine:

> I think that TVO, because of the huge amount of choice kids have now and the fact that they know how to use channel-changers, has lost some audience share. TVO is strong in preschool and good at shows that parents want their kids to watch, but as soon as kids get the channel-changers in their hands, they change to something that is not educational.[34]

Morris was adept at mixing educational content with more accessible fare, and envisioned a block of new after-school programs where young viewers "will want to hang out with the TVO vibe" as well as making sure "pedagogical information is slipped in."[35] Titled "TVOKids — The Crawlspace" ("It was shot in this tiny little studio the size of a shoebox"[36]), the new block aired from 3:30 p.m. until 7:00 p.m. Monday through Friday, and, in a TVO first, featured hosts between shows. Accused by some of ripping off YTV's successful program-jockey format, Mills pointed out that back in the U.K., hosted children's blocks had been in operation long before the advent of YTV. Morris recalls:

> YTV's presence was a factor. The difference was really that The Crawlspace catered to an overall younger group. They were mostly preschoolers and people sending in crayon drawings and stuff. There wasn't so much of that at YTV.[37]

As with YTV, hosted blocks not only helped fill time between shows and counted toward the Canadian-content quotas, but they also made young viewers feel a closer kinship to the station. Television executive David Schatsky told *Starweek* magazine in 1994 it was "like a club to which they belong. It provides a human link between the child and television; an outlet for kids to feel they're making contact and being heard, so in that sense it's a very good idea."[38]

In classic TVO fashion, videotaped auditions of potential TVOKids hosts were road-tested with kids, parents, and educators who filled out detailed reports on who they enjoyed most. Patty Sullivan had been working at TVO as an aspiring journalist before answering an internal job posting for a children's host. Her submitted videotape had ranked highest with the test audience and she was offered the role of solo host. During early rehearsals it was decided to add an on-air partner, and Kevin Brauch, whose audition scored second highest, was brought in. The new TVOKids premiered April 1, 1994.

Mills suggested that with great power came great responsibility. He suggested Patty and Kevin were cognizant of the responsibility for being the faces of TVOKids to so many young people. "[They] are aware of their influence on viewers. So, Patty and Kevin are very hip, very funny, and clever, but they appeal to kids' desire to be naughty, with a twinkle."[39]

At first the block was lumbered with older shows that were still playing out their prepaid runs at TVO. Sullivan recalls:

> We had a lot of antiquated shows when we started — we had *Polka Dot Door*, obviously. We had a show called *The Kitty Cats*, an odd show. We were doing a contest — count how many times the cat blinks. We didn't know what else to do. We needed new stuff.[40]

The addition of two new popular foreign shows to the schedule literally changed the fortunes of The Crawlspace overnight: *Ghostwriter* (1992), a popular U.S. series co-produced by the Children's Television Workshop and the BBC, and *Bill Nye the Science Guy* (1993), a KCTS/PBS production out of Seattle. Suddenly, TVOKids was competitive with YTV: "We even brought Bill Nye to do various meet and greets with kids in Toronto and other cities in Ontario. It became very, very popular."[41] *Starweek* magazine reported that Patty and Kevin received on average of fifteen hundred phone calls a day, and eight thousand handwritten letters a month. It was clear that younger viewers were keen to interact with this new incarnation of TVO.[42]

Later in 1994, TVO cancelled *Polka Dot Door*, *Bookmice*, and *Join In!*, the final three legacy kids' shows from before Peter Herrndorf's arrival — the Ruth Vernon era. The shows continued as repeats, but Mills began to clear the deck of the old-fashioned TVO properties that had been airing for over a decade. At first, they were replaced with modern British imports he was familiar with, including *Art Attack*, *Zzzap!*, *Tots TV*, and his own *Growing Up Wild*. He told *Starweek* magazine in 1995,

> TVO's mandate is to service all the children in Ontario, and our research showed that we were not doing enough for kids over 7. We have always done very well with the preschoolers, but we have just one hour a day for the older children and I'm very concerned that none of that is Canadian. I want TVO to develop some new flagship shows for this age group.[43]

Veteran TVO producer Clive VanderBurgh was engaged by Mills to develop an original, *Ghostwriter*–like program to call their own. Given

TVO's track record of spooky educational series for kids, programs like *The Adventures of Timothy Pilgrim* (1975) and *Read All About It!* (1979), along with the pedigree of VanderBurgh (*CUCUMBER*, *Today's Special*), this seemed like an easy layup. VanderBurgh was also a professor of children's television at Ryerson Polytechnic University (now Toronto Metropolitan University) and made full use of the research done at the school about modern children's viewing habits. From the very beginning, TVO had prided itself on the amount of research done to get concepts to pilot, and then pilots to series. VanderBurgh had spent years workshopping the two pilots of *Today's Special* before the full series went into production. Vanderburgh told *Playback* magazine in 1994,

> We talked to kids, we looked at the research at both TVO and Ryerson. We looked at the video games kids were playing and the TV shows they watched. We did deconstructions of the TV shows that appeal to kids to assess how many scenes, how many characters, what age group were the characters, what was the appeal of the show. We researched psychological and sociological aspects and analyzed books and comic books.[44]

Clive Endersby, who had written at TVO since the mid-1970s for everything from *Two Plus You* to *Today's Special* and *Dear Aunt Agnes*, collaborated with VanderBurgh on a thrilling adventure pilot that involved an eleven-year-old protagonist on a treasure hunt mixed up with a ghost. The two Clives were also masters at using TVO's often meagre budgets for maximum effect to create good-looking shows, doing a lot with a little. "Kids [are] able to target which shows were American and which ones were Canadian, and then which ones were cheap."[45] The result was the one-hour-long *McCabe Mysteries* (1995). Sadly, the pilot was not picked up, although it ended up airing on Halloween night in 1996.

One of the more popular segments of The Crawlspace was the Power Hour, an interactive hour of games and trivia that aired on the weekend. The hosts were encouraged to develop their own short interstitials like *The Bod Squad* and *Reading Rangers*, that aired alongside the channel's popular imports such as *Arthur* (1996), *The Magic School Bus* (1994), and *Pingu* (1980). Sullivan remembers the latter series attracting a demographic considerably older than its target:

> We took live phone calls on the show, and we would get university students calling because they were fans of *Pingu*. It was the craziest thing because our viewers were technically between eight and thirteen, but inevitably we'd get university kids calling, going "We love *Pingu*! We watch it!" It was just so crazy.[46]

From top left: TVOKids hosts Joseph Motiki, Patty Sullivan, Kevin Brauch, and Rekha Shah promote UNICEF boxes for Halloween.

Sullivan also noticed a much different reaction to the TVO brand when The Crawlspace hosts ventured outside of the GTA for public events:

> TVO was a big deal when you left Toronto. In Toronto and the GTA, you know, YTV and TVO kind of battled it out for eyeballs. But if you went to Northern Ontario or Sarnia or Sudbury or, wherever it was — "TVO, TVO, TVO!" That was just something. In that sense, we were still able to compete with YTV and all that stuff. And I think it was also because parents trusted us.[47]

110
Polka Dot Shorts (1995)

WHILE PLANS TO REBOOT *POLKA DOT DOOR* NEVER MATERialized, its ten-minute-long spinoff *Polka Dot Shorts* premiered in 1995. Created by Jed MacKay, it kept the iconic Polkaroo, giving him the ability to speak, as well as the long-suffering toys Marigold, Humpty, Dumpty, and Bear, although here they had grown up and were roughly the same size as the Polkaroo. New character Bibble was Polkaroo's pet. Life lessons such as co-operating, being truthful, and listening were explored, and every episode contained a reoccurring motif of someone finding a pair of polka dot shorts and exclaiming, "A great big pair of polka dot shorts! How did they get there?" after which the Polkaroo would reply, "I haven't the foggiest." Sweet, but certainly not as memorable as "… And I missed him, *again*?").

Polka Dot Shorts was clearly aimed at an even younger audience than *Polka Dot Door*, and there was grumbling from some older viewers who had grown up with Ted Coneybeare's iteration of *Polka Dot Door*. Initially the show included a wraparound segment featuring a host reading stories to children, but it was phased out to maximize the short run time.

The series chalked up an impressive 180 episodes, and ran until 2001, after which time many of the characters transitioned to another TVO preschool series, *Gisèle's Big Backyard* (2006). Many of the series performers had ballet or circus backgrounds, such as Charles P. Schott, who portrayed Bear. Voices of actors were later dubbed in, including *The Edison Twins*' Andrew Sabiston as the voice of Polkaroo, allowing the show to easily be versioned for foreign markets. *Polka Dot Shorts* was well received in the U.K., airing on Children's BBC (CBBC). After BBC's *Play School* had helped launch TVO in 1970 by inspiring the creation of *Polka Dot Door*, there is an appealing symmetry in its warm reception, bringing the whole enterprise full circle.

111
The Brainwash (1995)

BEGINNING IN 1995, YTV CONDUCTED AN ANNUAL RESEARCH report that soon became the industry standard, *The YTV Kid & Tween Report*, tracking lifestyles, attitudes, opinions, motivations, and consumption behaviours of nine-to-fourteen-year-olds across Canada. Similar in theory to Ruth Vernon's pursuit of educational and entertainment parity through targeted research at TVOntario, YTV's approach was enormous in scope but much more commercially driven. This vast research undertaking soon landed on a single word that best summarized the era, a unifying message that would inform the channel's headspace for the remainder of the nineties: "weird."

By the mid-1990s, YTV was dominating the youth space and was seen in an estimated seven million homes across Canada. Since it was forbidden for YTV to air any drama featuring a lead protagonist over the age of eighteen as a condition of its broadcast licence, and seeing as it was mandated that at least 60 percent of its output be Canadian, it was deeply invested in domestic productions, such as the Grogs specials and the YTV Achievement Awards that raised the profile of children on television. The network also took risks, including broadcasting the 1995 NBA Draft live on-air, out-scooping CTV and TSN, with PJ Phil providing courtside commentary.

The influence of YTV's program-jockey gambit was felt across the medium, with TVOntario and CTV aping the format. CTV's spin was called "BBS Master Control" and had even poached former PJ Jenn Beech from YTV. Over at Global Television, younger children aged nine to twelve were used for a hosted cartoon block entitled "Kids TV." In 1995, YTV added The Breakfast Zone (or B-Zone) hosted by the frenetic PJ Paul (Paul McGuire) for early-morning PJ mayhem. YTV's preschool block The Treehouse was now hosted by the Fuzzpaws puppets (operated and voiced by Marty Stelnick), PJ Krista

(Krista Jackson), PJ Todd (Todd Doldersum), and PJ Katie (Jennifer Racicot, named Katie as there had already been a "PJ Jenn"). Katie filled much of her airtime manipulating small plastic animals for a segment dubbed "PJ Katie's Farm," where she also provided the animals distinct voices and characters. The popularity of this segment led to the commissioning of a spinoff series, *PJ Katie's Farm* (1998), produced by Nelvana. The Fuzzpaws were also given their own series in 1998, as well as a plush toy line.

YTV's weekend block — now titled The Brainwash — was hosted by musician and puppeteer Ali Eisner as Carrie Funkwash (*Nanalan'*) and Shaun Majumder as Ed Brainbin. The Brainwash was produced by Kim J. Saltarski (B-Zone) and Atul N. Rao (YTV's *Snit*) and featured the hosts soliciting kids to send in lint. Rao recalled:

> We started the lint brain, and it became this national phenomenon. Kids sending dryer lint to YTV. And we kept putting it together to make this gigantic brain. Of course, we had to put a stop to it because there was nowhere to store it. We were getting letters from mothers saying the kids are wanting to help out with the laundry just so they can get some lint.[48]

112

The Anti-Gravity Room (1995)

IN 1993, ELEVEN-YEAR-OLD NICK SCOULLAR WAS A GIGANTIC comic-book aficionado who had his own public access television show *TALKCOMICS* in New York City, where he talked about comics and took live calls on-air. Producers at Fremantle, a U.K.-based production and distribution company, took notice and pitched it to YTV as a co-production that could get airplay in the U.S. on the fledgling Sci-Fi Channel.

YTV remodelled Scoullar's program as *The Anti-Gravity Room* (*AGR*), a magazine show looking at not only comic books, but also science-fiction films, video games, technology, and all things culty. Scoullar remained in NYC as a host, while YTV produced segments with Phil Guerrero (who was doing double duty as PJ Phil on YTV's The Zone) in Toronto and beyond (they would occasionally intersect at conventions and movie premieres).

It is hard to fathom, but no one in broadcasting was catering to the very large "nerd" demographic. TVOntario's *Prisoners of Gravity* (1989), a truly brilliant series in its own right, had tried its hand at populist genres but carried a highbrow literary air aimed at older viewers. *AGR* went wherever the hardcore fans were: *Star Trek* conventions, movie premieres, celebrity signings, software expos, etc. The show featured a veritable who's who of nerd-dom, including Kevin Smith, Alan Moore, Todd McFarlane, Stan Lee, Mark Hamill, Janeane Garofalo, and even a pre–Jennifer Lopez Ben Affleck. *AGR* producer Chris Greaves remembers the crew attending the San Diego Comic-Con before it became an overblown multi-genre media frenzy:

> The first time we went to San Diego by the way, the main floor was still comic book trading. Like, it was guys with milk crates trading comic books. That was the main floor. I think I saw Weezer play in a parking lot.[49]

Building a network of correspondents and interview subjects, *AGR* became an unmissable weekly event for genre fans of all ages, even if it was aimed at youngsters. The show was a massive success for YTV, attaining ratings between 350,000 and 400,000 per week, and close to two million on the Sci-Fi Channel in the U.S. "It was actually earning the network money!" recalls Greaves. After five seasons, *AGR* was spun off into *Warp* (1999), a slightly more comical look at the world of fandom, which broke the fourth wall by including behind-the-scenes footage of the crew. A similar YTV magazine-style series focused entirely on video games, *GamerZ* (1998), also starred Guerrero, and featured co-hosts Susan Quinn and Sarah Bywater.

113
Mr. Dressup Says Goodbye (1996)

MR. DRESSUP ULTIMATELY CAME TO AN END IN 1996, AFTER twenty-nine years on the air and the production of three thousand plus episodes. For star Ernie Coombs, it had been thirty-two years non-stop of playing the character who originated in *Butternut Square* (1964). Original Casey and Finnegan puppeteer and kindred spirit Judith Lawrence, with whom Coombs had an almost telepathic connection, retired in 1989, but Coombs felt a duty to carry on their gentle crusade as children's television grew louder and courser. Rather than risking trauma by having beloved puppets Casey and Finnegan depart between episodes, their goodbye was long and signposted for months. Even before Lawrence left, a new cast of puppet characters emerged to transition viewers away from the past: Truffles, performed by Nina Keogh; Chester the Crow (Karen Valleau); Lorenzo the Raccoon (Bob Dermer); Granny (Jani Lauzon); Annie (Ruth Danziger); and Alex (Jim Parker, Coombs's long-time touring co-star, see p. 200) all joined the show to give it a new dimension for the 1990s. But even when the show concluded in 1996, it was still fundamentally the same show as had premiered back in 1967.

While the world had changed dramatically, *Mr. Dressup* remained an immutable time-locked constant, not only an aberration in the dynamic world of

Guest Jim Parker rocks out with Mr. Dressup (Ernie Coombs) in the twilight days of *Mr. Dressup*.

television but the last connection to Fred Rainsberry's era of CBC. "We know our way is as right for our audience as the other shows are for theirs,"[50] Coombs once said when pressed why he didn't accelerate the pace of *Mr. Dressup*.

During his final weeks on-air, tributes for Coombs and the show poured in: "He's such a wonderful person," his old friend Fred Rogers told *Starweek* magazine. "I'm just delighted in his success."[51] Lois Lilienstein from the children's folk trio Sharon, Lois & Bram spoke for them all: "To all of us, Ernie Coombs is in the pantheon of greats. His personality resonates with gentleness, caring and kindness. We wish he could go on forever."[52] Bob Homme, the Friendly Giant and a fellow American caught in the Rainsberry draft, said, "We bounced off the same kind of shows that were popular when we both began. Our shows were different, but we saw our television audience as sitting in one of two or three small chairs so you could communicate directly to them."[53]

A two-and-a-half-hour "*Mr. Dressup* Holiday Special" aired on December 24, 1997, featuring Coombs cheering up children at SickKids Hospital in Toronto with songs and presents, alongside National Film Board shorts like *The Sweater* (1967), and cameos from Nina Keogh as Truffles and Alyson Court as Loonette from *The Big Comfy Couch* (1992). Coombs continued to tour his live *Mr. Dressup* show across Canada with Parker, but once *Mr. Dressup* left the airwaves, children's television was never really the same again.

114
Sesame Park (1996)

IN FALL 1996, THE CBC'S HEAD OF CHILDREN'S PROGRAMMING, Peter Moss, announced the arrival of a new, thirty-minute all-Canadian edition of *Sesame Street*:

> My own kids grew up on the original *Sesame Street*, but we decided it was time to put the pro-social messages of the show and its wonderful pedagogy — the skills of literacy and numeracy — into a Canadian context. There isn't a Canadian city where you can go more than about six blocks without finding a safe, green park. So, it became *Sesame Park*.[54]

Moss had come to the network after serving eleven years as artistic director of Toronto's Young People's Theatre, a creative hatchery for many talented Toronto performers and producers, founded in 1966 by Susan Douglas Rubeš, wife of Jan Rubeš. *Sesame Park* retained the magazine format of the mother series, with segments running an average of three and a half minutes long, as well as the series' iconic characters such as Big Bird, Cookie Monster, Grover, and Bert and Ernie.

The long incubation period for *Sesame Park* started back in 1972 with the creation of *Sesame Street Canada*, spearheaded by CBC's former head of children's programming Daniel McCarthy, who over the next decade recruited many of the show's production team from the thriving Toronto broadcast scene. Based on the success of his TVOntario math series *Math Patrol* (1977), Clive VanderBurgh was hired as an independent producer to create new content for *Sesame Street Canada* in 1978. For this assignment, his experience working with Ruth Vernon's curriculum-minded approach at TVO served him well. VanderBurgh recalls:

> They'd had a heck of a time getting any scripts approved, because there was no experience in Canada writing cognitively based segments. You know, *Mr. Dressup* and the other shows tended to be socially oriented as opposed to cognitively oriented, not so much math and spelling and key concepts. So, they had trouble. They were shocked when I submitted a bunch of scripts and they were all accepted, because normally they had trouble getting anything through. So, they hired me to write and compose and direct segments for a number of years.[55]

By 1981, the amount of Canadian content within an episode of *Canadian Sesame Street* was averaging almost fifty percent, and by 1987 featured three uniquely Canadian puppets created by the Jim Henson Workshop and operated by Noreen Young — Basil the Bear, Louis the Otter, and Dodi the bush pilot, named after pioneering children's author and broadcaster Dodi Robb (*Telestory Time*, *Polka Dot Door*). Additional characters were added each successive season.

In December 1990, "Basil Hears a Noise," a sixty-minute seasonal Christmas special, aired in CBC prime time, written by Barbara Nichol and featuring music and lyrics by VanderBurgh. Notably it featured the character of Elmo, who was slowly usurping Big Bird as *Sesame Street*'s most prevalent resident. The special opened with a dedication to Henson, who had passed away in May of that year.

By 1996, new episodes contained over 60 percent original Canadian content and the decision was made to retitle the program *Sesame Park*. The series ran until 2001, when Sesame Workshop (formerly the Children's Television Workshop) decided to cancel all international co-productions and produce everything in-house. Owing to the complexity of *Sesame Street*/*Sesame Park*'s entwined ownership of intellectual property, most of these segments have not been seen since they originally aired. However, the Christmas special "Basil Hears a Noise" was released on home video in 1993, with a more commercial title, "Elmo in Basil Hears a Noise: A Musical Adventure," with Elmo featured prominently on the cover.

115
Treehouse TV (1997)

ON NOVEMBER 1, 1997, YTV'S NEW SPECIALTY CABLE CHANNEL Treehouse TV began transmitting twenty-four-hour commercial-free programming aimed exclusively at a preschool audience. The licence for a dedicated preschool cable service had been competitive, with rival applications coming from the National Film Board of Canada, the CBC, Global Television, and Owl Communications, the publishers of *OWL*, *Chirp*, and *Chickadee* magazines. YTV obtained the licence based on its almost decade-long commitment to quality broadcasting, and the new channel was named after its morning preschool block The Treehouse, which was retired and rebranded YTV Jr. the following year.

This new venture, however, would forgo YTV's signature human or puppet program jockeys, opting for sentient toys instead. Since the channel was commercial-free, programming could be broken up by the Treetownies — Tansy (Kathleen LeRoux), Rosabelle (Denise Shaw), and the Treetown toys. Susan Ross, vice-president and general manager of Treehouse, explained, "The idea of a Treehouse was a springboard to enable us to create a magical place, Treetown, where the various characters representing the network lived — Tansy, Rosabelle, Cush, Osbert, Stu and others."[56] In the early days, Treehouse TV's marquee imports were *Barney & Friends* and *Blue's Clues* (1996), but the channel also gave a home to new and old Canadian shows, such as the final airing of *Today's Special* (1981) in Canada, *Ants in Your Pants* (1997), and *Little Bear* (1995).

Less than one month earlier, another specialty cable channel aimed at children and teenagers arrived in Canada: Teletoon launched on October 17, 1997, and broadcast primarily animated series. Headquartered on Bay Street in Toronto, Teletoon was owned by a group that included Astral Media (via the Family Channel), Shaw Communications (via YTV), and Canadian animation studios Nelvana and Cinar. The arrival of Teletoon further splintered YTV's nine-to-fourteen-year-old audience and created even more viewing options, just as youth culture became an increasingly substantial part of mainstream culture no longer contained in after-school or Saturday-morning programming blocks, or a box to be ticked on a regulatory to-do list. For the first time ever, there were whole television networks broadcasting 24/7, publishers, games divisions, movie studios, and commercial producers dedicated solely to creating original and compelling content for youth.

After the establishment of Treehouse TV, YTV Jr. debuted in the fall of 1998 in a new format that eschewed program jockeys for short-form original content that could serve as interstitials between programs (YTV Jr. remained commercial-free). The vice-president of programming for both YTV and Treehouse TV, Peter Moss, who had come to the network after serving as creative director of Toronto's Young People's Theatre, head of children's programming at CBC, and an executive producer at the Children's Television Workshop, began to retool YTV Jr.'s output so that it would better compliment the new Treehouse TV network. Moss offered the remaining PJs from YTV's Treehouse an opportunity to create their own short-form series. PJ Krista, PJ Katie, and PJ Simon (a.k.a. Jamie Shannon, a Grogs puppeteer) all pitched new programs — *My Special Book*, *Pet Squad*, and *Nanalan'* respectively. They were greenlit and went into production to become part of the YTV Jr. schedule the following year.

116
Keep It Weird (1998)

DARYN JONES, RISING STAR OF ROGERS TELEVISION'S CABLE 10 in Toronto, signed on as a regular host of YTV's The Zone, while the network's iconic PJ Phil Guerrero was slowly phased out due to his age and other work commitments (*The Anti-Gravity Room* and *GamerZ*). Based on Jones's cult man-on-the-street cable series *Buzz* (1997), The Zone added a new segment called "The Roving Eye," where he spent more time out of the studio and on location interacting with everyday kids and random celebrities. Snit, the beloved Zone co-host, had been sensationally blasted into outer space on Halloween day in 1997, but returned in 1999 as the host of his own block entitled "Snit Station" (Kendra FitzRandolph appeared as his sidekick, and Snit was played by Anand Rajaram), which replaced The Brainwash (1995).

When speaking to *Playback* magazine on the network's tenth anniversary in 1998, president Paul Robertson signalled a change in the network's branding, informed by research:

> We always knew we had to constantly evolve. The alternative is to risk having the kids think that you're last year's news. It's been typical at YTV that in 10 short years, there has been extraordinary innovation in our look, our presentation and the increased quality of programming. It was natural for us to take it up a notch. We had used "You rule" for five or six years. We felt that in a world where we were the only kid's network, "You Rule" was compelling. But with so many choices now available for the kids we felt we had to have something that would distinguish YTV and would capture kids' imagination. So based on our research, we came up with "Keep it Weird."[57]

In 1998, Shaw Communications secured full control of YTV, spinning it and other Shaw media assets (including Treehouse TV) into Corus Entertainment in 1999. In early 2000, PJs Phil and Paul were found to be not Y2K compliant and exited The Zone, and YTV altogether. They were replaced by comedian Pat Kelly and Jenny "Katie" Racicot, who had previously appeared as PJ Katie on The Treehouse. Looking back on his pivotal time at YTV, Snit's defining operator and voice Atul N. Rao reflected,

> YTV in those days was the Wild West. It was the freest. It'll never be like that ever again, and it was never like that ever before. YTV of the nineties, the late nineties especially, we got into areas and got into things ... TV still has never caught up, and it probably won't.[58]

117
Skinnamarink TV (1998)

WHEN SKETCH COMEDY INFILTRATED CHILDREN'S TELEVISION in the early 1990s, much lip service was paid to the broad influence of *Saturday Night Live*, but it wasn't until later in the decade that producers fully embraced the even more locally salted *Second City Television* (1976). Besides launching the stratospheric careers of John Candy, Eugene Levy, Catherine O'Hara, Martin Short, Dave Thomas, Rick Moranis, Harold Ramis, and Joe Flaherty, *SCTV*'s defining genius was in its concept — a fictional television station broadcasting in Melonville, a premise that allowed the troupe to riff on soap operas, commercials, newscasters, public service announcements, old films, and even mandated CanCon in the form of Bob and Doug McKenzie's Great White North (originally known as "Kanadian Korner").

As the target demographic became much more media literate, the conceit of sketch comedy for kids using a similar set-up became irresistible. *Skinnamarink TV* (1998) found kid-friendly singing trio of Sharon Hampson, Lois Lilienstein, and Bram Morrison operating a zany television station that aired a mishmash of genre spoofs. Their targets ranged from cooking to exercise shows, and even personalities, including a takeoff on Uncle Chichimus's old sparring partner Percy Saltzman in the character of weatherman Percy P. Tation. According to Morrison:

> There's a big, not so secret secret about *Skinnamarink TV* and we didn't even realize it at the time, and it's only in retrospect that we realized that it was a children's version of *Second City Television*.[59]

The trio relished playing multiple roles, while still engaging the audience through their music as they had their whole career. Hampson remembers that while the television industry might have changed in the late 1990s, Sharon, Lois & Bram had not:

> Music was always at the centre of what we did. Providing good quality music for our audience. In *Skinnamarink TV*, there were solos and duets and different combinations of us singing together, which happened more often than on *The Elephant Show* (1984).[60]

Skinnamarink TV ran for two seasons on CBC and released a Juno Award–winning album of the same name in 1998. Reflecting on the success of both Sharon, Lois & Bram television series, Hampson believes,

> People liked working on our shows. Someone used the word "wholesome" almost as if it is a dirty word, but I like that

> word. And I think that's why our shows were successful, [they were] wholesome. It was good people being nice to each other, being fun and kooky, all of that.[61]

118
System Crash (1999)

THE ADULATION OF *SCTV* CONTINUED IN 1999 ON YTV IN THE Josh Morris creation *System Crash*, showcasing a group of kids who use a media club to report on and lambaste life at their high school. Talking to the *Montreal Gazette*, Morris said:

> I'm a defender of shows made for kids that reinforce positive values and think kids' television is one of the highest quality and most innovative branches of television in the world, but it is not hermetically sealed. Children can still flick to WWF Wrestling, the news, or *South Park*.[62]

The subversive series acknowledged an increased media literacy among its core audience of ten-to-twelve-year-olds, the fabled "tweens" who became the most prized demographic of 1990s television programmers. Morris's vast experience working in the genre on everything from the didactic to the disgusting served him well in understanding what kids wanted to watch. Morris recalled,

> At the time, I think YTV was going through a bit of an identity crisis because on the one hand, they were trying to sort of mix the "eat your greens" kind of shows and the growth shows as one, and it didn't work. You could really only be one or the other. It would be very hard to have both.[63]

In 1998, Morris had begun pre-production on the suitably named sketch-comedy series *Gag Me*, his attempt to bottle *You Can't Do That on Television!*–style lightning for YTV as a triumphant return to the network after years rebuilding the children's department at TVOntario. Starting in 1998, YTV's Keep It Weird! campaign ushered in a wave of gross-out imagery and sounds based on the research collected by their annual *YTV Kid & Tween Report*. However, when a controlling share in YTV was purchased by Shaw Communications (also in 1998), just weeks before production was set to start, new management scrapped *Gag Me* and signalled that the network was moving away from the gross-out humour that had started to define it. Morris created the still edgy but less slime-ridden *System Crash* as its replacement, and local Toronto actor Nathaniel Siegler, a *Gag Me* holdover, was cast as Nathan Burnbaum, the series resident John Candy–vibes man.

> The humour on *System Crash* was a fair bit more sophisticated than *Gag Me*, with many of the sketches coming from classic Canadian TV. An interview bit in the style of Brian Linehan, a crime-reenactment show just like *Crime Stoppers*, and of course my recurring segment, Burnbaum Helps, which was an obvious nod to [Citytv's] *Silverman Helps*.[64]

Unfortunately, the new executive environment at YTV favoured the burgeoning Disney sitcom style of shows like *Student Bodies* (1997), *Breaker High* (1997), and *Radio Active* (1998) over Morris's postmodern *Degrassi*-meets-*SCTV*. Although not heavily promoted, modest ratings and word of mouth kept it alive for four seasons. Speaking of Morris's contribution to children's television, Siegler says: "He's a Canadian television legend that in my opinion doesn't get the credit he deserves." [65]

119
Nanalan' (1999)

AFTER A WILD DECADE THAT TOOK THEM FROM MERE HOI polloi birthday-party performers to revered Henson-status artists at the vanguard of Canada's budding children's network YTV, puppeteering duo Jamie Shannon and Jason Hopley — The Grogs — delivered one final televisual treasure before the twentieth century concluded.

Offered a shot at creating original three-minute interstitials for YTV Jr., the newly branded hostless preschool block on YTV, Shannon dug deep within his soul to take inspiration from warm and fuzzy memories of playing at his nana's house as a young child. He and Hopley created Mona, a curious three-year-old with an adventurous nature, and her co-conspirator in fun, a wise dog named Russell, or "Russer," belonging to Mona's grandmother, Nana. The title was a portmanteau of "Nana" and "Land," referring to the wonderous world that existed in Nana's backyard. "We both had these really quirky Nanas and fond memories of being in our Nana's house," Hopley told *The Globe and Mail* in 2024. "We also started trying to break apart what is really important for an almost-three-year-old and we realized that being a little kid in the world, everything is exciting. Those two things combined became what *Nanalan'* really was."[66]

The sweet and simple series harkened back to the very beginnings of television in Toronto, when CBC's first head of children's programming, Fred Rainsberry, enlisted entertainers like Bob Homme, Fred Rogers, and Ernie Coombs to come to Toronto. The shows they produced here — *The Friendly Giant* (1958), *Misterogers* (1962), and ultimately *Mr. Dressup* (1967) — favoured emotional growth over rote pedagogy. They fostered imagination and wonder, all through the lens of ordinary relatable things. "We just wanted to make a show that teaches emotional intelligence and how to experience your emotions,"[67] Shannon said in 2024.

Above: Jason Hopley as Nana and Jamie Shannon as Mona in *Nanalan'* (1999), Shannon's delightfully zen ode to memories of playing in his nana's back garden.

Below: Everyone loves their nana! Nana, Mona, and Russer (Russell) in *Nanalan'* (1999).

Like many of the best local puppet shows before it, much of *Nanalan'* was ad libbed and improvised. There were no special effects or computers; even the titles were cutouts on sticks. It celebrated practical puppetry in a way that recalled John Conway and Norman Jewison's joyous collaborative work on *Uncle Chichimus* (1952). Shannon operated and voiced Mona, while Hopley was Nana and Ali J. Eisner was Russell. YTV's Fuzzpaws creator Marty Stelnick appeared as Mona's mother, Mrs. Bea.

Nanalan' was later picked up by the CBC, which debuted longer, twenty-four-minute episodes in 2003. However, it wasn't until twenty years later, in 2023, when the show finally got its due, thanks to going viral on TikTok, where hashtag #nanalan garnered over 320 million views.[68] Shannon and Hopley "put the old band back together" and began filming new instalments of the series for YouTube, TikTok, Instagram, and the personalized video site Cameo. "I think the show resonates so well this time around because of its simple, pure essence," Shannon told Canadian Newswire in 2024 in a story announcing *Nanalan*'s partnership with the Canadian Mental Health Association (CMHA) to highlight the power of compassion.

Like so many other Toronto children's series, *Nanalan'* was ahead of its time. But there was wonderful symmetry with its appearance in 1999: At the end of the millennium, Toronto kids' TV had truly come full circle — starting and finishing with the extraordinary exploits of a little green puppet.

Acknowledgements

I WOULD LIKE TO SINCERELY THANK THE FOLLOWING INDIVIDuals and organizations for their inspiration, assistance, and unwavering support during the production of this book:

Sarah Tunney, Ellie Conroy, Aiden Conroy, Fiona and Eric Conroy, Catharine & Kevin Tunney, Nina Keogh (the godmother of Canadian kids' TV!), Agathon Fric, Peter Kenter, Paul Rainsberry, Dale Taylor, Steve Cichon, Beau Levitt, Clive VanderBurgh, Jennifer VanderBurgh, Stuart Hands, Steve Paikin, Noreen Young, Jeff Morris, Gary Eisler, Olga Kuplowska, Travis Doucette, Susan Mawhood (Murgatroyd), Louise Murgatroyd, Mike Cutting, Meredith Cutting, Meta and Paul Hoepfner-Homme, Christopher Coombs, Cathie LeFort, Greg Oliver, Olivier Côté, Natalie Coulter, Kris Stengele, Sharon Hampson, Randi Hampson, Bram Morrison, Christopher Greaves, Phil Guerrero, Jamie Shannon, Robyn Hall, Eric Bilodeau, Library and Archives Canada, Jim Huber, Dusty Langois, Gary Clement, Jed MacKay, Jeanne Beker, Risa Shuman, Clive Endersby, Barry Kent MacKay, Emily A. Uhrin, Ted Kulczycky and Serah-Marie McMahon, Martin Laba, Jean Mathieson-Guest, Karen Gifford, Rick Ambrozic, Carrie Loring, Jim Codrington, Bobby Dermer, Jim Parker, John Sobol, Charles Levi and Rachel Delle Palme, Steve Gaskin, Mikey Artelle, Linda Steele, David Moore, Patty Sullivan, Kevin Shea, Mr. Phillips (Fairmount Public School), Sue Sheridan,

Owen Gottlieb, Museum of Toronto, Heidi Reitmaier, Christine Elson, Bria Dietrich, Kamran Dadi, Nadine Villasin Feldman, Breanne Gimza, Davin Henson, Emma Stirling, Rex Hagon, Dick Derhodge, Atul N. Rao, Nathaniel Sielger, Rose Oushalkas and Christopher Dew, Rache Julkowski, Ariadne Dunn, Aubray Lynas, Sara Chan, Rick Upton, Judith Gilman, Gairey-Wayne Richardson, Beth Lowery, Marc Weisblott, Ben (@hwdsbedarchives), Morgan White, Justin Lee, Dave Hodgson, Moses Znaimer, Joel Goldberg, Carolyn Stewart, MZTV Museum of Television, "Toronto Mike" Boon, Blake Markle (The "Maths"), Stephen Ellis, Rick Watts, Derek Flack, Tim Shore, Scott Brian Woods, Gareth Grainger, Rob Preuss, Steven Kerzner (for confirming Ed the Sock was not based on Uncle Chichimus), Matthew O'Mara, Peter Van Rijn, Dave Keast, Robert McCallum, the amazing team at Dundurn (including Meghan Macdonald, Kathryn Lane, Jess Shulman, Laura Boyle, Janna Green, and Elena Radic), and to all of the followers, subscribers, viewers, and fans of @Retrontario. Stay tuned!

Also, the incredible Toronto television critics whose dedicated work on the beat provided immeasurable help while I rummaged around different eras — E.H. Hausmann, Sid Adilman, Blaik Kirby, Ron Base, Jim Bawden, Sandy Greer, Lousie Brown, and Bill Brioux.

And finally, to the many people who made these beloved television shows — a profound thank you on behalf of all your viewers for helping to make our childhoods extra special.

Notes

Epigraph

1 Rogers, *Beautiful Day in the Neighborhood*, 164.
2 McIntyre, "From Crass to Crash."

Introduction

1 VanderBurgh, *What Television Remembers*, 180.
2 Conroy, "About Retrontario."
3 "About Us," Museum of Toronto.
4 *Mr. Dressup to Degrassi*, Museum of Toronto.
5 Yeo, "TV Treasure Trove."
6 Dymond and Pevere, *Mondo Canuck*, 116.
7 Coulter, "'Missed Opportunity.'"
8 Obituary — Rainsberry.

1950s

1 Cole, *Here's Looking at Us*, 17.
2 Cole, *Here's Looking at Us*, 10.
3 Cole, *Here's Looking at Us*, 10.
4 Conway, interview.
5 Conway, interview.
6 Rainsberry, *History of Children's Television*, 7.
7 Jewison, interview.
8 Jewison, interview.
9 Jewison, interview.
10 Jewison, interview.
11 Rainsberry, *History of Children's Television*, 9.
12 "Uncle Chichimus, Hollyhock Kidnapped," *Toronto Daily Star*.
13 Rainsberry, *History of Children's Television*, 6–7.
14 Houle, "Uncle Chichimus."
15 Jewison, interview.
16 Conway, interview.
17 Harris, "Science Fiction TV."
18 Robb, interview.
19 Rainsberry, *History of Children's Television*, 174.
20 Rainsberry, *History of Children's Television*, 174.
21 Rainsberry, *History of Children's Television*, 12.
22 Rainsberry, *History of Children's Television*, 47.
23 Rainsberry, *History of Children's Television*, 16.
24 Rainsberry, *History of Children's Television*, 17.
25 Chapman, interview.
26 Chapman, interview.
27 "Old Testament Stories," *CBC Times*.
28 Spivak, interview.
29 McKay, *Puppetry in Canada*.
30 Rainsberry, *History of Children's Television*, 64.
31 Homme, interview.
32 Fairley, *Look Up — Way Up!*, 26.
33 Homme, interview.
34 Homme, interview.
35 Fairley, *Look Up — Way Up!*, 64.
36 Fairley, *Look Up — Way Up!*, 63.
37 Coneybeare, interview.

38 Coneybeare, interview.
39 Homme, interview.
40 Homme, interview.
41 Lunn, "Friendly Giant Who Won't Be Hurried."
42 Charles, "Childwatch."
43 Kenter, *TV North*, 61.
44 "Fables of La Fontaine," *CBC Times*.

1960s

1 Krantz, interview.
2 Krantz, interview.
3 Krantz, interview.
4 Krantz, interview.
5 CTV News, "About CTV News Toronto."
6 "No More Quiz Wealth," *Toronto Star*.
7 "No More Quiz Wealth," *Toronto Star*.
8 Robb, interview.
9 Braithwaite, "Professor's Fadeaway."
10 Gollom, "Uncle Bobby Still Performs."
11 King, "Send in the Clown."
12 Brioux, "Today at brioux.tv."
13 Dempsey, "Uncle Bobby Meets Some Fans."
14 Bawden, "Kids Loved Uncle Bobby's TV Show."
15 MacKay, B.K., interview.
16 Gollom, "Uncle Bobby Still Performs."
17 MacKay, B.K., interview.
18 Crosby, interview.
19 King, *The Good Neighbor*, 144.
20 King, *The Good Neighbor*, 141.
21 Chapman, interview.
22 Chapman, interview.
23 Gibbons, interview.
24 Chapman, interview.
25 Rogers, interview.
26 Coombs, interview.
27 Adilman, "No More Kidding Around."
28 Coombs, interview.
29 Coombs, interview.
30 Gilchrist, interview.
31 Gilchrist, interview.
32 Conroy, "History of the Mr. Dressup."
33 Cole, *Here's Looking at Us*, 160.
34 Gibbons, interview.
35 Coombs, interview.
36 Gilchrist, interview.
37 Yost, interview.
38 Kenter, *TV North*, 149.
39 Yost, interview.
40 Stewart, *Here's Looking at Us*, 256.
41 Coneybeare, interview.
42 Gilchrist, interview.
43 Gilchrist, interview.
44 Hausmann, "Bananas."
45 Kenter, *TV North*, 10.
46 Kenter, *TV North*, 2.

1970s

1 Rainsberry, *History of Children's Television*, 184.
2 "TV Listings," *Starweek*, 1969.
3 Scott, "TV's Finest Route Is Sesame Street."
4 Scott, "TV's Finest Route Is Sesame Street."
5 Scott, "TV's Finest Route Is Sesame Street."
6 Scott, "TV's Finest Route Is Sesame Street."
7 Scott, "CBC Stuck with Sesame Street."
8 Scott, "CBC Stuck with Sesame Street."
9 Stoffman, "Sesame Street Won't Be Canadianized."
10 Stoffman, "Sesame Street Won't Be Canadianized."
11 Stoffman, "Sesame Street Won't Be Canadianized."
12 Nash, *Prime Time at Ten*, 127.
13 Chapman, interview.
14 Ide, *Transparent Blackboard*, 9.
15 Ide, *Transparent Blackboard*, 52.
16 Novakowski, interview.
17 Ide, *Transparent Blackboard*, 52.
18 Novakowski, interview.
19 Ide, *Transparent Blackboard*, 53.
20 Derhodge, interview.
21 "Polka Dot Door Themes," TVOntario.
22 Teachman, "Polka Dot Door."
23 Ide, *Transparent Blackboard*, 227.
24 Kenter, *TV North*, 22.
25 *School Broadcasts K–8*.
26 Patrick-Roberts, interview.
27 Harpur, "For Heaven's Sake."

28 Allan, "CBC Television Series, 1952–1982."
29 Elder, interview.
30 Evans, interview.
31 VanderBurgh, interview, 2024.
32 Gottlieb, interview
33 Sobol, interview.
34 Yost, interview.
35 Shuman, interview.
36 *School Broadcasts K–8.*
37 Novakowski, interview.
38 "Children's TV," *Toronto Daily Star.*
39 "TV Listings," *Broadcast Week*, 1975.
40 "TV Listings," *Starweek*, 1975.
41 VanderBurgh, interview, 2024.
42 Novakowski, interview.
43 Farrell, "How Young View TV."
44 VanderBurgh, interview, 2024.
45 Kirby, "Supershow Not Really Super."
46 Kirby, "Supershow Not Really Super."
47 Ide, *Transparent Blackboard*, 129
48 Cole, "Reiner Schwarz 1948–2014."
49 "TVOntario," Canada Modern.
50 Ide, *Transparent Blackboard*, 135.
51 Ide, *Transparent Blackboard*, 147.
52 Sobol, interview.
53 Ide, *Transparent Blackboard*, 149.
54 VanderBurgh, interview, 2024.
55 VanderBurgh, interview, 2024.
56 Elston, "Math Patrol [comment]."
57 VanderBurgh, interview, 2024.
58 Carr, "OECA Is Getting to Everybody."
59 *School Broadcasts K–8.*
60 *School Broadcasts K–8.*
61 Ide, *Transparent Blackboard*, 56.
62 Ide, *Transparent Blackboard*, 229.
63 Boiteau, interview.
64 Donaldson, "Star Trek to Literacy."
65 Donaldson, "Star Trek to Literacy."
66 Donaldson, "Star Trek to Literacy."
67 Houle, "Zachary Houle Interview with Jeremy Pollock."
68 Donaldson, "Star Trek to Literacy."
69 Donaldson, "Star Trek to Literacy."
70 Endersby, interview.
71 Teachman, "Read All About It," 21.
72 Teachman, "Read All About It," 21.
73 Houle, "Zachary Houle Interview with Jeremy Pollock," 252.
74 Houle, "Zachary Houle Interview with Jeremy Pollock."
75 Kuplowska, "Read All About It! in Mississippi," 3.
76 Ide, *Transparent Blackboard*, 134.
77 Lundy, *Camp TVOntario.*
78 Adilman, "CFTO Mute about Mutt's New Series."
79 Base, "Two Kids and a Dog."
80 Hawkes, "Teaching Old Dogs New Tricks."
81 Kitching, "Rocker Who Wrote."
82 Boeckh, "Entertaining the Kids."
83 Cutting, interview.
84 MacKay, B.K., interview.
85 MacKay, B.K., interview.
86 Grainger, interview.
87 Gollom, "Uncle Bobby Still Performs."
88 CBC Archives, "The Canadian TV Channel."
89 Shea, interview.

1980s

1 Rainsberry, *History of Children's Television*, 123.
2 Giorno, "De Grassi, the Story Behind the Name."
3 Bawden, "CBC's Sunday Kid Series."
4 Greer, "Parents Shouldn't Use TV as a Scapegoat."
5 Schuyler, *Mother of All Degrassi*, 162.
6 "TVOntario Summer Academy [brochure]."
7 Shea, interview.
8 "Archived – Public Notice CRTC 84-138," Government of Canada.
9 VanderBurgh, interview, 2024.
10 VanderBurgh, "Pre-School Pilot Proposal."
11 VanderBurgh, "Pre-School Pilot Proposal."
12 VanderBurgh, "Pre-School Pilot Proposal."
13 VanderBurgh, interview, 2024.
14 VanderBurgh, "Pre-School Pilot Proposal."
15 Krantz, interview.

16 VanderBurgh, interview, 1983.
17 VanderBurgh, interview, 1983.
18 Godard, "Today's Special Yesterday's Production."
19 McBride and Shields, "Nobody's Second Banana."
20 "Molding Healthy Viewing Habits," *Starweek*.
21 *School Broadcasts K–8.*
22 "Read All About It!," Rick's TV.
23 Endersby, interview.
24 Bunch, "Down at Fraggle Rock … In Yorkville."
25 Jones, *Jim Henson*, 581.
26 Jones, *Jim Henson*, 607.
27 Levitch, "Gaggle of Fraggles."
28 Stein, "Count Writes a Haiku."
29 Rainsberry, *A History of Children's Television*, 215.
30 Taylor, "Maestros."
31 Adilman, "CBC's Fraggles Rocking the Ratings."
32 Jones, *Jim Henson*, 609.
33 Conroy, "How Scarborough Once Had the Largest McDonald's."
34 Sobol, interview.
35 Segarini, "Bob Recalls the Tale of Chops Dorfman."
36 Morrison and Hampson, interview.
37 Morrison and Hampson, interview.
38 Morrison and Hampson, interview.
39 Morrison and Hampson, interview.
40 Bardoel, "Sharon, Lois and Bram Riding High!"
41 Bardoel, "Sharon, Lois and Bram Riding High!"
42 Bardoel, "Sharon, Lois and Bram Riding High!"
43 Morrison and Hampson, interview.
44 Morrison and Hampson, interview.
45 Morrison and Hampson, interview.
46 Bawden, "CBC Puts Big Boot to Friendly Giant."
47 Bawden, "CBC Puts Big Boot to Friendly Giant."
48 Daller, "Dinner Date."
49 Rainsberry, *History of Children's Television*, 90.
50 Greer, "It's a Hoot!"
51 Greer, "It's a Hoot!"
52 Greer, "Small Screen."
53 Greer, "Spirit Moves Him."
54 Fasick, "Turning Culture Shock into TV Drama."
55 Fasick, "Turning Culture Shock into TV Drama."
56 Greer, "Small Screen."
57 Posesorki, "Aunt Agnes Sets Out."
58 Posesorki, "Aunt Agnes Sets Out."
59 Cuff, "TVOntario Budget Cuts."
60 Scrivener, "Two Faces of Aunt Agnes."
61 Quill, "Aunt Agnes Finds Real Christmas Spirit."
62 Greer, "Coup Degrassi."
63 Greer, "For the Family."
64 Blackadar, "TV Expands in a Family Way."
65 Shea, interview.
66 "Kids Just Wanna Have Fun," *Prince George Citizen.*
67 MacKay, interview.
68 MacKay, interview.
69 Bawden, "See How They'll Run."

1990s

1 Adilman, "The Reason *Road to Avonlea* Endures."
2 Vyhnak, "NOISEmakers."
3 Vyhnak, "NOISEmakers."
4 Vyhnak, "NOISEmakers."
5 Trotz and Livesley. *Penguin Guide to Children's TV and Video,* 50–51.
6 Taylor, interview.
7 Brown, "Stations Join the PJ Party."
8 Taylor, interview.
9 Shannon, interview.
10 Hume, "Let's Get Physical."
11 Hume, "Let's Get Physical."
12 "TVTALK: Ready or Not Probes Rejection," *Toronto Star.*

13 Chisholm, "Ready to Educate and Entertain."
14 "Ready or Not Creator Says Public Ready," *Cornwall Standard Freeholder.*
15 Kastner, "He's No Dud."
16 Zerbisias, "TVO Stands by Its Strategies and Tactics."
17 Bawden, "Ruth-less TVO."
18 Bawden, "Ruth-less TVO."
19 Kadima, interview.
20 Taylor, interview.
21 Guerrero, interview.
22 Taylor, interview.
23 Guerrero, interview.
24 Taylor, interview.
25 Stelnick, interview.
26 Kadima, interview.
27 Rao, interview.
28 Kadima, interview.
29 Guerrero, interview.
30 Taylor, interview.
31 Morris, interview.
32 Brown, "Squawkbox."
33 Staff, "Ontario Scene."
34 Cuthbert, "TVO Postings Spell."
35 Cuthbert, "TVO Postings Spell."
36 Morris, interview.
37 Morris, interview.
38 Brown, "Stations Join the PJ Party."
39 Brown, "Stations Join the PJ Party."
40 Sullivan, interview.
41 Morris, interview.
42 Brown, "Stations Join the PJ Party."
43 Brown, "Win Some, Lose Some."
44 Cuthbert, "To Research or Not to Research?"
45 Cuthbert, "To Research or Not to Research?"
46 Sullivan, interview.
47 Sullivan, interview.
48 Rao, interview.
49 Greaves, interview.
50 Brown, "We Love You, Mr. Dressup."
51 Adilman, "No More Kidding Around."
52 Adilman, "No More Kidding Around."
53 Adilman, "No More Kidding Around."
54 Brown, "Star Gazing in Sesame Park."
55 VanderBurgh, interview, 2024.
56 Ross, interview.
57 Leger, "YTV Celebrates 10 Years."
58 Rao, interview.
59 Morrison and Hampson, interview.
60 Morrison and Hampson, interview.
61 Morrison and Hampson, interview.
62 Greenaway, "Teenage Angst Gets Its Own TV Show."
63 Morris, interview.
64 Siegler, interview.
65 Siegler, interview.
66 Miller, "Inside the Strange Resurgence of Nanalan'."
67 Miller, "Inside the Strange Resurgence of Nanalan'."
68 Miller, "Inside the Strange Resurgence of Nanalan'."

Bibliography

"About Us." Museum of Toronto. n.d. Accessed October 1, 2024. museumoftoronto.com/about-us/.

Adilman, Sid. "CBC's Fraggles Rocking the Ratings." *Toronto Star*, February 17, 1983: B1.

Adilman, Sid. "CFTO Mute about Mutt's New Series." *Toronto Star*, October 11, 1979: G3.

Adilman, Sid. "No More Kidding Around." *Starweek*, December 23, 1995: 16.

Adilman, Sid. "The Reason *Road to Avonlea* Endures." *Toronto Star*, March 31, 1996: B8.

Allan, Blaine. "CBC Television Series, 1952–1982." Queen's University Film and Media, n.d. Accessed January 31, 2024. queensu.ca/filmandmedia/other-resources/cbc-television-series-1952-1982.

"Archived – Public Notice CRTC 84-138." Government of Canada. June 11, 1984. crtc.gc.ca/eng/archive/1984/pb84-138.htm.

Bardoel, Isabella. "Sharon, Lois and Bram Riding High!" *Sunday Star*, September 23, 1984: C8.

Base, Ron. "Two Kids and a Dog — That's Canadian Drama." *Sunday Star*, October 21, 1979: B1.

Bawden, Jim. "CBC Puts Big Boot to Friendly Giant." *Toronto Star*, December 18, 1984: B1.

Bawden, Jim. "CBC's Sunday Kid Series Prove There's No Place Like Homegrown." *Toronto Star*, December 8, 1985: G2.

Bawden, Jim. "Kids Loved Uncle Bobby's TV Show." *Toronto Star*, May 24, 2007.

Bawden, Jim. "Ruth-less TVO." *Toronto Star*, June 12, 1993: SW72.

Bawden, Jim. "See How They'll Run." *Toronto Star*, September 28, 1991: S4.

Blackadar, Bruce. "TV Expands in a Family Way." *Toronto Star*, August 27, 1988: J1.

Boeckh, Sherry. "Entertaining the Kids, with a Little Help from Their Friends." *Toronto Star*, November 25, 1972: A14.

Boiteau, Denise, interview by Greg Oliver. 2019.

Braithwaite, Dennis. "Professor's Fadeaway." *Globe and Mail*, June 3, 1963.

Brioux, Bill. "Today at brioux.tv: the Podcast — Meet TV Pioneer Trevor Evans, a.k.a. 'Kiddo the Clown.'" brioux.tv, March 3, 2021. brioux.tv/blog/2021/03/03/today-at-brioux-tv-the-podcast-meet-tv-pioneer-trevor-evans-a-k-a-kiddo-the-clown/.

Brown, Louise. "Squawkbox." *Starweek*, August 13, 1994: 6.
Brown, Louise. "Star Gazing in Sesame Park." *Starweek*, October 19, 1996: 41.
Brown, Louise. "Stations Join the PJ Party." *Starweek*, May 21, 1994: 6.
Brown, Louise. "We Love You, Mr. Dressup." *Starweek*, March 2, 1996: 13.
Brown, Louise. "Win Some, Lose Some." *Starweek*, April 15, 1995: 72.
Bunch, Adam. "Down at Fraggle Rock … In Yorkville — The Muppets Take Toronto." *Spacing*. February 18, 2014. spacing.ca/toronto/2014/02/18/fraggle-rock-yorkville-muppets-take-toronto/.
Carr, Bob. "OECA Is Getting to Everybody." *Broadcaster*, August 1980: 6.
CBC Archives. "The Canadian TV Channel That Was Just for Kids in 1979." CBC, February 11, 2020. cbc.ca/archives/the-canadian-tv-channel-that-was-just-for-kids-in-1979-1.5446626.
Chapman, Francis, interview by Fred Rainsberry. September 14, 1982.
Charles, Nancy. "Childwatch." *Montreal Gazette*, November 3, 1979: 4.
"Children's TV." *Toronto Daily Star*, January 20, 1963: 42.
Chisholm, Patricia. "Ready to Educate and Entertain Young Teens." *Maclean's*, June 17, 1993.
Cole, Stephen. *Here's Looking at Us: Celebrating Fifty Years of CBC-TV*. McClelland & Stewart, 2002.
Cole, Susan G. "Reiner Schwarz 1948–2014." *Now Magazine*, September 3, 2014. nowtoronto.com/music/reiner-schwarz-1948-2014/.
Coneybeare, Rod, interview by Fred Rainsberry. December 20, 1982.
Conroy, Ed. "About Retrontario." Retrontario, 2008. retrontario.com/about/.
Conroy, Ed. "The History of the Mr. Dressup TV Show and Its Connection to Toronto." blogTO, July 17, 2022. blogto.com/film/2021/06/history-mr-dressup-toronto/.
Conroy, Ed. "How Scarborough Once Had the Largest McDonald's in the World." blogTO, May 27, 2023. blogto.com/eat_drink/2016/02/scarborough_once_had_the_worlds_largest_mcdonalds/.
Conway, John, interview by Fred Rainsberry. November 23, 1982.
Coombs, Ernie, interview by Fred Rainsberry. September 28, 1982.
Coulter, Natalie. "'Missed Opportunity': The Oversight of Canadian Children's Media." *Canadian Journal of Communication* 41, no. 1 (February 2016): 95–113.
Crosby, Laurel, interview by Fred Rainsberry. September 22, 1982.
CTV News. "About CTV News Toronto." n.d. Accessed August 11, 2024. toronto.ctvnews.ca/about-us.
Cuff, John Haslett. "TVOntario Budget Cuts Hit Children's Shows, Educational Programs." *Globe and Mail*, May 28, 1987: D3.
Cuthbert, Pamela. "To Research or Not to Research?" *Playback*, October 10, 1994.
Cuthbert, Pamela. "TVO Postings Spell." *Playback*, July 18, 1994.
Cutting, Meredith, interview by Ed Conroy. June 2022.
Daller, Kate. "Dinner Date." *Starweek*, April 13, 1985: 74.
Davis, Michael. *Street Gang: The Complete History of* Sesame Street. Penguin Books, 2009.
Dempsey, Lotta. "Uncle Bobby Meets Some Fans with a Message from Santa." *Toronto Star*, November 10, 1969.
Derhodge, Dick, interview by Ed Conroy. August 18, 2024.

Donaldson, Gordon. "Star Trek to Literacy." *TVO Plus* 1, no. 5 (1979): 8.
Dymond, Greig, and Geoff Pevere. *Mondo Canuck: A Canadian Pop Culture Odyssey*. Prentice Hall Canada, 1996.
Elder, Don, interview by Fred Rainsberry. January 19, 1983.
Elston, Brian. "Math Patrol [comment]." *Mathematical Fiction*, n.d. Accessed July 7, 2024. kasmana.people.charleston.edu/MATHFICT/mfview.php?callnumber=mf245.
Endersby, Clive, interview by Ed Conroy. August 24, 2024.
Evans, Trevor, interview by Fred Rainsberry. October 8, 1982.
"Fables of La Fontaine." *CBC Times*, April 13, 1958: 5.
Fairley, Grant D. *Look Up — Way Up! The Friendly Giant: The Biography of Robert Homme*. Silverwoods Publishing, 2016.
Farrell, Ann. "How Young View TV." *Toronto Star*, July 4, 1975: D1.
Fasick, Laura. "Turning Culture Shock into TV Drama." *Broadcast Week*, April 20, 1985: 8.
Gibbons, Robert, interview by Fred Rainsberry. August 27, 1982.
Gilchrist, Stuart, interview by Fred Rainsberry. August 3, 1982.
Giorno, Frank. "De Grassi, the Story Behind the Name." *Accenti*, June 28, 2010. accenti.ca/de-grassi-the-story-behind-the-name/.
Godard, Peter. "Today's Special Yesterday's Production." *Toronto Star*, February 22, 1986: F9.
Gollom, Mark. "Uncle Bobby Still Performs for His Supper." *National Post*, March 6, 1999: B13.
Gottlieb, Owen, interview by Ed Conroy. October 2024.
Grainger, Gareth, interview by Ed Conroy. August 25, 2024.
Greaves, Christopher, interview by Ed Conroy. August 29, 2024.
Greenaway, Kathryn. "Teenage Angst Gets Its Own TV Show." *Montreal Gazette*, March 13, 1999: 39.
Greer, Sandy. "Coup Degrassi." *Starweek*, January 17, 1987: 5.
Greer, Sandy. "For the Family." *Starweek*, November 5, 1988: 95.
Greer, Sandy. "It's a Hoot!" *Starweek*, November 2, 1985: 8.
Greer, Sandy. "Parents Shouldn't Use TV as a Scapegoat for Personal Shortcomings, says Noted Educator." *Starweek*, May 31, 1986: 20.
Greer, Sandy. "Small Screen." *Starweek*, January 18, 1986: 17.
Greer, Sandy. "Small Screen." *Starweek*, April 26, 1986: 16.
Greer, Sandy. "The Spirit Moves Him." *Starweek*, April 27, 1985: 6.
Guerrero, Phil, interview by Ed Conroy. October 2012.
Harpur, Tom. "For Heaven's Sake." *Starweek*, June 13, 1987: 5.
Harris, Alfred. "Science Fiction TV." *CBC Times*, March 8–15, 1953.
Hausmann, E.H. "The Bananas — Something Very Much Different, as Children's Shows Go." *Starweek*, January 4, 1969: A3.
Hawkes, Cheryl. "Teaching Old Dogs New Tricks." *Starweek*, October 20, 1979: 10.
Homme, Bob, interview by Fred Rainsberry. August 19, 1982.
Houle, Zachary. "Uncle Chichimus." TV Party, n.d. Accessed July 1, 2024. tvparty.com/lostchichimus.html.
Houle, Zachary. "Zachary Houle Interview with Jeremy Pollock." In *TV Party! Television's Untold Tales*, by Billy Ingram. Bonus Books, 2002.
Hume, Christopher. "Let's Get Physical." *Starweek*, February 27, 1993: 6.

Ide, Ran. *Transparent Blackboard — TVOntario: A Memoir.* Lugus Publications, 1994.
Jewison, Norman, interview by Fred Rainsberry. March 15, 1983.
Jones, Brian Jay. *Jim Henson: The Biography.* Ballantine Books, 2016.
Kadima, Nicolas, interview by Ed Conroy. October 4, 2024.
Kastner, Kathy. "He's No Dud: Dudley the Dragon Is Joined by Moppets, Puppets and People in Adventures that Help Children Discover the World Around Them." *Toronto Star*, October 2, 1993: SW4.
Kenter, Peter. *TV North: Everything You Wanted to Know About Canadian Television.* Whitecap Books, 2000.
"Kids Just Wanna Have Fun." *Prince George Citizen*, January 13, 1990.
King, Maxwell. *The Good Neighbor: The Life and Work of Fred Rogers.* Abrams Press, 2018.
King, Paul. "Send in the Clown." *Starweek*, March 19, 1983: K6.
Kirby, Blaik. "Supershow Not Really Super." *Globe and Mail*, January 11, 1975: 31.
Kitching, Heather. "The Rocker Who Wrote One of the Greatest Canadian Folk Songs of All Time: The Littlest Hobo Theme." Roots Music Canada. November 26, 2022. rootsmusic.ca/2022/11/26/the-rocker-who-wrote-one-of-the-greatest-canadian-folk-songs-of-all-time-the-littlest-hobo-theme/#google_vignette.
Krantz, Ron, interview by Fred Rainsberry. September 27, 1982.
Kuplowska, Olga. "Read All About It! in Mississippi." *The Org* employee newsletter, TVOntario, June 24, 1983.
Leger, Louie. "YTV Celebrates 10 Years by Keeping It Weird." *Playback*, November 2, 1998.
Levitch, Geral. "A Gaggle of Fraggles." *Starweek*, January 22, 1983: 5.
Lundy, Charles, Wendy McNaughton, Larry Zack, and Nancy Hill. *Camp TVOntario — What If... A Leaders Handbook.* TVOntario, 1979.
Lunn, Janet. "The Friendly Giant Who Won't Be Hurried." *Canadian Weekly*, 1966: 8–9.
MacKay, Barry Kent, interview by Ed Conroy. September 23, 2024.
MacKay, Jed, interview by Ed Conroy. August 19, 2024.
McBride, Peter, and Roy Shields. "Nobody's Second Banana." *Starweek*, August 16, 1980: K4.
McIntyre, Grant. "From Crass to Crash Kids' Television Writer/Producer Has Done It All." *Globe and Mail*, March 20, 1999: 10.
McKay, Kenneth B. *Puppetry in Canada: An Art to Enchant*. Ontario Puppetry Association Publishing, 1980: 140.
Miller, Mira. "Inside the Strange Resurgence of Nanalan', the Decades-Old TV Show Aimed at Toddlers." *Globe and Mail*, February 8, 2024. theglobeandmail.com/arts/article-inside-the-strange-resurgence-of-nanalan-the-decades-old-tv-show-aimed/.
"Molding Healthy Viewing Habits." *Starweek*, September 10, 1983: 10.
Morris, Josh, interview by Ed Conroy. October 16, 2024.
Morrison, Bram, and Sharon Hampson, interview by Ed Conroy. September 23, 2024.
"Mr. Dressup to Degrassi." Museum of Toronto, n.d. Accessed October 1, 2024. museumoftoronto.com/collection/from-mr-dressup-to-degrassi/.
Nash, Knowlton. *Prime Time at Ten.* McClelland & Stewart, 1987.
"No More Quiz Wealth to Share Stan Francis Finds New TV Niche." *Toronto Star*, June 10, 1961: 26.
Novakowski, Vera, interview by Fred Rainsberry. January 4, 1983.
"Obituary — Rainsberry, Dr. Frederick B." *Toronto Star*, April 10, 1996: D16.

"Old Testament Stories with Puppets." *CBC Times*, February 24, 1957.
"Ontario Scene." *Playback*, March 14, 1994.
Patrick-Roberts, Marnie, interview by Travis Doucette. *An Interview with Marnie Patrick Roberts.* YouTube, December 20, 2013. youtu.be/COmsEp7iQSA?si=LdYGf1bgSbMurnyh.
"Polka Dot Door Themes." TVOntario internal report, 1982–83.
Posesorki, Sheri. "Aunt Agnes Sets Out to Make Children Think." *Globe and Mail*, January 11, 1986: 8.
Quill, Greg. "Aunt Agnes Finds Real Christmas Spirit." *Toronto Star*, December 20, 1989: B2.
Rainsberry, F.B. *A History of Children's Television in English Canada, 1952–1986.* Scarecrow Press, 1988.
Rao, Atul N., interview by Ed Conroy. September 29, 2024.
"Read All About It!: Interview with Series Writer Clive Endersby." Rick's TV, n.d. Accessed August 21, 2024. rickstv.com/tvo/read.html.
"Ready or Not Creator Says Public Ready for Risqué TV Series." *Cornwall Standard Freeholder*, October 14, 1994.
Robb, Dodi, interview by Fred Rainsberry. October 18, 1982.
Rogers, Fred, interview by Fred Rainsberry. May 15, 1983.
Rogers, Fred. *A Beautiful Day in the Neighborhood: Neighborly Words of Wisdom from Mister Rogers.* Penguin Random House, 2019.
Ross, Susan, interview by Ed Conroy. 2013.
School Broadcasts K–8 [programming guide issued to schools]. TVOntario, n.d.
Schuyler, Linda. *The Mother of All Degrassi: A Memoir.* ECW Press, 2022.
Scott, Patrick. "CBC Stuck with Sesame Street." *Toronto Daily Star*, July 21, 1970: 39.
Scott, Patrick. "TV's Finest Route Is Sesame Street." *Toronto Star*, February 7, 1970: 39.
Scrivener, Leslie. "Two Faces of Aunt Agnes." *Toronto Star*, November 22, 1987.
Segarini, Bob. "Bob Recalls the Tale of Chops Dorfman and the Edison Twins, the Insanely Talented David Celia, and the Heavenly Voice of Rumer from England." Segarini: Don't Believe A Word I Say, May 22, 2021. bobsegarini.wordpress.com/2021/05/21/bob-recalls-the-tale-of-chops-dorfman-and-the-edison-twins-the-insanely-talented-david-celia-and-the-heavenly-voice-of-rumer-from-england/.
Shannon, Jamie, interview by Ed Conroy. 2012.
Shea, Kevin, interview by Ed Conroy. August 12, 2024.
Shuman, Risa, interview by Ed Conroy. October 17, 2024.
Siegler, Nathaniel, interview by Ed Conroy. October 20, 2024.
Sobol, John, interview by Ed Conroy. September 17, 2024.
Spivak, Michael, interview by Fred Rainsberry. October 4, 1982.
Stein, Jessica Max. "The Count Writes a Haiku: Jerry Nelson (1934–2012)." Jessica Max Stein website, April 9, 2013. jessicamaxstein.com/the-count-writes-haiku-jerry-nelson-1934-2012/.
Stelnick, Marty, interview by Ed Conroy. September 23, 2024.
Stewart, Sandy. *Here's Looking At Us: A Personal History of Television in Canada.* McClelland & Stewart, 1986.
Stoffman, Daniel. "Sesame Street Won't Be Canadianized." *Toronto Daily Star*, September 25, 1970: 26.

Sullivan, Patty, interview by Ed Conroy. September 19, 2024.
Taube, Michael. "Ontario's Circle Square Ranch an Emblem of Childhood Nostalgia." Troy Media, July 18, 2023. troymedia.com/lifestyle/ontarios-circle-square-ranch-an-emblem-of-childhood-nostalgia/.
Taylor, Bill. "Maestros, a Little Traveling (Matt) Music, Please." *Starweek*, December 24, 1983: 61.
Taylor, Dale, interview by Ed Conroy. June 17, 2024.
Teachman, Goody, Joan Prowse, and Kay Duggan. *Read All About It: Summative Evaluation of the Learning System in a Classroom Setting.* TVOntario Office of Project Research, August 1981.
Teachman, Goody, and Kay Duggan. *Polka Dot Door: Summative Evaluation, Parent Survey.* TVOntario Office of Project Research, 1982.
Trotz, Frank, and Jack Livesley. *The Penguin Guide to Children's TV and Video.* Penguin Books Canada, 1993.
"TV Listings." *Broadcast Week*, January 20, 1975: T5.
"TV Listings." *Starweek*, November 8, 1969: A14.
"TV Listings." *Starweek*, January 10, 1975: 48.
"TVOntario." Canada Modern, n.d. Accessed June 12, 2024. canadamodern.org/tvontario-tm80/.
TVOntario Summer Academy. June 1980.
"TVTALK: Ready or Not Probes Rejection." *Toronto Star*, June 27, 1993: 6.
"Uncle Chichimus, Hollyhock Kidnapped." *Toronto Daily Star*, January 20, 1954: 1.
VanderBurgh, Clive, interview by Ed Conroy. August 22, 2024.
VanderBurgh, Clive, interview by Fred Rainsberry. January 12, 1983.
VanderBurgh, Clive. "Pre-School Pilot Proposal." November 17, 1980.
VanderBurgh, Jennifer. *What Television Remembers: Artifacts and Footprints of TV in Toronto.* McGill-Queen's University Press, 2023.
Vyhnak, Carola. "NOISEmakers." *Starweek*, May 4, 1991: 86.
Yeo, Debra. "A TV Treasure Trove: New Museum Exhibition, 'Mr. Dressup to Degrassi,' Explores Revolutionary Kids' Programming." *Toronto Star*, July 6, 2023: C6.
Yost, Elwy, interview by Fred Rainsberry. January 14, 1983.
Zerbisias, Antonia. "TVO Stands by Its Strategies and Tactics." *Toronto Star*, October 15, 1994: H8.

Image Credits

CBC, back cover (*top*), 25, 39, 47, 57, 81, 226
Cichon, Steve, 68, 175
City of Toronto Archives, 59, 85, 123
Conway, John, from Mikey Artelle, *John Conway and Uncle Chichimus*, 15; from Mikey Artelle's Puppetry Archives, 19
Derhodge, Dick, 115
Endersby, Clive, 167
Fred Rogers Institute, 72, 74, 76
Keogh, Nina, 33, 46, 104, 113, 197, 249
Museum of Toronto, 4
New Hobo Productions Inc. (© 2025, used with permission), 173
Parker, Jim, 200, 295
Retrontario, 7, 11, 26, 50, 64, 69, 82, 89, 105, 129, 138, 177, 179, 199
Shannon, Jamie, 261, 306 (*top & bottom*)
Sharon, Lois & Bram Archive, 223 (*top & bottom*)
TVOntario, back cover (*bottom*), 109, 116, 128, 139, 142, 149, 151, 152, 158, 160, 161, 168, 190, 198, 203, 204, 209, 217, 235, 247, 270, 289
WildBrain, 188, 239
YTV Canada Inc. (all rights reserved), 244, 259, 273, 277, 279, 282

Index

Characters listed in the index are indicated by an asterisk next to their name. Cast information can be found under show titles.

About the Author

ED CONROY is a cultural historian, writer, producer, and founder of Retrontario.com who was born and raised in Toronto. His work on Canadian pop culture and history has appeared in the *Toronto Star*, *Toronto Life*, and blogTO, among others. A sought-after media commentator, Ed has been featured on CTV, CBC, TVO, Global, Zoomer, and iHeartRadio Canada, and he has collaborated with Canadian Heritage/Patrimoine canadien, the City of Toronto, Reel Canada, and the Toronto Museum. He is a lifelong television enthusiast, and his earliest memory is being terrorized by an episode of *Doctor Who* featuring giant spiders, which had immediately followed a short Paddington Bear animation on TVO. He now lives in Scugog with his wife and two children, and he is dedicated to preserving and celebrating Canada's media history in analogue and digital formats, online and beyond.

Please visit imagination.retrontario.com to share your memories, lodge complaints, meet fellow nostalgists, and learn even more about the golden age of Toronto kids' TV!